THE BAD MAN
OF THE WEST

The hanging of Curly Tex for the murder of a fellow cowboy; tried, convicted, and hanged under the direction of Col. Charles Goodnight. The Negro in the background was an important witness. (drawing by Frank Anthony Stanush)

THE BAD MAN
OF THE WEST

by

GEORGE D. HENDRICKS

Drawings by FRANK ANTHONY STANUSH

The Naylor Company
Book Publishers of the Southwest
San Antonio, Texas

First Edition 1942

Revised and Enlarged Edition 1950

Revised and Enlarged Edition 1959

Revised and Enlarged Edition 1970

Dedication

TO the place
    and the time
    and the spirit
    that never were
    anywhere else
    before nor since
    nor ever will be again.

— PREFACE —

The fact that this book has gone through four editions and has been in print since 1941 will speak for itself. Such a phenomenon is explainable in the nature of the subject. The several hundred men whose lives this study encompasses were exceptional men in a unique area in a singularly transitional era. There occurs, from time to time in the history of mankind, a restless transitional period in which there is a kind of bursting at the seams and which requires daring men to expand their horizons, physical and otherwise. We are probably in such an era in the latter half of the twentieth century.

Survival of man in outer space requires extra special equipment. Not only is it physical equipment, but it is also psychological and emotional equipment. Especially is this true in the early stages of man's conquest of outer space. Survival on the early Western frontier required a different set of physical equipment, a new insight and philosophy, and an innovation in emotional attitudes. Especially was this true when the West was first settled.

Outer space will require — as a result of these forthcoming new equipments, psychology, and emotional outlooks — a correspondingly new set of law, customs, taboos, and mores. No doubt, human society will bungle and fumble in developing them — just as our forebears have always done in moving into new and exotic environments. There will be bad men of outer space, just as there were bad men of the West. Their actions and techniques may not be identical, but the underlying human motivation will at least be similar. It is still true, as I conclude at the end of this study, that there never was and never will be another one *exactly* like the bad man of the West (because he was the sum-total product of his own time, place, and ancestry); but it is high time we recognize the human motivations that drove him to his reckless life for what they were and are and always will be. My whole point here is that I treat of a timeless subject with universal truths.

The significant factual and philosophical causes underlying the appearance and the passing of the Western bad man are probably less understood than any other phase of Western pioneer life. The actual facts have too frequently been distorted and deliberately exaggerated. To winnow facts from legends as presented in secondary sources is indeed quite difficult, but I have spared no efforts to check and double-check all the evidence, and then to portray this unique bad man for what he really was. Because

vii

of the semi-analytical approach required in such a comprehensive study. the reader will appreciate the obvious necessity for the reoccurrence of certain facts, as the viewpoint varies during the progressive development of this story.

My obligations for the material are as numerous as are my sources. Grateful acknowledgments to both authors and publishers are indicated in the body of the text and in the BIBLIO-GRAPHY given in the APPENDIX. Photographs were obtained from several sources, but especial acknowledgment is due the N. H. Rose collection of San Antonio, Texas.

My indebtedness to others is a heavy one. Among these, but not to the exclusion of still others, should be mentioned Mody C. Boatright, J. Frank Dobie, William MacLeod Raine, Captain John R. Hughes of the Texas Rangers, Mr. Joe Naylor and his wife Mrs. Rita Naylor, the many patient librarians, the several custodians of old public records and newspaper files, and the few remaining old-timers who were always ready to help clarify the facts. To all of these, I wish to express my very deep gratitude.

The first edition of this book came out in 1941, when I was a buck private in the 132nd Field Artillery at Camp Bowie, Texas. Movie rights were sold on that edition to Twentieth Century-Fox Film Directors, Harry Sherman and Dick Dickson. Many a western bad-man motif found in the book has been employed in movies and in television since that transaction.

Since that time much water has passed under the bridge, and the world will never again be the same. The second edition of the book came out in 1950, shortly before I received the doctorate at The University of Texas; in this edition I attempted to weed out a few sophomoric expressions.

The third edition came out in 1959. In this present fourth edition I have attempted to bring the subject up to date, as the general public seems to be more interested in the bad man of the west than it ever was. I think this is a very healthy sign.

I have always owed much to my father and mother, Mr. Jake J. and Mrs. Gypsie Hannah Hendricks, for their continued encouragement. And now I have five new sources of inspiration. There is Peggy, my wife; and there are our children: David, Jake, Cindy, and Helen. To know them is to realize that further expatiation is superfluous.

George D. Hendricks

North Texas State University, Denton, Texas
October, 1969

TABLE OF CONTENTS

ix

LIST OF ILLUSTRATIONS

xiii

— FOREWORD —

Not only did the "bad man of the old West" blaze his name across the front pages of pioneer life and secure for himself a lasting place in America's folklore, but also his experiences are now furnishing the foundation for many of the best movies of our own day. He gained this recognition not because he was bad but rather because he was a man of swift and decisive action. The thought and action of the bad man was matched and excelled only by such pioneer peace officers as the Texas Rangers, whose very existence the bad man helped to make necessary.

There is much to be said in favor of the chivalry, the generosity, and the fighting spirit often displayed by the Western bad man. Unfortunately, too often, this has been the only side of his life displayed to the youth of our country. We must remember that the Western bad man was also bad, and at times very bad. We have for a long time needed a book that would picture the Western bad man for what he really was, and at the same time explain the underlying causes for his actions and his very existence.

Mr. Hendricks, in his book, has now made just that contribution. In *The Bad Man of the West*, he has told the actual and the whole truth about this bad man.

Capt. John R. Hughes

> — CAPT. JOHN R. HUGHES
> *Texas Ranger, from 1887 to 1915 and captain for 22 years. (The above foreword was written for the 1941 edition of this book.)*

xv

TEXAS RANGER CAPTAIN JOHN R. HUGHES

He entered the service 1887, was appointed Captain
July 4, 1893 by Governor Hogg, was retired from
active duty Jan. 31, 1915. He died June 3, 1947.

"The Boss of the Texas Border"

1. MAJOR WM. BRADY, Sheriff, and son ROBERT of Lincoln County, New Mexico. Sheriff Brady was killed and son Robert shot in the mouth by "Billy the Kid" and his gang, April 1, 1878. 2. PALS 3. La Paloma, original bar of Billy the Kid days, Lincoln, New Mexico. 4. Courthouse and window from which Billy the Kid shot Bob Ollinger, the guard, as he approached Lincoln, New Mexico. 5. Main Street, Lincoln, New Mexico.

CHAPTER I

MOTIVES AND INFLUENCES AFFECTING THE BAD MAN

CATTLE! GOLD! SILVER!

GOLD

Gold! Gold! Gold!
Bright and yellow, hard and cold,
Molten, graven, hammered and rolled;
Heavy to get, and light to hold;
Hoarded, bartered, bought and sold,
Stolen, borrowed, squandered, doled;
To the very verge of the church yard mold;
Price of many a crime untold —
Gold! Gold! Gold! Gold!

— Thomas Hood

 am an individual more important to myself than anyone else," thought the bad man of the old West, if he reasoned or excused himself at all. "Cattle, gold, and silver were created for man to use. I am a man. I must therefore provide for and protect myself with these things. I shall look for the most practical means of doing it!" But these means were not always ethical.

The bad man lived on the Western frontier, where personal safety depended upon the use of firearms, and where law and order did not really exist until he himself made them necessary. Lee Sage, who called himself "The Last Rustler," in his book by the same name, said, "I believe the spirit of man builds the

1

spirit of the country he lives in. The world was created for man. As he orders it, so it will yield."

It was easy, if not necessary for his sustenance, so the bad man thought, for him to drift into crime, and that sometimes without punishment. Lee Sage, in speaking of a scrape he got into in Montana, said, "My old trouble in that country had died down. It don't take them long to forget things, if there ain't some special person to keep nudging it on."

PRODIGAL NOMADS

Another reason why the wild West was wild was the very character of its inhabitants — they were nomadic. In the mountains of the Northwest, Southwest, and far West, mining settlements sprang up overnight and decayed with the rapid exhaustion of the deposits. For example, today you can drive to a quiet little village named Central City, nestled in the lofty and majestic mountains of Colorado. It's almost a ghost town with only a few hundred inhabitants, but you can readily see that once upon a time it must surely have been a teeming hive of some 20,000 respectable citizens, and probably a number of cardsharks, ne'er-do-wells, and bad men. They will show you the old barroom in the famous, historic Teller House where is still painted the "face on the barroom floor" and where the poem of the same name was inspired. They will show you the Glory Hole, a seemingly bottomless pit from which has been taken $80,000,000 in gold. But now, it's just a hole. You can look around at entire blocks of six-storied empty buildings.

At Tombstone, Arizona, now a city of one or two thousand, they will show you the saloon and dance hall where Curly Bill and his band used to drink their red-eye on Saturday nights, and they will tell you all about Ed Schieffelin's miraculous discovery of the silver lode. They will also tell you in wide-eyed, awesome fashion about how all the twenty thousand good people of the old Tombstone took to cover when the three Earp brothers who were then U. S. Marshals and their bad-man pal Doc Holliday sprung around the corner of Fly's photo gallery into the O. K. Corral to meet five of the Cochise County rustlers.

"Oh, it was a bloody battle!" the old-timers will tell you. "Yes-siree, I can just see them three tall brother officers, Wyatt, Virgil, and Morgan Earp swaggerin' along abreast with them little knots bulgin' on their jawbones and that there determined look

His (Clay Allison's) favorite amusement was to ride into a town, alone, with six-shooter in each hand, shoot out lights and windows and empty the streets of populace, daring any and everyone to come out. (See page 36)

FRANK ANTHONY STANUSH

in their steel blue eyes. Fact is, I hardly knowed one from 'tother. They wuz all three about the same size, tall handsome fellers, all blond and blue-eyed. No, I reckon I could have picked out Wyatt — there was somethin' about his manner that always showed he was the leader. And hobblin' alongside of 'em was that tubercular invalid, that riproarin' Doc Holliday. They say he used to be a dentist in Dallas, Texas, but lost all his customers on account of his illness. Then he started gamblin' and drinkin' and you know what that led to in them days. Why, they say he was the coldest-blooded killer west of the Mississippi!

"Yessir, I can just see them Cochise County rustlers — Ike and Billy Clanton, Frank and Tom McLowery, and Billy Claiborne over there in the O. K. Corral saddlin' their hosses. Here come the Earps and Holliday around the corner and then the fireworks start! Pop! Boom! Pop! Quicker'n you can say Jack Jehosephat each side has already shot seventeen times apiece.

"When the smoke clears away, I can just peep through and see Virgil and Morgan Earp have been plugged in their arms and legs; Doc is just scratched; Wyatt is untouched! Doggondest feller! He seems to have worn some mighty good luck piece! Thirteen out of their seventeen shots have found rustlers! Doc has disgustedly thrown away his double-barreled sawed-off shotgun during the fight and whipped out his six-gun which is still steamin'!

"Now, I'm lookin' at the rustlers. Ike Clanton and Billy Claiborne have hightailed it durin' the fight, leavin' their three compadres killed — only three of their seventeen shots have found officers. You bet, it was some affair, I'll tell you!"

But now, Tombstone, Virginia City, Central City, Bannack, and other once important mining centers where bad men were once shot down on Main Street are peaceful ghosts of their former selves.

On the Western frontier practically nothing was taxable. There were no farms. The means to provide an adequate and efficient staff of officers were not available. On the Plains the cattle center was ever moving Westward — it was really a "hell on wheels." From San Antonio and Austin to Abilene, Ellsworth, Ogallala, and Dodge City — from this "worst town on earth" westward to Las Vegas and Santa Fé, and from thence to the virgin Southwest of Arizona at Tombstone and of Nevada at Virginia City, we have followed the sporadic "hell on wheels" set going by

4

the bad man of the West. In each of these towns the bad man felt his "oats" until encroaching civilization drove him to newer and greener pastures. Such towns as these were usually the junctions of railroads from the North and East with the long trail drives from the South and West. There was no agriculture; practically nothing taxable; practically no police force — it was every man for himself.

CONFLICT, BETWEEN THE RACES

Then, too, the West was wild because of the conflict between the races. White men killed so many Indians and Mexicans that the phrase, "Mexicans don't count," became trite. The old-timers said, "Stranger, stay shy o' that there Wild Bill Hickok. 'Specially when he's drunk as a skunk. Why, he's killed eighty-five men, not countin' Mexicans and Indians!"

The bad man became so hardened that the value of human life cheapened in his estimation. Having slain a few of another race, it grated less on the white bad man's conscience to kill one of his own.

Judge Roy Bean, "The Law West of the Pecos," was trying a friendly Irishman named Paddy O'Rourke for shooting a Chinaman. Tradition has it that the Irishmen built the Southern Pacific Railroad from the East and the Chinamen from the West coast. They met at Langtry, Texas, where Judge Roy Bean appointed himself as "The Law West of the Pecos." It just so happened that the Irishman was a good customer at Bean's 'bar,' where the Judge dealt justice with his six-shooter hand and beer with other. The Judge solemnly thumbed through his entire books of statutes and came to the conclusion, "By gobs, I don't find a word in these here books about shooting a Chinaman, so I hereby declare the Chinaman contraband and the case is dismissed! Have a drink of beer, O'Rourke!"

Besides, reasoned the judge, was it the fault of his friend if the fool Chinaman didn't duck when he was shot at?

But most of all the six-shooter made the wild West wild. It was cheap and efficient and fatal; everybody had one, or two, just as he wore boots. It was a land of extreme individualism, necessitated by its very nature and by the newness and sparseness of its civilization. Honest men came West to work and build their fortunes on minerals, cattle, or their proceeds; and the bad men followed in their tracks to prey on them and build their own fortunes without having to labor as patiently as the honest man.

"G. T. T."

Also, the West was a refuge for the desperado. The first principle in the code of the West was that no questions should be asked of newcomers. Many a debtor or 'wanted' man in the East or South before the Civil War, in order to prevent being taken into custody, would hang out a sign on his door, "G. T. T." — "gone to Texas," where no questions would be asked. Certainly the connotation associated with the phrase did not apply to all emigrants to Texas, but doubtless to an appreciable percent of them.

One needs but to examine the record of Judge Parker in the Territory of Oklahoma to comprehend the extent of its wildness. The Indian Territory of seventy-four thousand square miles had no general civil law whatever, and was a refuge for all types of criminals. Parker was judge of the first court of justice with jurisdiction over Oklahoma and the Indian Territory. The court was at Fort Smith, Arkansas; but it had jurisdiction over the Indian Territory. During his twenty-one years as judge of this court, he sentenced more murderers than any other American judge. He tried 13,500 cases; 9,500 of the accused were either convicted or pleaded guilty. Of these, 344 were convicted of crimes punishable by death, 174 of the convictions being for murder. He sentenced 172 to death, and 88 were hanged during his term of office.

In the Territory of California between 1848 and 1854 during the gold rush there were 42,000 murders; 1,600 killed by Indians en route to California across the plains; 5,300 perished by want and accident and killed by Indians in the Territory; 2,200 wrecked and lost at sea en route; 1,400 suicides; 1,700 became insane through hardships. No one will deny that the old West was wild!

The lawlessness of the newly formed West, frontier conditions, natural topography and plant life of the West, all encouraged the bad man to "Go West" to continue his depredations. From the Mississippi to the Rockies, the many miles of fenceless rolling plains with fine prairie grass four to six feet tall in places, the dense foliage of river bottoms and forests furnished a natural hideout for the bad man and have been described as the paradise of the desperado. The next-to-impassable mountain and canyon of lava flow and blinding alkali could and did hide whole herds of cattle and settlements of rustlers.

WHEN IN ROME, DO AS THE ROMANS!

Among rough associates in rough settlements the Western bad man probably felt little pang of conscience in his misdeeds. Judge Nathaniel P. Langford, who lived in the Territory of Idaho and whose experience qualified him to speak, writes in his memoirs, *Vigilante Days and Ways,* that in the Territory, until the vigilantes exterminated the vicious Henry Plummer gang, seventy-five per cent of the population were of the outlaw type. And as for the Western mining towns, too, Langford knew them well:

> This human hive, numbering at least ten thousand people, was a product of ninety days [Virginia City, Montana]. Into it crowded all the elements of a rough and active civilization. Thousands of cabins and tents and brush wakiups, thrown together in the roughest form, and scattered at random along the banks, and in the nooks of the hills, were seen on every hand . . . Gold was abundant, and every possible device was employed by the gamblers, the traders, the vile men and women that had come with the miners to the locality, to obtain it. Nearly every third cabin in the towns was a saloon where vile whiskey was peddled out for fifty cents a drink in gold dust. Many of these places were filled with gambling tables and gamblers, and the miner who was bold enough to enter one of them with his day's earnings in his pocket, seldom left until thoroughly fleeced. Hurdy-gurdy dance-houses were numerous, and there were plenty of camp beauties to patronize them. There too, the successful miner, lured by siren smiles, after an evening spent in dancing and carousing at his expense, steeped with liquor, would empty his purse into the lap of his charmer for an hour of license in her arms. Not a day or night passed which did not yield its full fruition of fights, quarrels, wounds, or murders. The crack of the revolver was often heard above the merry notes of the violin. Street fights were frequent, and as no one knew when or where they would occur, every one was on his guard against a random shot.

It was at another and similar Virginia City (Nevada) that Samuel Clemens, later to be known as the immortal Mark Twain, came with his brother, who was to be secretary to the provisional governor of the Territory of Nevada. Samuel himself became a reporter for the *Virginia City Enterprise*. According to him, one day his boss editor had to leave town hurriedly on unexpected business and left him in charge. He had to get out the paper all by himself practically. There were several pages to fill up and he was perplexed as to what to fill them up with. Somebody bought a new wagon and he wrote about two and a half columns about that. Someone else discovered a new silver lode and he wrote about a page concerning the new find. Finally, in exasperation, he wrote six or eight scorching editorials about the mayor, the preachers, the sheriff, and other public characters. At last the job was done and every inch of the paper was filled in!

Upon the editor's return, he was promptly faced with three libel suits, four threatening letters, and two duels. Naturally he fired Samuel Clemens, who went from there to San Francisco and from there to the Sandwich Islands (Hawaii) because of similar altercations.

At any rate the description of Virginia City might just as well be applied to Dodge City, Ellsworth, Hays City or Abilene, Kansas; Ogallala, Nebraska; Bannack or Lewiston, Idaho; Holbrook, Galeyville, or Tombstone, Arizona; Tascosa or Towash, Texas; or even Dawson, Alaska. These were either mining settlements or cow-town junctions or trail drives with railroads. Today they are quiet villages or do not even exist (Tascosa, Galeyville, and Towash have grown up in weeds), but back in the turbulent roarin' 70's men were shot down on their main streets!

It is small wonder that in the company with all this prodigal vice on the Western frontier and with the protection afforded by nature, the outlaw was strongly influenced to do wrong. The habitat of the West presented a powerful incentive to the outlaw to depredate.

VICTIMS OF CIRCUMSTANCES

Doubtless there were, and still are, many potential bad men spending a prosaic life at a desk or a plow. Had they been subjected to a similar environment, they might just as easily have been as notorious a character as Jesse James himself. When you look at that first little incident, or big one, that inflamed the bad man's anger and made him want to "get even" with somebody; and when you put yourself in his place, you can come nearer understanding his actions. As a matter of fact, very few bad men claimed they were bad men — nearly all of them said, "I was forced into this situation. I am a victim of circumstances. I am just an average man who's been treated wrong, and I'm not going to let anybody trample over me, my kin, or my rights!"

Jesse James, like many another bad man, was a product of the Civil War. I strongly suspect that you or I would have started off the same way that he did. He lived on a peaceful Missouri farm, caught in the ravishing clutches of the unofficial Civil War, between Quantrill's Missouri Border Guerrilla men and the Kansas Jayhawker 'Regulators.' The 'Regulators' found that Jesse's folks sympathized with the South so they ravished his home, whipped him, tried to hang his stepfather, and jailed his mother. Brother Frank had already run away to join Quantrill's border ruffians. It is not difficult to understand why Jesse left home and joined Quantrill's men. Many of us, under similar conditions, would likely have acted in the same way.

The trouble with Jesse and Frank was that after the Civil War they couldn't settle down; they had to go on and on "gettin' even." Few bad men knew when to stop. Even after they became hardened criminals, one can hardly blame the Jameses for wanting to "get even" with those "dirty, cowardly Pinkerton detectives" whom the "evil" railroads sent spying on their home. Why, the detectives even threw a bomb into the James home, killing Jesse's little seven-year-old half-brother, tearing his mother's arm off, and burning the home. And how did the railroads get their land for a right of way in the beginning? Why, they got it from innocent farmers frequently for a mere song and sometimes at the point of a gun! Of course, the James boys struck back at the Pinkertons and the railroads. You, too, would have wanted to use some method of "getting even" with these forces. In this respect, the James boys were not by themselves. Missouri farmers and ranchers for miles around had suffered from the same unscrupulous methods used by the railroads of that day. In fact, most of the people in half the state of Missouri and many of the people throughout the country sympathized with the Jameses. That's one reason why they were permitted to continue robbing trains successfully for nearly fifteen years without punishment. They had friends, a lot of them, who were willing to help them, hide them, and warn them. Of course, these conditions changed many years ago. The railroads changed their earlier methods and improved their services until they have become an indispensable part of our national life. We simply could not get along without them. The people, consequently, changed their attitude toward the railroads on the one hand and toward the outlaw on the other hand.

The average person today knows less about William Clarke Quantrill than about Jesse James, Sam Bass, or Billy the Kid; yet Quantrill was probably the worst all-time bad man this country will ever know. He organized and led a band of four-hundred and fifty cutthroat ruffians and Southern sympathizers, completely ransacking, burning, and pillaging the whole town of Lawrence, Kansas; and he lined up eighty Yankees at once and had them executed at a single command. He s a past-master instructor for men like Jesse and Frank James i. che art and science of outlawry. He must have been thoroughly evil — all through. Yet, though apparently naturally depraved, he was a peaceful school teacher before the Civil War. He continued peaceful even until the Jayhawkers of Kansas slew his older brother. From that time on, Quantrill became the blood-lusty personification of old Lucifer himself. He wrote his name in flaming red across the crime-stained history of this country inflicting more terror in Kansas, Missouri, and other central states than ever known before or since his time.

Polk Wells was a daring, fearless desperado robber whose exploits would cover volumes. He tells his own story in his autobiography, written while he was in an Ohio penitentiary. His sensitive feelings were hurt and his anger aroused by his cruel stepmother and older stepbrothers. "Ever since my first encounter with Joe [his stepbrother] I have always been ready — too ready, perhaps — to fight when there was a reasonable excuse for doing so." Polk's nature, like many another bad man's was essentially sensitive, and he carried around on his shoulder a chip which was easily unbalanced.

Lee Sage's father left his mother and married another. Lee never forgave his father. He ran away from home while a youth and later rebuked his father for being a cad. He said that the least thing may be the firecracker of a turbulent career. When he lost his horse, for example, he changed from Indian life to driving cattle to Mexico. "I was heartsick. I've often thought since if I hadn't lost Wolf [his horse] my whole life might have been changed. Sometimes the smallest thing in a man's life leads him another way. I didn't love nothing nor nobody, but my horse was part of me."

Tom Hill, a Tombstone bad man, ran away from home at the

tender age of twelve. Wild Bill Hickok did the same at fifteen. Hickok's father had died. Sam Bass' parents died and he quarreled with his cruel Uncle Dave Sheeks, from whom he departed to fight the world. Sam's education was very slim, but he could read just enough to get enthusiastic about a train robbery by the Reno brothers up north in Minnesota, and he lacked the restraining hand of his parents. Sam's real trouble probably started with his racing and betting on his Denton Mare, at Denton, Texas, where he lived for some time. He began betting on the mare and that created the desire for big money.

Two of the earliest American desperadoes were Micajah and Wiley Harpe. Micajah was heavy-set, about six feet, with black, short, curly, uncombed hair which flopped over his lowering forehead. Upon his full face were written gory, lustful, bloodthirsty, cold-blooded passions. He killed for convenience. Brother Wiley was not as large as Micajah, slight in weight, under six feet, straight-black haired. His face was scrawny, weazened, meager, downcast, and wolfish. The two wore drab cloth and dragged their hungry women and children through Kentucky, Tennessee, and Virginia from 1780 to 1800, begging food and killing their benefactors. After numerous escapes and incognitos, they were found and hanged. Said Wiley, according to Emerson Hough: "My parents had not much property, but they were intelligent people; and my father was an honest man, I expect, and tried to raise me honest, but I think none the better of him for that. My mother was of the pure grit; she learned me and all her children to steal as soon as we could walk and would hide for us whenever she could."

Billy the Kid blamed cruel treatment by his stepfather Antrim for his always wanting to "get even" with just anybody who trod upon his small toes. At the age of twelve, the Kid began his career of lawlessness. Most boys at that age or earlier have some "hero" whom they positively worship. He had one, a fine young man. The Kid's folks had just moved into a small Western town from back East. (He himself was born in New York City.) Some mashers had bothered his mother and his "hero," a perfect stranger, who stepped up and intervened in her behalf, thus dispersing the villains. Billy followed his "hero" around town admiring his every move. A drunk bumped into the "hero" and began fighting him, whereupon twelve-year-old Billy the Kid jumped astride the drunk and stabbed him to death. There were no ex-

11

tremes the Kid wouldn't go to for a real friend of his, and there were no extremes he wouldn't go to against his enemies! He ran home to his mother after the affray; she hid him for a time, but advised him to run away when some officers approached the place.

Thus, probably it was more frequently than not adverse home conditions that instigated the bad man's career. Many desperadoes lacked parental guidance through their impetuous youth.

AN EYE FOR AN EYE

One of the strongest human emotions is vengeance. Frequently the bad man's first criminal act was instigated by this motive. A friend of Billy the Kid's named George Coe swore vengeance against Sheriff Brady of Lincoln County, New Mexico, for cruel treatment at the time of his arrest upon a charge of which he was innocent. Sheriff Brady was a Murphy partisan in the Murphy-McSween feud and had just cooked up some excuse to jail Coe, who he knew was sympathetic with McSween. About this incident, Coe wrote in his memoirs, *Frontier Fighter*:

> I groaned with agony at the thought. They took horse hobbles and tied my feet together under the horse's belly (a common method of preventing escape). At the same time they bound Scurlock's feet in the same manner. Then, with bed-cord, they tied my hands together after circling my arms about Scurlock's waist. Talk about suffering! That was the most horrible three hours that anyone ever had to endure. I know, for I've been shot twice, had my leg broken in two places, and *could* say more, but that's enough. A slow, drizzling rain had begun to fall, making the night more hideous. The cords on my wrists tightened up as they wet through, adding to my misery — if that were possible. That ride was hell!

Coe swore to get revenge upon Sheriff Brady and his cohorts because of this treatment if it was the last thing he did. This ride was the chief thing that induced Coe actually to join up with Billy the Kid and fight the Murphy-Riley-Dolan faction of the Lincoln County War.

The Dalton brothers were an impetuous clan of outlaws whose daring and nerve were unquestioned in Oklahoma and Kansas. The very name of Dalton held people of the Midwest in awesome fear. Bob, Grat, and Emmett Daltons' first criminal movement came after they had been refused amounts due them as Osage policemen. They were especially bitter against organized law and legal injustice since their brother had been killed while serving as an officer. They were a hot tempered tribe and of a vengeful nature.

Many a bad man became so during the evil reconstruction era of the South after the Civil War, and no one will deny that conditions were such that would arouse indignation in the proud Southern gentleman during those turbulent times.

George Freeman was a friend of George Coe and an associate of Billy the Kid. His first offense was the killing of a newly freed Negro.

Bill Longley was probably the second worst bad man Texas has known — he was an "official nigger killer." He took delight in riding horseback into "holy-roly" Negro meetings dressed in a white hood with both his six-guns blazing, slaying a few blacks and laughing at the others diving for cover.

John Wesley Hardin was probably the *worst* bad man Texas has even known. He was reputed as having killed forty-three men in all. The Texas Rangers dubbed him the "World's Champion Desperado." He had a fiery temper and an itching finger. It is easy to understand (though not easy to justify) why he acted as he did when as a boy he was confronted by a big black, recently-freed, bully Negro threatening little "Wes" with a good "walloping." Little Wes went straight home and procured the family six-shooter and soon thereafter one less bully Negro existed in animate form, but from then on John Wesley Hardin was a wanted man.

The same happened to Doc Holliday, whose first offense was the slaying of a newly freed impudent Negro. Later, however, Doc's dentist practice died out and it was really gambling and drinking that led to his demise as a respectable citizen.

Little Al Jennings, probably the smallest bandit, weighing about 120 pounds and being barely over five feet tall, but at the same time one of the toughest hombres and nerviest bank and train robbers of old Oklahoma, became a bandit primarily to avenge his brother's death and the loss of his own attorneyship. The objects of Jennings' personal retaliation were some men whom he blamed for his own misfortunes. He tells his own story in *Beating Back*, of how he accomplished his retaliation.

So strong is the motive of vengeance for injury to one's own self that Clay Allison, a bad man of the Washita country in New Mexico, beaten by three men and left for dead, spent six months tracing them all over the entire Western part of the United States, finally killing them all. There never was another Clay Allison, nor will there ever be. He was a man among men, and he had a most unusual sense of humor.

Still others gave various reasons for their wrong doings. George Ives was considered honest until the temptation to steal government mules in his charge at Walla Walla, Washington, presented itself. Bob Zachary gave drinking, card playing, and bad company as the causes of his own downfall. Langford Peel gave ingratitude of the people he had befriended and helped when in need as his primary motive for desperadoism. Joseph A. Slade is said by many to have been a good man until his employment by the Overland Stage Company, when he felt it his duty to gain a reputation for fierceness. Many small Western townships or stage companies would hire the man in the vicinity with the toughest reputation as their sheriff or shotgun messenger or station keeper in order to instill fear into lesser desperadoes and thereby prevent robberies of their valuable property. Joseph A. Slade was one of the most feared men in the West. He really ran his stagecoach station and there were no attempts at robbery while he was on hand.

Such are many of the varied reasons for the first misdeeds of the bad man, and it usually happened in his youth. His first serious mistake was all too often condoned by even the best people of the community. Unfortunately, this eventually led to other misdeeds until finally society turned against him and refused to accept his gestures at reformation. Then, he couldn't quit. The important lesson to youth is that, regardless of how seemingly justified it may be, one should *never make the first mistake.*

GET RICH QUICK

It was true that a hard-working Western pioneer could make a living, but really big and easy money was seldom to be had. By hard labor and thrifty habits, a Charles Goodnight might become extremely wealthy, or by continuous perserverance and a piece of good luck an Ed Schieffelin might locate a silver mine and become immensely wealthy. But there were relatively few men at that time like these.

Few honest men of the Old West had the business ability

and the stamina and courage to drive herds upon herds upon herds of cattle over the old Chisholm trail, first blazed by the half-breed Indian Jesse Chisholm; and few had sense enough to keep their money instead of getting drunk at Dodge City after a long trail drive and gambling away their earnings or profits or "giving" it to some fair Cyprian. But Charles Goodnight was just such a person. He made money and kept it to reinvest it wisely. He became immensely wealthy.

Few miners were lucky enough to find a lode of silver such as did Ed Schieffelin. His friends had told him if he didn't clear out of that God forsaken corner of Arizona, the Apaches would scalp him and his "mine" would be his tombstone. He pshawed them away and said when he found his mine he would take their advice and name it "The Tombstone." He found the silver, lay low from the Indians, established his claim, and pretty soon the news spread and a settlement sprang up. They named it "Tombstone" after his mine and Schieffelin became a wealthy man. But there were very few Charley Goodnights or Ed Schieffelins.

Of course, anybody who knew how could hunt buffalo and make money, but it took somewhat of an expert to make the profession pay. Wild Bill Hickok once remarked to U. S. Marshal Wyatt Earp that he expected to make $5,000 in eight months hunting buffalo. Uncle Billy Tilghman, who was a veteran peace officer in Oklahoma during its wild days (he was killed in action at the age of seventy-five by a drunken prohibitionist after serving as officer for five decades), established the record with 3,300 buffalo hides between September 1 of one year and April 1 of the next. These hides brought from $1.25 to $5.00 apiece. However, the profits of this peculiar profession were offset by the danger of Indians on the warpath because of the extermination of their food supply, the buffalo. Furthermore, the profession itself was short-lived as the millions of these prairie-roaming animals lasted only twenty-five years of this wholesale slaughter.

The farmers of the Southwest made little. His biographer, Wayne Gard, says that Sam Bass was once talking to two of his boys, Frank Jackson and Jim Murphy, "What do you reckon that old farmer would have said if I had told him I was Sam Bass and had showed him a few twenties? I'll bet I could have broken his eyes off with a board. I'll bet he hasn't had twenty dollars this year. That's the way with most of these old farmers;

they never have any money. I never expect to work any more, unless it is before a shotgun or something like that."

Frequently no work at all was available to the cowhand. Lee Sage tells us, "I found no sale for honest elbow grease. So I and my big lazy pal drifted into cattle rustling."

The cowboy got on an average from $30 to $50 per month, the stage driver $62.50 or thereabouts, the shotgun messenger $150, the ordinary ranger only $50 and never much over $100, the Mexican and Indian interpreter for Army forts $75 to $100, a deputy or marshal about $100 to $150 — only these small amounts for being a target and fighting desperate men in a hazardous country.

These amounts seem almost nothing in comparison with the $169,500 the Dalton brothers robbed from banks, express offices, and trains at Pawnee, Gordon, Cimarron, Southwest City, Derby, Spearville, and Woodward. Compare these salaries with the loot of $10,000 taken by Burt Alvord, Bob Downing, and Billy Stiles from a train in Cochise County, Arizona. Jesse and Frank James and their cousins, the three Younger brothers, got $2,000 apiece at just one robbery at Oterville. Sam Bass' gang took $60,000 in $20 gold pieces of '77 mintage from a Union Pacific robbery at Big Springs, Nebraska. There were probably quite a few of the many hard-working cowboys on the Western range, making only $30 a month, who thought it would be mighty nice to make a big haul like the Jameses or the Daltons; and the thought might have become a real temptation to a still fewer number of these cowboys. We treat here only of the motive, the desire to get-rich-quick — and not of the justification of either the motive or the act.

Besides, robbing a train or a bank was said to be easy. The James boys said that the people being robbed were so scared that they acted like trained seals. Little Al Jennings, who could stir up more dust than Noah's flood could settle in forty days, also commented on the ease of train robbing (taken from his memoirs, *Beating Back*):

> People were so dazed that they acted like trained dogs. Really, robbing a train is easy. The element of surprise favors the robbers. The hard and dangerous part comes afterward, when the trainmen start up the marshals and vigilantes, and the whole country seems roused against you.

Judge N. P. Langford of the Territories of Idaho and Montana knew the Henry Plummer gang well, through personal contact. He had even been threatened by them, and he knew how they worked, especially how they robbed stagecoaches (from *Vigilante Days and Ways*):

> Several of the most daring exploits occurred on the route between Virginia City and Bannack, a region admirably adapted to their purposes. Its frequent streams, canyons, mountain passes, rocky ledges, willow thickets, and deep embosomed valleys, afforded ample means of concealment, and advantages for attack upon passing trains, with very few chances for defense or escape. The robbers had their established points of rendezvous on the road, and worked in concert by a system of horseback telegraphy, as unfailing as electricity . . . Whenever it was known that a person with money was about to leave by coach, a private mark was made upon the vehicle . . .

Too often it was not until the bandit had committed several robberies and had aroused suspicion or indignation that he encountered great difficulties. It was not until the James-Younger gang had made ten or twelve successful major robberies over a period of about fifteen years that they finally met their Waterloo at Northfield, Minnesota. It was not until the Daltons had already made at least four such robberies looting $169,500 altogether that they were nearly all killed at Coffeyville, Kansas. After a seeming laxity for some time, Texas finally demanded that her Rangers gather as a reception committee for Sam Bass and his gang at the quiet little village of Round Rock.

BRAND BURNING

Nor was it, in the early days of the open range, difficult to rustle cattle. A slight disturbance would stampede a herd; a gunshot and a whoop would scatter them pell-mell and enable the rustlers to drive off part of the herd. Buyers could be found who were eager to pay half price for stolen cattle without asking any questions. Brand burning, or changing brands, was not unusual. A *V* brand, for example, could be changed into a diamond, or a heart, or a *P* to an *R,* or an *O* to a *Q,* or an *I* into a *P. R. T,* or *B.*

Conditions on the frontier, then, made the commission of crime relatively easy, provided the outlaw had a swift, powerful, enduring horse. Such horses were readily procurable through theft, and when the outlaw "lamped a good horse, he had it, if it did cost a man or two," according to Lee Sage. A horse corral, usually quite flimsy, was easily emptied in the dark of the night, frequently without detection. A good horse was indeed a coveted thing of value. Emmett Dalton told how he felt about his horse in his record *When the Daltons Rode*:

> The outlaw's horse was favored among its kind when it came to good treatment and conserving attentions. Man and animal composed a Centaur. Almost literally the outlaw's mount was his legs, swift to strike, swift to retreat, dependable in the long runs. Unusual care was lavished upon him; if from no sentimental reason, certainly for safety. He was, fed before the man ate. His feet were zealously shod. He suffered no saddle sores, and the slightest ailment was immediately doctored. After the first hard run from a raid the animal's strength was conserved. One lived close beside his horse, night and day. Quite naturally a bond grew between the two. I used to talk to Ginger and to the sorrel as if they were human members of our band.

In robbing, the bad man of the West had very little difficulty until the after-effects set in, but the bad man was probably concerned with the present more than the future.

CUT THEM CARDS, MISTER!

Gambling at monte, faro, seven-up, or a horse race or foot race brought easy money and often quick death to the Western bad man. The cardshark or crooked gambler sooner or later met a grim man who wouldn't be cheated nor bluffed out of his money. Nearly everyone gambled — officers, outlaws, and respected citizens included. Frequently when a sleight-of-hand expert shifted a card, the fireworks started. Many a bad man began his career at the monte table. The Gardner-Biby war in Texas was started because of a horse race. John Wesley Hardin, himself badly shot, tried to kill Phil Sublett of Trinity, Texas, over a bowling-contest stake of fifty dollars. His biographer and pal, Buck Walton, quoted bad man Ben Thompson:

> Fatal difficulties arise from cause and no cause; men are killed in their own difficulties and in those of others. I have a son and I had rather follow him to the grave than see him con-

tract the habit of gambling. Yet I continue in that line of life; but so help me God, I never have and never will countenance and assist, encourage or influence any boy, youth, or man to engage in the hell-earning business, which I will probably follow until I am dead. . . .

[In gambling] my life was of never so much value to me that fear of losing it would deter me from maintaining my rights.

DEAD OR ALIVE!

Big money, though sometimes not easy, could be made by the bad man through rewards. It is asserted that Tom Horn was offered $600 and "Buckshot" Roberts $100 a head for dead rustlers, the source of the money being probably big cattlemen of a belligerent cattle faction in a feud. Also certain early cattle kings of Texas, disgruntled at their treatment by Marshal Wyatt Earp of Dodge, offered as much as $1,000 for a dead Wyatt Earp. It is not unusual that men of all shades of character would jump at the chance of collecting a reward of $12,000 for a Chacon or $10,000 for a Jesse James. In fact, so many of them did that the desperadoes in question grew beards and became lost in the crowd and confusion. It is said that Jesse James became distrustful of his best friends. That he might well have been was later evident, because Bob Ford, a distant relative of his, shot him in the back while he was hanging a picture in his own home — for no other reason than to get the $10,000 reward, of which he collected only about $100, the rest supposedly going to crooked politicians.

Sam Bass said, " I have gone back on everybody." He knew even his pal, Jim Murphy, had bargained with the Texas Rangers information about him, or at least suspected as much.

A friend of Bill Longley once "captured" Bill, collected a fee of $1,500, and then threw down on the jailer to let Bill escape. They later divided the booty. Thus Bill collected his own reward.

Ike Stockton collected $2,000 for turning his outlaw compatriot over to officers — a distinct violation of the outlaw code. The brother of an outlaw compatriot, upon finding out about the trick Ike had played, looked Ike up and shot him dead.

Easy money came easy and went fast with the bad man. In the long run he paid for it, usually with his own red blood.

DAMN YANK AND JOHNNY REB

In some cases the bad man's actions were due to his loyalty to a group. Some of the groups in conflict were

North vs. South
Republicans vs. Democrats
Unionists vs. secessionists
Texas cowboys vs. Northern Kansas marshals
Rebels vs. Yankees, carpetbaggers, and reconstruction Negroes
Kansas jayhawkers vs. Missouri border guerrillas.

Although the intensity of their hatred is revealed only by close study of the feuds and fights they made, it is apparent why these six sets of factions mutually warred. They were outgrowths or hangovers of the Civil War.

So strong was Cole Younger's (Jesse James' cousin) sentiment for the South that, while robbing an Arkansas stage, he returned a man's possessions upon learning he was a fellow ex-Confederate.

One of the most classic examples of duels fought because of political differences was that between Sheriff Pinkham of Boise City (Idaho) and Ferd Patterson. Pinkham was an ardent Republican and Unionist; whereas Patterson, having been reared among the bloody men of the border state of Tennessee and having lived in secessionist Texas, was a hot-headed sympathizer with the Southern cause. Patterson had already killed a Captain Staples in Portland, Oregon, over a political scrape. The Captain was an ardent Unionist who demanded that everyone drink a toast to Lincoln and the Union's Arms. Patterson alone refused. Later the same evening the two met and exchanged profanities and six-gun slugs. Staples came out second in the affray. Patterson was acquitted in the subsequent trial on the plea of self-defense.

Patterson was ordinarily a soft-spoken, courteous pacifist, except when in his cups; and then he became a raving, bloodthirsty demon, remembering every insult he ever received and taking it out on the nearest insulter. He and other drunks took over a brewery one day and unionist Sheriff Pinkham arrested them. Everyone expected Patterson to kill him either right then or at least later, but he kept his peace by just biding his time and remembering the insult. Sheriff Pinkham and Patterson had Unionist and Secessionist followers respectively. Their followers urged each one to combat the other, that they would back their leader up. Finally it happened. In a saloon Patterson had become well oiled in some powerful tarantula juice when he heard Pinkham and his friends singing away on a refrain from

John Brown, "We'll hang Jeff Davis on a sour apple tree!" Pinkham was also well in his cups. Patterson stepped from a saloon upon its porch, and turning to his right, stood face to face with Pinkham. The deepening scowl of the antagonist met the fearful glare of the opponent's bloody eyes. Patterson hurled a degrading epithet at Pinkham, "Draw, will you?"

"Yes," Pinkham retaliated with a curse, "I will." He then drew his revolver and was just cocking it and drawing a bead when Patterson with the rapidity of lightning drew his own six-gun, cocking it in the act and firing as he raised it. The bullet found Pinkham's shoulder blade; and, receiving a severe nervous wound, the sheriff fired too soon and his bullet missed Patterson. Patterson's second cap failed to fire, but before the wounded sheriff could recock his pistol, Patterson had shot him again, this time near the heart. Pinkham reeled down the porch steps and fell on his face, a dead man.

Naturally Pinkham's Unionist friends demanded Patterson's conviction and execution. Another sheriff by the name of Robbins arrested Patterson and kept him in custody. For several days afterward everybody in Boise City feared a small Civil War. About seven hundred Unionists met out of town and planned a vigilante hanging bee for Patterson, but Robbins got busy and appointed about two hundred Secessionists as deputies to guard the prisoner. Robbins handled the situation nicely by appeasement to both parties and a "fair" trial was held, in which Patterson was acquitted.

However, very soon afterwards Patterson, just as he arose from a barber chair, confronted one Donahue, a friend of Pinkham's and a Unionist, who gave him some of his own medicine, shooting him two or three times before he reached his own gun; and that was the end of Patterson.

RIGHT MAKES MIGHT

Other groups mutually warring in the Old West were

Vigilantes vs. rustlers and robbers
Vigilance Committee of San Francisco vs. The Hounds and Sidney Coves.

In newly-formed San Francisco the Hounds and Sidney Coves were a group of professional cutthroats, organized criminals; and

21

they literally ruled the roost. Men, women, and children lived in constant dread and fear of them, until a large group of fearless respectable citizens organized the Vigilance Committee of San Francisco. In a vigilance committee, ordinary men became much braver than when they were on a jury of twelve. In a vigilance committee, they were among the pack; the pack was the individual, and the member became a nonentity. A member could yell out, "Hang the murderer!" or "Pipe down, you thief, no back talk!" without being detected or without fear of consequence. On a jury of twelve men, the individual was often afraid to render a conviction for fear the victim's friends would waylay him.

REMEMBER THE ALAMO

Still other groups to which the bad man owed allegiance were

Texans vs. Mexicans
Palefaces vs. Indians
Cattlemen vs. sheepmen
Bullwhackers vs. cowboys
Miners vs. buffalo hunters
Cattle barons vs. squatters
Keelboaters vs. flatboaters on the Mississippi.

The Texas gringos hated the 'greasers' ever since Goliad, Alamo, San Jacinto, and the Mier Expedition. What little Texan hasn't been told of the drawing of the black beans by the unfortunate members of the Mier Expedition? What Texan to this very day doesn't thrill to the battle cry, "Remember the Alamo!"

But there are few Texans who have read Robert Hancock Hunter's first-hand account of the battle of San Jacinto. Here is the story of that eventful day as told by a man who was actually there:

The next day which was the 21 [of April, 1836], [Mexican] General Coss, past on down threw Harrisburg, & Major McNutt gave orders not to fire a gun, but be quiet. One of the boys below camp a peace fired a cros at them, and coses men fired at us & wounded one of our men in the ancle, & they set fire to the town & burned down the steam mill. Coss went down to crost the bridge 2 or 3 hours befor it was burnt. Santa Anna had come up from New Washington & camp on the rige. When Coss got in to Sant Annas Camp, a bout 3 o'clock in the evening, we hered a cannon fire, & a nother & a nother. Three fired in [succession], & stopt, about 2 minutes a nother fired, & the little twin sisters commenced . . .

Between sun down & dark, a currer come up & brought the word, & by times in the morning we were under way for the Battle ground a bout 8 miles distant. We got thear a bout 11 o'clock. We went out to the Battle ground & looked at the ded Mexicans, where there cannon stud. For a bout 12 or 15 feet the Mexicans lay 3 or 4 deck. They did [not] git to fire there cannon but 3 times. Our men shot them down as fast as they could git to the gun. Our men took there gun loded, turned it on them & shot them with there own gun & they give up. General Houston gave orders not to kill [any] more but to take prisners, Capt. Easlen said Boys take prisners, you know how to take prisners, take them with the but of your guns, club guns, & said remember the Alamo remember Laberde [Goliad], and club guns, right & left & nocked there brains out. The Mexicans would fall down on there knees, & say me no Alamo me no Laberde [Goliad]. There was a mudy laggune a bout 4 or 5 hundred yeards south of the Battle field a bout 15 or 20 yeards wide, & the Mexicans broke. They run for that laggune & man & horse went in head and years to the bottom, a bout 18 feet boly [boggy] mud. It was said that Sant Anna money chest was throwed in there, & a parsel of us boys went and cut out some poles 6 or 7 feet long, probed down to finde the money & we could not finde bottom, & got some poles 10 or 12 feet long. We could feal the ded horses, & expect men, but no bottom, & we gave it up. That laggune was full of men & horses for a bout 20 or 30 feet up and down it, & non of them ever got out. I think there bones are laying there yet.

Such phrases as "Remember the Alamo" and "Mexicans don't count" (especially the latter) are forgotten in our present "good neighbor policy" toward Latin America.

THE TEWKSBURYS ARE DRIVING SHEEP OVER THE
RIM OF THE MOGOLLONS!

The cattlemen said that their cattle could not and would not eat grass after sheep had munched it to the roots; hence, the cattleman's animosity for the sheepherder. Witness the worst feud Arizona has ever known. It raged out below the Mogollon foothills under the Tonto Rim of bloody old Arizona. It was the sheepmen Tewksburys vs. the cattlemen Grahams. Zane Grey based his novel *To the Last Man* on this feud and Earle Forrest's book *The Dark and Bloody Ground of Arizona* tells all about it. "The last man" actually was Jim Roberts, a deputy and partisan of the Tewksburys. He was the last man to emerge alive on either side of the vendetta. Edwin Tewksbury, a half-breed Scotch-Indian, was the last man of either the Grahams or Tewksburys to come out in one piece from either side. The story of his life makes our horse-opera movies seem insipidly tame. All told, there were seventeen known persons killed, seven unknown, three lynched. The cattlemen had little love for the sheepmen.

FREAK WAR

Very unusual, almost freakish, disputatious groups of the old West were rival newspapers, railroads, business establishments, and even whole townships. Warring newspapers were exemplified by the Tombstone (Arizona) *Epitaph* and *Nugget*, with the *Epitaph* supporting the United States Marshals, the Earp brothers, and their "law and order party" versus the *Nugget* supporting Johnny Behan and Billy Breakenridge, county officers, and the outlaw element under the Clantons, John Ringo, and Curly Bill Brocius. Sententious editorial epithets were mutually hurled from one paper to the other.

Ben Thompson and ten other "good Texans" received $20,-000 for changing from the Santa Fé Railroad to the Denver and Rio Grande Railroad side in a feud between the two railroads. Naturally, Ben denied the receipt, but he was broke and downcast before the event and bloated afterward. Ben Thompson was that one-man wave of destruction from down Austin, Texas, way. Austinites actually made him city marshal one time because of his toughness. They actually hailed him as a conquering hero and favorite son upon his return from San Antonio where he had just slain a San Antonio bad man. Obviously his lurid career brought him employment by the railroads to frighten the other side of the feud.

Business rivalry between McSween's and Murphy's general stores enhanced the Lincoln County (New Mexico) war. Another bit of business entering into this feud was that pertaining to the Fritz insurance policy disputed between the two factions. And here is precisely where Billy the Kid became immortal in the annals of this country's flaming outlawry. He was the leader of the McSween faction.

Most singular in the annals of American feuds was the Stevens County (Kansas) vendetta between Hugoton and Woodsdale, two whole townships at war. Bloody battles were fought between citizens of these communities between 1886-1887. Ed Short, representing Woodsdale and known as a killer, was thought a fit man to go after bad man Robinson of Hugoton. Both were official town marshals. The legalities concerning this feud were so intricate that when investigations were made by Federal authorities, it became impossible to convict anyone on either side — a most atrocious miscarriage of justice. Collecting witnesses alone for a trial cost the U. S. Government over one-hundred-thousand dollars. It was long and bitterly fought, resulting in absolute failure of the ends of justice. Not one of the murderers of either side has ever been punished. Eventually the two towns were abandoned, the county disorganized by the legislature, population decimated, farms abandoned or sold, and anarchy gave back its own to the wilderness.

In some cases, especially where the participant was a hired fighter, the bad man was impersonal and mercenary in his allegiance to these groups; in others his connection to his party was either sentimental or necessary. George Coe actually found it safer to side in with Billy the Kid and the McSween faction in the Lincoln County war than to remain a neutral and be suspected by both sides of being a sympathizer with or even a spy for the other side.

MY BUDDY!

We beat our drums slowly and played the fife lowly,
And bitterly wept as we bore him along;
For we all loved our comrade, so brave, young, and handsome
We all loved our comrade although he'd done wrong.
                                        — From Cowboy Lore.

Diminutive bandit Al Jennings (in *Beating Back*) once said, "To desert a friend, to go back on an ally, was the blackest sin of the outlaw's decalogue."

Indeed, this was one of the vital parts of the unwritten code of outlawry. Probably the greatest majority of outlaws were faithful to their friends and would not have revealed their identities or crimes to anyone for anything. One of the strongest motives stirring the bad man into action was loyalty to a friend or relative —

25

the feeling of duty to aid him or to avenge his mistreatment at the hands of an enemy.

The supreme test of loyalty to brother was met by the three Younger brothers (Jesse James' cousins) at Northfield, Minnesota. They had tried to rob a bank there but were completely surprised by an impromptu reception of usually docile citizens. A young college student, home during a holiday, noticed the gang and aroused the merchants up and down the street. They all quietly armed themselves and waited for the Jameses and Youngers to emerge from the bank, when they let the bandits have it. After being hunted extensively, the Younger brothers stuck by each other until all three, Cole, Jim, and Bob, were shot down and captured, while Jesse and Frank made a phenomenal escape. They broke through a heavy line of fire; and after riding breakneck closely pursued through dense woods, they dived from a high cliff into a lake and hid under some thick foliage until it was safe to venture forth. Although wounded, they quietly walked along country lanes, picked up a stray horse here and there, and when questioned by farmers, they would ask "Have you seen anything of the James boys? We're scouts for the posse after them."

This escapade ended the James gang; it was their Waterloo. After fifteen years of successful looting of banks, stages, and trains, they were at last finished. Frank went to California as a Mr. Woodson; and Jesse to Tennessee, posing as a Mr. Howard. They robbed no more.

The supreme test of loyalty to brother was also met by the Dalton brothers at Coffeyville. Two of them might have escaped after their bank-robbing enterprise failed, but they went back to help their fellows who had been mortally wounded. Later, after four bandits and four citizens were dead or dying, twenty-year-old Emmett Dalton, already wounded, turned his horse back from complete safety and rode through a hail of bullets to attempt to rescue his brother Grat. In so doing, he was himself severely wounded by one of the bullets showering around him and was captured. He subsequently spent several years in a penitentiary. He lived, however, to become a decent citizen, married, and wrote his memoirs in the book, *When the Daltons Rode,* which has been made into a movie. In fact, he appeared not long ago on the radio program, "We, the People."

There were some bad men who attached themselves as bodyguards to a close friend. Charley Duchet stuck with Tom Graham throughout the Pleasant Valley Feud (between the Graham cattle faction and the Tewksbury sheepmen). Likewise Doc Holliday, bad man that he was, attached himself to Marshal Wyatt Earp, following him from Dodge to Tombstone and saving his life a number of times. The Texas cowboys had little use for U. S. Marshal Wyatt Earp, who was Yankee in sentiment and who wouldn't let the cowboys "cut up" in Dodge after their long trail drives. Earp would make the Texans park their irons before going on sprees. Naturally they didn't like the idea since their six-shooters were part of their language and helped them relieve their ecstatic spirits when under the influence of old Bacchus. Wyatt Earp said he would never forget the first time he ever saw Doc Holliday. He walked straight into a saloon, looked up, and saw about twenty drunk cowboys with pistols drawn — pointing right at him — Wyatt really thought that was his end. He began to say his prayers to himself when from a distant corner a nervous, rasping voice commanded the cowboys, "Drop your guns or I'll fill your belly so full of hot lead you'll think you've swallowed a volcano."

The doc supplemented this admonition with quite a few opprobious diatribes apropos of the occasion, and when it came down to pure ornamental cussing, Doc was probably gifted above all other sons of men.

Instantly the pistols dropped and Earp's two Buntline specials were out like a whip and the disgruntled cowboys dispersed. From then on, Doc Holliday was Earp's pal.

Billy the Kid became strongly concerned with the welfare of his ranch boss Tunstall. Tunstall and the Kid's mother were two of the very few people who ever treated the Kid with human kindness. He would have jumped into a fire for his boss. Tunstall was friendly with McSween, and McSween was Murphy's business enemy. Murphy dispatched about a dozen ruffians to murder Tunstall because he was interfering with his plans. They caught him alone riding horseback from his ranch to town and brutally beat him up, literally stomped him to death. Billy the Kid was the first to discover the body. He swore right then and there to get vengeance on each and every foul murderer of his beloved and kind employer. He found out who they were and one by one picked them off. Like George Coe, the Kid had also suffered at the hands of Sheriff Brady, who was a Murphy partisan. He bet Coe his pistol against five cents that he would get even with the

Sheriff before Coe did. He won the bet. He shot the Sheriff clean through the heart.✓

At bloody Tombstone Billy Claiborne, the same that fled from the O. K. Corral when the U. S. Marshal Earp brothers and Doc Holliday made it too hot for him, swore vengeance for the death of his fellow rustler John Ringo, one of the leaders of the Cochise County rustlers. Billy supposed Ringo's death was caused by Buckskin Frank Leslie. Actually, Ringo committed suicide. He was found barefooted, sun-baked, and blistered — miles from any house or springs, his body resting against the trunk of a tree. His pistol was still in his hand. He had fired it through his head and splattered his brains all over the tree trunk. His horse was found several miles away. It was generally accepted that he died by his own hand. He was of a sullen, morose disposition, a pessimist. He probably stopped on a prairie and his horse wandered away. He must have walked until blisters came on his feet and he became crazed from heat and thirst, deciding to end it all. He was heard several times to say he would probably end up that way, that he feared no man — that someone might save himself the trouble of ending Johnny Ringo.

But Billy Claiborne was strongly attached to John Ringo and it was rumored that Leslie had been at odds with Ringo for some time and that Buckskin Frank had killed him. Little Billy voiced his opinion and it got around to Buckskin that Billy was gunning for him. So Buckskin, who was at the time tending bar in his establishment, calmly laid down his cigar, loaded his pistol and struck out for Billy. He knew it was simply a question of killing or being killed. He knew further he could plead "self defense" since Billy had threatened him, and he had witnesses who would testify as much. Buckskin Frank found Billy Claiborne walking in the opposite direction with his back to Buckskin. He observed the code of the West. It is said that even a rattlesnake warns before it strikes. He called out pleasantly, "Hello, Billy!"

Billy turned, recognized his assailant, started for the draw, but expert pistoleer Buckskin Frank had the edge on him. He shot Billy just once, went back for his cigar and then to the sheriff's office, and gave his still hot gun over to the officer, saying, "Be careful, this thing's still loaded."

Naturally, he was acquitted, since the opponents were both armed, the killer had been threatened, he had given a warning — a fighting chance, the two had "met" face to face in broad daylight. It was a "killing" and not a "murder."

Strange indeed was the bond of affection between the Cochise County (Arizona) rustlers and deputies Breakenridge and Behan. Several times John Ringo appeared in court to relieve embarrassment of these deputies, and Curly Bill even aided them in collecting taxes. In fact, they were the first taxes of any large amount ever collected in Cochise County, and there is little doubt that anyone would refuse to pay Curly Bill.

Although Sam Bass was pumped severely by the Texas Rangers to reveal the identity of his comrades while on his deathbed, he remained true to his friends. He would not tell them who they were nor what they had done. The Rangers thought more of Sam for that. Like many another bad man, Sam would have done anything for a real friend.

STOOL PIGEONS

However, not all outlaws were entirely loyal to their comrades. Harry Tracy and his friend Merrill, a couple of twentieth-century desperadoes on the West coast, escaped from the penitentiary in Washington State not many years ago, but when Tracy found Merrill of no further use to himself, he killed him.

Tracy then played the fox that eluded the bloodhounds for nearly a year, barely escaping trap after trap set by dozens of sheriffs. He obtained his food and clothing from farm houses, posing as a beggar. His career ended at Creston, in Lincoln County, Washington. He had spent the night at farmer L. B. Eddy's house. A posse of about seven men surrounded Tracy, who broke desperately through the barn to a large boulder, shooting twice on the run. He made for a wheat field but stumbled when a posseman's bullet hit him. As the posse reached the outlaw, they heard a single shot and then silence that screamed. They found the body of Harry Tracy, who had committed suicide rather than surrender with the odds to hang.

Likewise, Ben Cravens of Oklahoma induced a young outlaw named Welty to undertake a robbing expedition, but once their task was completed, Cravens, having no further use for Welty, shot him full in the face and left him for dead. Strangely enough, Welty lived to see Cravens put in jail.

The first principle in the code of the outlaw was explained by Emmett Dalton, the youngest and sole survivor of the Dalton brothers (from *When the Daltons Rode*):

29

His [the outlaw's] code is one of survival morals . . . One of these basic taboos is not to give the other fellow away; to protect a comrade even at cost of death. For the squealer becomes the worst enemy of his associates, and retaliation is apt to be very swift and final.

But there were thieves without honor. They would sell out a friend's liberty to gain their own. There were a few bad men who bartered with officers information about their fellow bad men for their own personal liberty or immunity from prosecution by law. Among them was Ike Stockton, who collected a $2,000 reward for turning his outlaw compatriot over to officers. The outlaw's brother got immediate revenge on Ike. He shot him dead. Likewise, one outlaw named Dillingham and another named Red Yager betrayed the rest of Plummer's gang to a vigilance committee in Montana.

If it hadn't been for Jim Murphy, the Texas Rangers might never have intercepted Sam Bass. He sent a telegram to Austin to the Rangers with whom he had previously bargained to be stool pigeon on Sam. Bass strongly suspected Jim of being a double-crosser and threatened to kill Jim himself, but Frank Jackson, another member of the gang, intervened. Jim telegraphed the Rangers, "For God's sakes, meet us at Round Rock." Obviously he was getting desperate. After hard riding and much ado, the Rangers did get there and woe it was to Sam and his gang. Jim kept in the background when the fireworks began, heaving a sigh of relief.

Three Rangers, Connor, Harrell, and Ware, were there as a reception committee for Bass, Jackson, and Barnes. Sheriff Grimes of Round Rock went up to the three outlaws who were in a store buying tobacco and was going to arrest them for carrying guns, not knowing their identity. He felt of Bass' clothes and asked him, "That's a gun, isn't it?"

Whereupon the three bandits whirled and shot Grimes about six times. Another sheriff, Moore, came running and entered the store blazing away through the thickening smoke. He shot Bass' long and ring fingers off his pistol hand, and at the same time received one shot in his lung. The outlaws retreated through the door only to meet the three Rangers on the run. Sam Bass was fatally wounded by several bullets; Ranger Dick Ware took deliberate aim and shot Seaborne Barnes through the head. Outlaw Jackson coolly took Barnes' ammunition belt, helped

Bass on his horse, and rode out of town in a hurry, shouting to a little girl swinging on her front gate to get back in the house. Jackson escaped and showed up years later in Arizona as a Mr. Downing. Bass died at a farmhouse near Round Rock. Jim Murphy, the squealer, looked on the shooting sheepishly from a safe distance.

What happened to Jim later is interesting: he died an accidental death — one of the two or three bad men encountered in this entire investigation (including about two hundred and fifty) to die accidentally. Some deadly poisonous eye medicine trickled down his face to his lips.

The Dunn brothers bartered with Marshal Frank Canton information about the Dalton brothers. Ike Clanton gave information to Wyatt Earp concerning Cochise County (Arizona) rustlers. Billy Stiles was a past-master double-crosser. Through him and Burt Alvord, Arizona Ranger Captain Burton Mossman finally captured the Mexican desperado Augustine Chacon, one of the two or three most colorful bad Mexicans of all time.

These squealers were usually killed by outlaws through vengeance. They usually double-crossed their friends to escape jail or enjoy freedom from prosecution by law.

THEY WON'T TAKE ME ALIVE!

The desire to escape capture is one of the strongest motives of the bad man. Frequently an outlaw would not kill or murder anyone until he felt it necessary to prevent being taken by police, for in many cases he knew this meant death on the scaffold. It is doubtful whether Sam Bass, the Daltons, the Jameses, or the Youngers ever killed a man until at bay; certainly they did not murder for the sake of bloodshed. It was this kind of outlaw that found a sympathetic public, not the cold-blooded murderer.

Many a desperado swore never to surrender his guns to anyone. According to Wayne Gard, Sam Bass once said, "I never expect to give up to nobody."

The bad man preferred being a target with a small chance for freedom than surrendering with the odds to hang.

Sometimes the bad man killed to prevent witnesses from testifying against him at trial. According to U. S. Deputy Marshal Fred Sutton (in *Hands Up!*), Prairie Dog Dave once said to a man whose horse he had stolen, "Do you still accuse me of stealing your horse?"

"Yes, I do, and unless you pay for it I am going to have the law on you," was the man's reply.

Prairie Dog, for that was his only known name, thereupon killed the man; and, in order that there would be no accusing witnesses, he killed the other three men listening to the conversation and left the four lying in the road where it took place.

Judge Langford of the Territory of Idaho and Montana told about methods used by the vicious Henry Plummer's gang (*Vigilante Days and Ways*):

> Insensible to all appeals for mercy, and ever acting upon the cautious maxim that 'dead men tell no tales,' the only chance for escape from death for those whom they assaulted was in their utter inability to do them injury. Human life regarded as an obstacle to their designs, was of no more importance than the blowing up of a safe, or any other act which stood between them and their prey.

DISHONORABLE DISCHARGE

Once jailed and told of his death sentence, the bad man was willing to resort to the more brutal means of escaping. Although the bad man had formerly risked his life with very little thought, it suddenly became very dear to him. It may have been that he feared a death of disgrace and dishonor, of being branded a knave, whereas he may have considered death in being pursued as an honorable, heroic death — on the field of battle, so to speak. Grant Wheeler, train robber of Arizona, shot himself through the head rather than surrender to officers. We treat here only of the desire for freedom; later, in describing the bad man's technique, we shall treat of his method of escape.

SEEING RED

The impetuous bad man acted on the spur of the moment, leaping before he looked. Actions of this sort indicated his violent, temperamental anger. Polk Wells, for example, shot a cowboy outfit's cook for allowing perspiration and dirt to mix with the dough for their biscuits. A Texas bad man named Bill Palmer killed another named Bill Mann because he pulled all the cover off of Palmer on a cold Texas winter night when one of those blasting, freezing northers swept down.

Clay Allison, whose sense of humor we've mentioned before, floored a Las Vegas dentist who had pulled the wrong tooth, and promptly extracted four of the dentist's own, saying, "Now, let that be a lesson to you!"

Bad man Ben Thompson of Austin, Texas, when sober, was the very personification of sartorial elegance. He was especially proud of his brand new silk top-hat, all black and shiny. A drunken cowboy once saw him swaggering down the street all dressed up to beat the band and decided he would have some fun with "that city dude." He walked up to Ben and knocked his hat into the street. As Ben was sober himself and seeing that the cowboy wasn't and as he appreciated a joke as well as the next fellow, he just laughed, picked up the hat, and went on about his business. But the cowboy thought it was so funny that he repeated the stunt. This time it made Ben sore. He whaled away and with all expedience shot the cowboy's ears off. The inebriate was taken into a near-by store and when informed of the identity of his assailant, "Why do you know who that was? Why, that was the notorious Ben Thompson whose hat you knocked off" — when he heard that, he fainted away in a cold swoon. It was said that the occurrence cured him of the liquor habit.

Texas' bad man Bill Longley murdered a Preacher Lay, on whose farm he had been working and who knew Bill's character but not his identity. The Preacher had warned Bill's girl friend that Bill was a no-good tramp, so Bill shot the preacher. He killed another man simply for beating him in a card game. Both the Parson and the other man were unarmed. This was plain "murder" — not a mere "killing." There was nothing fair about either affair — neither of Bill's opponents had a "fighting chance." Bill was later brought to justice for these misdeeds and hanged — in fact, he was hanged twice, but that's another tale.

John Wesley Hardin, "World's Champion Desperado," so the Texas Rangers called him, killed an Indian brave for stealing his silver-mounted saddle. Further it was told that Hardin, irritated by snoring from an adjacent hotel room, fired his six-gun, ending the snoring and thus providing a good night's sleep for all. At another time, a prison guard grabbed some food away from Hardin at the Huntsville, Texas, prison. Enraged, Hardin promptly threw a boot with an iron tap, hitting the guard in the head. He claimed that he would not have killed still another man, a Deputy Charles Webb, had it not been for malicious gossip of people telling each of the two that the other meant bodily harm to him. As usual, each party believed the worst about the other, and in a moment of flighty anger they came to angry words and then to pistol shots.

That Billy Thompson (Ben's brother) killed Sheriff Whitney in Dodge City, Kansas, just "to get him a sheriff" has been avowed by some but questioned by others.

At Tombstone, businessman Bradshaw killed his own business partner McIntyre in a fit of wrath for ridiculing his taste in clothes. Bradshaw bought a beautiful, gorgeous shirt with bright red, blue, green, yellow, purple stripes. Not knowing much about tailoring or exquisite foppery, he took the shirt seriously and was quite proud of it. Everyone he met hooted and yelled in boisterous guffaws, saying, "Where on earth did you get that natural camouflage for a rainbow?"

Bradshaw, vexed considerably by all this ribaldry and derision, declared that the next man who made fun of his shirt he would shoot on the spot. The next man was his own business partner McIntyre, who performed incredible contortions, howling in unholy glee, finally emitting between his gurglings and gyratings his death sentence, "Where did you get that shirt?" Bradshaw, insane with anger, shot McIntyre full in the mouth, which was wide open with roaring levity.

Al George shot a butcher who had waved a paper at George's pony, making the pony scared and its owner angry.

At Galeyville, Arizona, which is now a patch of weeds, Pat O'Day objected so strenuously to "doing a hornpipe" at the point of Cherokee Jack's Colt that he considerably indented Cherokee's head with a near-by sledge hammer, just to "learn him a lesson."

Mike Fink, the Mississippi River bully, tried to whip little Sheriff Ned Taylor for refusing to laugh at his joke. Fink said, "Why don't you laugh at my joke, shrimp?"

Little Taylor quietly replied, "It ain't funny."

Fink scowled, "You'll laugh or I'll know the reason why!"

With that, little Sheriff Ned Taylor turned in and gave big Mike Fink the worst beating he ever had, and after that Fink confined his jokes to his own personal friends.

Thus, at times the bad man demonstrated that he was greatly susceptible to uncontrollable, flighty anger.

HORSEPLAY

Other spur-of-the-moment, physically violent actions illustrated his grotesque sense of humor. Red Buck, a member of the Doolin gang, said he liked to shoot a man "just to see him fall." Slim Kid, a confederate of Henry Starr, past-master Oklahoma bank robber, wanted to kill someone on each raid so that he could put another notch on his gun. It has been asserted and denied that on the spur of the moment Billy the Kid killed a stranger cowboy just because he was working for his enemy land baron John Chisum, that he killed four Mexicans just to see them kick, and that he said when questioned why he killed a keeper of an Overland Stage station named Bernstein, "Well, I needed the horses; and besides, he was a Jew."

Such almost incredible acts are lacking in proof and are probably folklore. It is doubtful that even such hard cases as Billy the Kid, a man with twenty-one "credits," could kill with such lack of motivation. Perhaps there were hidden or more serious ulterior motives. Such men were certainly not the characters, neither angelic nor demonic, that romantic sentimentalism has created in the retrospect of a distant and disproportionate limelight.

However, it would be fallacious to judge the milieu of the Western frontier by today's standards. Doubtless, unusual things *did* happen in an almost incredible environment.

A man named Hinds brought Bill Longley and John Wesley Hardin together, presenting each as the other's enemy in a crafty manner, hoping to see gunplay just to determine who was the quicker on the draw. Such a motive is not altogether improbable. Today people often say, "Boy, oh boy, if we could just see a fight between Jack Dempsey at his best with Joe Louis at his best. What a fight *that* would be!" But Mr. Hinds was disappointed; Longley and Hardin became friends at the meeting instead of enemies.

A traveling drummer loudly complained of Miss Nellie Cashman's beans (Tombstone), whereupon a tall miner unlimbered his forty-five, stepped over the drummer's table, saying, "Stranger, eat them beans." With sudden gusto, the salesman's appetite improved.

According to Burns (in *Tombstone*), Curly Bill said to Jim Wallace, "I reckon I'll jest kill you fer luck." He was prevented from so doing, however.

Boone Helm, one of Henry Plummer's gang of the Northwest, Clay Allison, and Ben Thompson are supposed to have ridden horseback into courtrooms (at different times and places) and demanded with opprobious profanity what was wanted of them. It is said that the court decided in each case that nothing, after all, was wanted of them indeed. Thus by physical violence inspired by spur-of-the-moment whims the bad man demonstrated, in some respects, his grotesque sense of humor.

Also by tricks, pranks, and practical jokes he displayed his peculiar sense of humor, much of which might be termed colloquially as "horseplay."

For example, Prairie Dog Dave hadn't seen a female of his species for several weeks and when he came to Dodge City and saw the British Blondes in a show there, he simply went to pieces. Beside himself, he ripped out his forty-fives and belched ten exuberant shots through the ceiling.

At the same "worst town on earth" a cowboy was trying to cut a few capers with a dance-hall cutie, but the music was too slow to suit his tempo, so he punctured the piano with five vicious bullets. Another cowboy who had lost his wages in a bad gambling house there emitted his displeasure by unlimbering his six-shooter and banging away at the check rack of the faro bank. While bullets, cards, red, white, and blue chips, and people splashed and flew in all directions, he turned on the defenseless roulette wheel and perforated the 'goose' of the game of keno and with his last missile shot out the lights and escaped in the ebony darkness.

Billy the Kid on one occasion tested the nerve of his fellow bad men by secretly placing several cartridges into the campfire while they were boasting of what they had done and what they would do to old Sheriff Brady. When the shots went off, the Kid sat with his legs crossed laughing immensely at his compatriots who rapidly took to cover.

There never was another Clay Allison and never will be. He was not a rustler, a thief, a bushwhacker, a murderer, a robber, nor an officer — he was merely a killer of bad men. He had a most unusual sense of humor. His favorite amusement was to ride into a town, alone, with a six-shooter in each hand, shoot out lights and windows and empty the streets of populace, daring any and everyone to come out. He varied the performance at Canadian, Texas, by adding the Lady Godiva touch to his ride, wearing only his boots and ten-gallon hat.

It is maintained that Clay, being escorted to court by a Sheriff Rhinehart, hit upon the brilliant idea of shooting the sheriff's hat full of holes so that he could report being under fire. He then filled the hat full of stinking water, dirt, and a dead skunk's tail and made the sheriff wear it into court with him.

Clay once slipped Ranger Captain Arrington's forty-five from its holster, but the Captain did not appreciate the joke and commanded Clay to return the gun at once. Clay agreeably complied. At another time he lined up a group of men and an adolescent boy, and, desirous of entertainment, commanded them to dance a "durned good hornpipe," which they did, neither very gracefully nor graciously. When satisfied, Clay let them adjourn, whereupon the youth returned with a shotgun and said, "Now, mister smart aleck, it's your turn to dance!" Clay appreciated the point and danced, clubfoot and all. He was greatly pained doing the hornpipe with his clubfoot, but he went right ahead. He respected the boy's nerve but not his own judgment. He said next time he wouldn't "fool with a kid — they got no better sense than to shoot somebody!"

Allison and a few other friends, several sheets in the breeze, decided they did not relish some articles in the *Cimarron* (New Mexico) *News and Press,* so they went over *en masse* and with sledge hammer wrecked the place. Clay piled up some of the half-printed papers the next morning and made the rounds of saloons selling each paper for twenty-five cents.

Mace Bowman was a man of some reputation. He and Clay got well along in their cups and decided to have some innocent fun. They met in a saloon and got into a heated argument. As the vituperation waxed more acrid and the cuss words became sharper, bystanders gave them more room. At length, they placed their six-shooters on the bar, backed away ten feet, and at the word *go* from the bartender leaped for their guns. Allison beat Bowman, who calmly struck a heroic pose, tearing open his shirt, revealing a brawny and hairy chest, and yelling, "Shoot and be damned!" Clay then hugged him, saying he couldn't shoot a thus-and-thus as brave as that, and ordered a drink for his health. Spectators suspected this act as being histrionic, but they knew it for a certainty when later it was ascertained that the performance was repeated in all the saloons in town.

Marshal Fred Sutton tells us that bandit Henry Starr enjoyed jokes on sheriffs. After robbing a bank, single-handed, and retiring to a farmhouse, incognito, he was enjoying supper with a hospitable farmer when the telephone rang. The farmer answered, and with receiver in hand informed Starr it was the Sheriff, desirous of information about the robber. "What shall I tell him?" Starr replied, "Tell him the robber is at your house eating supper and for him to come on out and get me."

The farmer nearly swallowed his tongue, but complied. Starr leisurely finished his meal, paid for it, and went on.

Frank Chaney, approached by a posse not quite a hundred feet away, whispered to Henry Starr, pointing at one of the possemen: "That hombre is so thin if he'd shut one eye he'd look like a needle." Henry Starr said he had to clap his hand over his mouth to keep from laughing out loud, which would have been disastrous for the two outlaws at that time.*

In a similarly grave situation were Bud Smith and Jeff Ake. Jeff tells about it himself (in *They Die But Once*):

> Bud Smith was a big awkward feller, always a-laughing. When the fellers come up, Bud throwed down on one like I did, and in a minute I heard him a-laughing. I asked him what the hell was the joke. Bud kept a-laughing and he says, 'Well I'm just figgering how this hatchet-faced———— of a————is a-going to look when I shoot his eye out.'

Down in Texas around San Antonio they still talk about bad man J. K. (King) Fisher of Uvalde County. He also had a sense of humor. He placed beside a public road sign not far from his abode, "This is King Fisher's road. Take the other!" And it is said that people usually did precisely that.

Much has been made of Curly Bill's going to church at Charlestown, Arizona. Upon his appearance, several of the congregation started to leave and Parson Tuttle hesitated; but at the firm insistence of Curly the services resumed their normality except that Parson Tuttle was forced to sing hymns for two hours to please Curly, who then passed the plate and turned in the largest collection in the church's history. Next day Justice Burnett opened court on Curly Bill, much in the same manner as that of Judge Roy Bean, and fined him $25 for disturbing the peace. Curly said no more church for him; it was too expensive.

---

* These examples are typical of only one grim aspect of frontier humor, too often misconstrued by psychologists and literary critics. The best and most definitive analysis of frontier humor is Mody C. Boatright's *Folk Laughter on the American Frontier*, The Macmillan Company, 1949.

A Dodge City minister centered a sermon on the conversion of Prairie Dog Dave until the latter wailed in a loud voice that at last he was willing to have his sins expurgated and, like the minister, was ready to meet his Master, ripping out his Colt and firing promiscuously. Of course, the parson took the panes with him as he went through the nearest window. Dave disgustedly remarked that he reckoned he was about as ready to meet his Master as was the minister right there and then.

John Wesley Hardin wagered a glass of beer that if he shot at a man close enough without hitting him, he would jump eleven feet. He won the bet. At another time he was hurriedly forced out of Dodge in his night clothes. Tom Carson and two other deputies were sent after him, whom he waylaid, disarmed, and returned to their bailiwick in B. V. D.'s thirty-five miles away, in a July sun on a bald prairie.

Ben Thompson was another bad man who respected courage in a youngster. Instead of shooting one, in a card game, he decided to buy him a drink when the little gamecock yelled, even while looking down the business end of Thompson's guns, "Shoot and be damned!"

Thompson's humor was perverted. His escapades were legion, but at the same time irritating. Under the influence of continued libations from the bottle, he decided to have the bartenders serve all Negro customers in that end of the bar reserved for the whites. Had any other man in the state of Texas done this, there would have been a riot. Back in the 70's during reconstruction of the South, no one could get away with that sort of thing but someone like bad man Ben Thompson.

On another occasion, he loaded his six-guns full of blank cartridges and burst out upon the stage of a variety theatre on Congress Avenue in Austin during a performance and in wild-eyed devilish glee emptied the blanks at the audience just to see the people fairly wreck the place in their frantic efforts to escape alive. He later explained laughingly that the theatre had been drawing trade from his own saloon.

On still another occasion, he broke up a stockmen's convention at Fort Worth in a similar fashion. Big, two-fisted men, accustomed to danger and thoroughly familiar with firearms and their uses, looked around at the door which Thompson had just slammed. There stood the killer with both guns blazing away at the stockmen, who knocked over tables, chairs, and each other diving for cover. Of course he had blank cartridges, but how were they to know that? Familiarity with the six-gun does not breed contempt for it. It is claimed that Thompson even shot up his own gambling joint in Dodge City once.

Cunningham states that Bill Longley's sense of humor was practical and showed good judgment:

> Mr. Baker, I've got a confession to make. I'm not really kinfolks with you [he had claimed his name was Baker]. I'm that hell-roaring Bill Longley you've heard so much about. I like a warm climate as much as the next man. But this weather is more than warm — it's' getting hot! I'll be leaving you! [Longley had found that sheriffs were on his trail.]

Quantrill, leader of the Missouri border guerrillas, was known to shout and laugh above the din of battle and roar of his men's guns. Jesse James was said to have his little joke, as we shall see in the Corydon bank robbery. But his brother Frank was the personification of taciturnity. He never wisecracked, seldom even laughed, was usually serious.

Jovial Sam Bass immensely enjoyed showing off to his friends and pretending he was robbing. Once while feeling unusually jocular, he sprang to his feet and shouted, "Now if that tree was some old banker, I'd jerk out my pistol and slip up to him this way and jab it into his countenance." He then went through the motions of robbing the bank. "Throw up your props, Cap!"

"I tell you boys the old fellow would jump back and say, 'Here are the boys. I guess you want some money.' "

Sam then went toward a tree with a sack in one hand and pistol in the other, rasping out, "Hurry up, old man, we are in a hurry."

This performance, according to Jim Murphy, the one of his gang who later betrayed him, caused much merriment among his men, states biographer Wayne Gard.

One of the traditions of the cow-towns of Kansas was that the boys would gather around some favorite, strip him, and then clothe him in a brand new, elegant foppery. This was usually taken in good grace. Wild Bill Hickok was once a victim of this custom.

The verity of some of these anecdotes concerning the bad man's sense of humor and especially his actions when in heated, violent anger you may question. He could not get away with just any and everything. He had to comply with the code of the West, or else the citizens would rise in arms against him. There was a limit beyond which even men like Clay Allison or Ben Thompson could not go even in their environment; however, there is no question that the bad man had a peculiar, and usually perverted, sense of humor which prompted some of his extraordinary actions.

Anyone familiar with the deadliness of the six-gun, and especially the old-timers, fail to see anything funny about the bad man's facetious escapades. Their accounts may sound humorous superficially, but they were not in reality. Again, familiarity with the six-gun does *not* breed contempt for it.

REDEYE

It was once in the saddle I used to go dashing,
It was once in the saddle I used to go gay,
First to the dram-house, then to the card-house
Got shot in the breast, I am dying today.

Look in the Appendix of this book at many of the descriptions of the bad men of reputation and they will show that while sober they were quiet, polite, and reserved in demeanor, but that when intoxicated they were the embodiment of the "fury of hell." Today we say that drinking and driving do not mix; then it might well have been said that drinking and the six-gun made a deadly combination. Frequent libations from the bottle caused many a mortal duel in the old West. There were a few bad men who realized this fact and who were abstainers or temperate drinkers; others seemed to enjoy constant potations from the bottle of tarantula juice.

On the night of August 19, 1895, out at El Paso, Texas, a young eleven-year-old Western Union delivery boy called "Jack" entered a saloon with a telegram for bad man John Wesley Hardin. Hardin took the message and tipped the boy. He put his hand on the boy's head and pointed to a great big glass of whiskey he was drinking and said, "Son, you see that? Take my advice and don't ever touch that stuff. It'll get you into trouble every time."

The boy answered that he wouldn't. That same night John Wesley Hardin was shot in the back by an enemy named John Selman in the same saloon, while Hardin was shaking dice. Hardin was saying, "Four sixes to beat . . ." but that's as far as he

41

got. He gripped the table railing and fell to the floor dead after having lived about forty-two hectic years and having killed about forty-three men.

That same little Western Union messenger boy grew up to be one of the finest men I have ever known. He was once the President of what is today Texas Womens University at Denton — Dr. L. H. ("Jack") Hubbard, for whom Hubbard Hall is named.

Yessir, in the old days the boys wanted something, as one old-timer put it, that would bite and scratch as it went down, just like barbed wire.

But they couldn't go Snakehead Thompson's brand. This particular brewer acquired his name from the fact that he flavored his whiskey delicately with rattlesnake heads and red pepper to make it more potent. When this was learned by the buffalo hunters whom he served at his make-shift bar, he made a hasty, involuntary exit punctuated by dust flying from forty-five slugs a few feet from his heels.

The drunkard bad man was usually in a greater number of personal scrapes and was more irascible and uncontrollable in his cups than was the temperate imbiber.

It was by means of liquor that the Manning brothers of El Paso induced a bad man named Johnson to attempt an assassination of Marshal Stoudenmire. Likewise, some enemies of Wild Bill Hickok plied a tinhorn gambler Jack McCall with a product of Bacchus to instill the courage in him to assassinate Hickok at Deadwood, Dakota.

"Most common killings," as one old-timer put it, "were caused by boozed cowboys."

I'M ROUGH AND I'M TOUGH

There is something alluring and glorifying to the bad man in the idea of being "the cock of the walk" or "a man among men."

Wild Bill Hickok started out with a false, exaggerated reputation, but he lived up to it. Practically no one ever knew James Butler Hickok until he was twenty-four years of age, but during the next and last fifteen years of his life he immortalized himself as the most colorful character in the entire history of the flaming West. It all started in July of 1861 at the Rock Creek Station of the Overland Stage Company in Jefferson County, Nebraska. Young Hickok was just a flunky there, handling the mules and horses. The bare facts, which have been long disputed, seemed to have been that he took it upon himself to "defend" Mrs. Wellman while her husband was away, from a vicious station operator named McCanles, for whom Hickok had formerly worked and to whom Wellman owed money. McCanles came to collect; Hickok intercepted him in the front room of the Wellman house. McCanles brought his young son with him and two friends by the names of Woods and Gorfdon. McCanles left his three companions in the buggy and came alone to the house. After exchanging epithets, Hickok slunk behind a curtain and shot McCanles through the heart. Woods and Gordon heard the shot and came running to the house. Hickok then shot Woods, giving him his death wound, and grazed Gordon, who escaped in spite of several more missiles flung in his direction.

The story of the killing of these two men, who were probably unarmed, spread from mouth to mouth and increased in leaps and bounds until the "vicious McCanles gang" mounted to eight vile ruffians, bent upon murder! From then on unheralded James Butler Hickok became the notorious Wild Bill Hickok.

Joseph A. Slade, manager of one of the Overland Stage Company's stations, wanted a bad reputation and achieved one, but he abused it, and thus brought about his own downfall. He indulged in too much liquor, too much indiscriminate and promiscuous shooting and killing, and was finally hanged by impromptu vigilantes.

The motive for gaining a fierce reputation alone prompted the famous duel between "Chunk" Colbert and Clay Allison; "Chunk" already had the fame of having about a dozen notches on his gun, but he felt that if he killed the one and only Allison, his glory would be perpetuated. A more detailed account of the duel will be given in subsequent chapters.

The same is true of the gun fight between Joe Grant and Billy the Kid. In 1880 in old Fort Sumner, New Mexico, a Texas bad man named Joe Grant came gunning for Billy the Kid merely to increase his lurid reputation and add another great big notch on his gun. He cultivated the Kid and his gang of rustlers for a while, but when in his cups his tongue loosened, betraying his true purpose in being with them.

One day in Sumner's popular Hargrove's saloon, Grant got thoroughly stewed and started "playing" with a gun he had taken from a bystander.

"Let me see it," said Billy the Kid. He took the gun and, unknown to Grant, twirled the cylinders so that at the next attempt at firing the hammer would fall on the empty cylinder. As a matter of safety Western men usually carried only five bullets in their six-guns, leaving the hammer resting on an empty cylinder, so that the jarring of riding or even walking would not throw the hammer against a percussion cap and set the gun off. Had he carried six bullets, it would have been quite possible for the frontiersman to find his foot accidentally shot.

The Kid handed back the pistol to Grant. About that time a friend of the Kid's named James Chisum came into action. The cattle baron John Chisum was the Kid's avowed enemy. Now here was Grant's chance. He pretended to mistake James Chisum for John and remarked, "I'm going to kill that 'thus-and-so' right now!"

Of course, the Kid interfered, saying, "You fool, that's James Chisum, not John."

Grant, pretending to be enraged (he didn't need to pretend intoxication), turned on the Kid himself, and pulled the trigger. Of course, the hammer fell on the empty cylinder. In his split-second moment of surprise the Kid drew his own gun and shot Grant through the head.

The Kid had used his head as well as his finger — he had out-guessed Grant. Grant's reputation went out as its owner went out.

In both cases — "Chunk" Colbert vs. Clay Allison and Joe Grant vs. Billy the Kid — the motive was merely to gain a reputation and put another notch in the seeker's gun and in both fights the challenger lost his life and his reputation.

GUN NOTCHES

It was usually the kind of bad man who reveled in his notches that gloated over his reputation, although there were few men who did so. When Fred Sutton asked Luke Short, a bad man bartender who shuttled back and forth from Kansas to Texas, why he put notches on his gun, he replied, "When you come right down to it, I don't know. It's kind of a habit, I guess."

Henry Starr, the unparalleled Oklahoma bank robber, probably offered Sutton the most satisfactory and reasonable explanation why some gunmen cut notches in their weapons: "A skilled workman is proud of his tools. Watch a barber honing and fondling his favorite razor. It's the best razor in seven states, if you believe him, and he'll brag about how many thousand faces it has shaved, the wonderful steel in its blade and how it holds its edge. Or listen to a conductor or engineer bragging about his watch that never varies a hundredth part of a second; or a carpenter talking about that saw he has had for nineteen years.

"Well, a six-shooter is the working tool of the outlaw and the fellows who chase him, and a darned sight more important to him than the razor to the barber or the watch to the engineer, for his life hangs on it. A good six-shooter costs about forty dollars, and if you want to go in for ivory, stag horn, silver or gold mountings, you can go up a lot higher. A fellow gets into a hole and it downs the other fellow, he's proud of it. He gives it a notch for remembrance. By the time there are six or eight notches on the stock he is a killer. He's likely to be case-hardened by then and drop a man just to add another notch. Maybe he's jealous of somebody that's got fourteen notches on his shooting iron. It gets to be a kind of contest, like a fellow getting a lot of medals."

It was customary that the gun notches, literal, pretended, or creditable, of the desperado were inherited by his killer who sought the reputation. That is, according to this custom, Pat Garrett, the New Mexico sheriff, would have been justified in cutting twenty-two notches in his gun — one for killing Billy the Kid and twenty-one for the men the Kid had killed — that is, if Pat Garrett had been the kind of braggadocious bad man sheriff some of them were.

But outlaw Emmett Dalton said, on the other hand (in *When the Daltons Rode):*

> Personally I have met hundreds of bad men, hard men, shooting men, killers, both peace officer and outlaw. And I have yet to see the first notch on any of their six-shooters. I have, however, seen fake bad men ostentatiously file dummy notches.
> Men who killed other men, I observed, did not boast of it. They did not advertise their prowess, aggressive or defensive, by cutting a notch on a gun. It is a fiction-writer's elaboration.

And Wyatt Earp spoke for the peace officers (in an interview by Stuart Lake):

> I might add that I never knew a man who amounted to anything to notch his guns with 'credits,' as they were called for men he had killed. Outlaws, gunmen of the wild crew who killed for the sake of brag, followed this custom. I have worked with most

45

of the noted peace officers — Hickok, Tilghman, Sughrue, Masterson, Bassett, and others of like caliber — have handled their weapons many times, but never knew one of them to carry a notched gun.

It does seem reasonable that the bad man, as a rule, would not care to have people estranged from and suspicious of himself, especially his friends. They probably would be if he sported a notched gun.

Of course, the bad man didn't count Mexicans or Indians; "everybody" shot *them,* as the saying went. It was white men only, dead white men, to the frontiersman's credit, that made his reputation and became his herald as a bad man. For example, Jeff Ake's Uncle Bate was supposed to have killed seventy-five Mexicans in Texas, and he was not even considered as a "bad" man.

It appears that no one can be certain as to the correctness of the numbers given credit to the various bad men, but it seems that many of them were exaggerated. The best single example is afforded in Bat Masterson, one time intrepid law officer in that "worst town on earth," Dodge City, Kansas, but later in his life a New York newspaperman. To oblige a gun collector, Bat (then in his New York City newspaper office) went down to a pawn shop and bought a secondhand pistol and carved twenty-two notches thereon. The wide-eyed collector cooed and gurgled with ecstasy at the mere sight of the twenty-two notches. As a result, his "killings" increased from twenty-two to twenty-seven to thirty-seven from one teller to another. Bat later admitted his caprice with large enjoyment, and his old associate frontier marshal Wyatt Earp insisted that his record was only four, giving the names and places involved. And here's exactly how it all happened, according to Wyatt (as told to Stuart N. Lake):

Bat Masterson was a brave man. As a peace officer he deserved all the celebrity he ever had, but as a killer his reputation has been greatly exaggerated. Old stories credit Bat with having killed twenty-seven men. The truth is, he never killed but four in his life.

I knew Bat when he was a kid in Wichita and he and I were bosom friends in Dodge. I hunted buffalo with him when he was hardly big enough to handle a rifle and I've been with him on many a round-up after outlaws. I shared the same home with him in Denver after my Tombstone days were over and kept up a correspondence with him until his death a few years ago in New

York. I know his career from beginning to end.

Bat killed his first man in Sweetwater, Texas, when he was eighteen years old. While he was serving as a civilian scout with the army, a dance-hall girl in Sweetwater took a shine to him. A cavalry sergeant named King grew jealous. When King went into the dance hall one night and saw Bat and the girl dancing together, he drew his gun. The girl saw him first and threw her arms around Bat to protect him. King's bullet killed her and, passing through her body, wounded Bat in the thigh. As the girl fell, Bat put a bullet through King's heart.

When I was marshal of Dodge in 1877, I went out with a posse to hunt some train robbers who had held up a Santa Fe express at Kinsley, and in my absence Ed Masterson, Bat's brother, acted as marshal. Some Texas cowboys were raising cain in a dance hall, and Bat and Ed went to quiet the disturbance. At the door, Jack Wagner, one of the cowboys, shot and killed Ed Masterson. As Ed reeled out into the street, Bat killed Wagner. When Alf Walker, the ringleader of the cowboys, came rushing out of the hall with a six-shooter Bat shot him twice. Walker ran up the street and through a saloon and dropped dead in an alley. Bat went into the dance hall and opened up on the other cowboys, but they piled out through the windows and got away!

The next man on Bat's list was Updegraft. Bat showed me the message he received in Tombstone and it was not from his brother. It didn't say what kind of trouble Jim Masterson was mixed up in. It only said that Peacock and Updegraft were threatening to kill him. Bat had had a quarrel with Jim and was hardly on speaking terms with him at the time but he took the first stage out of Tombstone to go back to Dodge and help his brother. That was the old frontier's brand of loyalty. These four, King, Wagner, Walker, and Updegraft —are the only men Bat ever killed, and there has always been a doubt whether Updegraft died of pneumonia or the wound from Bat's bullet.

There is something alluring in being "cock o' the walk" even to the mild-tempered soul. The reputation of being a fighter was at once helpful, dangerous, and necessary to the fighting man. Even officer Wyatt Earp realized that once he backed down or turned away from a fight, thus evading the issue, his reputation as a law officer would be ruined and he might as well turn in his badge. His long, continued success as an officer may have been due to his philosophy — he never looked for nor evaded trouble. Bat Masterson said that Wyatt must have disarmed from fifty to one hundred bad men at one time or another, never evading the issue. He always avoided shooting wherever it was possible. If a cowboy, drunk or otherwise, started to reach for his shooting irons, Wyatt wouldn't shoot with his Buntline specials; he would merely "konk" the cowboy over the head with the barrel of the Buntline, take his guns, and go lock him up in the local hoose-gow. He built up quite a reputation in this way as a peace officer. But Wyatt realized that he was a target: he returned to a Judge Fitzgerald a final decision against accepting an appointment as an officer of the law in Arizona, due to a petition by its citizens, saying (according to Stuart N. Lake):

> It would give me satisfaction to return to Arizona as United States Marshal, but it would make trouble. Every braggart in the Territory would be gunning for me, simply to run up a reputation. You and I know the stripe too well to believe otherwise. I'd have to shoot, or be shot; and there are a lot of newcomers over there who wouldn't appreciate that. The old-timers will understand why I'm turning down the job.

There is something vain about the make-up of a man. If you don't believe it, just look in any barbershop. Furthermore, he wants a reputation of some kind. With the bad man, it was the reputation of being the worst of the bad men, even though he sometimes would not admit it. Jealous Bill Longley once derided John Wesley Hardin's reputation, which he said was gained in a one-sided manner; and Hardin was never a man to give himself the worst of any report that he made. The outstanding quartet of Texas bad men of the '70's were Longley, Hardin, Ben Thompson, and King Fisher, and you can bet there was little love lost among them. Each one of them probably thought, "Oh yes, they're pretty tough customers, but just ask anybody who's the toughest and he'll tell you I am!"

As for the bogus bad man, whom we've barely mentioned thus far; he loved a reputation and that's all he lived for.

In a way, there is a conflict in the bad man. He wanted to have the reputation of being dangerous when on the warpath, yet he wanted to be a hero, a Robin Hood, loved by all — that is one reason for his generosity.

MISCELLANEOUS

Some of the motives activating the bad man were peculiar to a particularly unique situation.

1. WYATT EARP as he appeared in 1886. 2. VIRGIL EARP as he appeared in 1887. 3. MORGAN EARP as he appeared in 1880. 4. COL. WM. BREAKEN-RIDGE 1892. 5. This is a group of Dodge City, Kansas, gun-fighters, in 1870, from an old photograph taken in Kansas City in 1871. Reading from left to right, they are, top row: W. H. Harris, Luke Short, Bat Masterson. Sitting: C. Bassett, Wyatt Earp, McNeal, and Neal Brown. 6. BAT MASTERSON. 7. JESSE CHISHOLM, "Father of the Chisholm Trail."

1. Bird's-eye view of Tombstone, Arizona, 1880. 2. Main Street of Dodge City, Kansas, in 1878. a familiar scene to all old cowmen, and especially to the old-time Trail Drivers of Texas. 3. The building where cross-mark is seen, is the famous Oriental Gambling House, Tombstone, Arizona, where Doc Holliday often dealt faro. Upper story was the doctor's office where Billy Clanton was carried and died, after the famous battle with the Earps. The old stage was in daily use between Tombstone and Bisbee, and had an important part in the Bisbee massacre. 4. ELLSWORTH, KANSAS, at the time Ben Thompson took his shotgun and treed the town. The Drover's Cottage shown in the immediate foreground was the center of business activity on the northern end of the Chisholm Trail. It was originally built in Abilene in 1867. When that town went dead, it was moved to Ellsworth. At the top of the shipping season as many as two thousand whiskey-drinking, pistol-toting Texas cowboys nightly crowded this row of shack saloons, dancing halls and gambling houses. Of course, it was an exciting town!

1. BILLY STILES AND WIFE, Naco, Sonora, Mexico, March 9, 1902. In Spanish on photo, "*Un recuerdo para mi querida mama de su hijo y hija*, Maria Stiles. William Stiles." In English, "In remembrance of my mother, from her loving son and daughter." 2. BILLIE HILDRETH (seated), cowboy from John Slaughter ranch, and BURT ALVORD, Deputy Sheriff, Tombstone, Cochise County, Arizona. 3. BOB DALTON as he appeared May 9, 1889. Killed at Coffeyville, Kansas, Oct. 5, 1892. 4. GRAT DALTON, at age of 24. He was 33 when killed at Coffeyville, Kan., Oct. 5, 1892.

1. BIG-FOOT WALLACE, as he appeared, on streets of San Antonio, according to the old-timers in the late seventies and eighties. Kindly furnished the Rose collection by Witte Memorial Museum. 2. JOHN SELMAN, 1878 as he appeared just after the Lincoln County War in New Mexico. Afterwards he killed Bass Outlaw, and John Wesley Hardin. Then he was killed by George Scarborough in 1896. He was soldier of the C. S. A., 1861-65. 3. JIM COURTWRIGHT, Union Scout, frontier character and man slayer. Killed by Luke Short in personal encounter in Ft. Worth, February 8, 1886. 4. SHERIFF FRANK M. CANTON of Johnson County, Wyoming. 5. The man on right is JOHN BLEVANS. Other two are his cousins. John Blevans was prominent in the Pleasant Valley War, only survivor of three brothers who took part in the fight with Sheriff Commodore Perry Owens, in Holbrook, Arizona, September 4, 1887. The fight took place at the Blevans home. Andy Blevans (known in Arizona as Andy Cooper), and Sam Houston Blevans, were killed by Sheriff Owens, while John was only wounded.

1. TOM HORN. 2. This is GERONIMO, who was also known by his Indian name, Cow-a-ar-tha, meaning "Yawner." He was not a chief, as generally supposed, according to best information, but was extremely crafty and suspicious, with unusual ability as a warrior. 3. VICTORIO, Apache Chief. 4. THE APACHE KID (in center) and two of his pals at their hillside home, Arizona, in the 80's.

1. DALLAS STOUDENMIRE, City Marshal of El Paso, Texas, in 1881. Killed by Jim Manning in 1882. 2. Small man on left is CHAVEZ, a murderer, who escaped jail at Tucson, Ariz., and was killed by Sheriff Wakefield in the Santa Rita Mountains. Large man is AUGUSTINE CHACON, murderer, sentenced to hang in 1897, who also escaped, but was later captured, and hanged November 23, 1902. 3. JUDGE ROY BEAN, a portrait by Leach & Co., Llano, Texas. 4. This photo of JUDGE ROY BEAN, Law West of the Pecos, made by Assistant-Foreman Hall of Pecos High Bridge Gang in 1902, was preserved by Pastor Grover Lee, who was employed on bridge, added it to the Rose Collection, 1937. 5. MRS. LANGTRY.

1. J. H. (Doc) HOLLIDAY, as he appeared in the early eighties. 2. WILLIAM CLARKE QUANTRILL, famous Missouri Guerrilla Chief during the Civil War. 3. SAM BASS at the age of Sixteen, in Indiana, before he came to Texas. 4. BEN THOMPSON. 5. JESSE JAMES, age 17. 6. JOHN WESLEY HARDIN. 7. The last photo made of WILD BILL, in 1876. 8. WILLIAM H. BONNEY alias Billy the Kid who was killed by Sheriff Pat Garrett, in the old Pete Maxwell house, Ft. Sumner, New Mexico, 1881. The chain across his shirt belongs to the watch presented to him by Dr. Henry F. Hoyt who states that fact in his book,

1. MANNING CLEMENTS, Sr. 1879. Ranchman, on Deep Creek, McCulloch County, Texas. Killed at Ballinger, Texas, March 29, 1887. 2. Looking up Congress Avenue, 1876. State capitol at head of avenue. See page 100. 3. HENRY STARR, Oklahoma's King of Bank Robbers.

1. CAPTAIN HECK THOMAS, a Deputy United States Marshal for thirty-five years, in Indian Territory and Oklahoma. He died at Lawton, Oklahoma, August 15, 1912. 2. LEE SAGE. 3. CRAWFORD CROSBY alias Cherokee Bill, member of the Bill Cook gang. 4. AL JENNINGS, lawyer, outlaw, writer and evangelist of note. 5. THEY ARE FRIENDS NOW — (left) COL. E. D. NIX, U.S. Marshal Oklahoma District. (Center) AL JENNINGS, bank and train robber. (Right) CHRIS MADSEN, Deputy U. S. Marshal, who delivered Al to the penitentiary, in early days. Photo made by N. H. Rose, official photographer N. F. A., at their November 1937 Convention in Houston, Texas. 6. BILL TILGHMAN Chief of Police, 1912, Oklahoma City, Okla.

1. BELLE STARR, riding her famous black horse, America's most noted female bandit, the gamest who ever rode the range, and first white woman to locate in Oklahoma Territory. 2. "CATTLE ANNIE" and "LITTLE BREECHES," members of Oklahoma outlaw gangs, who were captured in 1894, by U. S. Marshals Burke and Tilghman, and sent to Reform School, Farmington, Mass. After their release Cattle Annie returned and lived a respectable life but nothing more is known of Little Breeches. 3. ROSE OF THE CIMARRON, member of the famous Doolin gang.

1. Famous White Elephant Bar, San Antonio, Texas, in the eighties, on north side of Main Plaza. 2. WM. P. LONGLEY, copy of an old faded photograph, made just before his execution at Giddings, Texas, Oct. 11, 1878. 3. JOHN KING FISHER, when he was Deputy Sheriff of Uvalde County, Texas, who was killed with Ben Thompson, in the old Jack Harris theatre March 11, 1884, San Antonio, Texas. 4. The Double "O."

1. JOHN S. CHISUM. 2. HOLE IN THE WALL GANG OR WILD BUNCH. Left to right, standing, Bill Carver and Harry Logan. Sitting: Harry Longabaugh, Ben Kilpatrick, and George Parker alias Butch Cassidy. (Photo by John Schwartz, at Ft. Worth, December 1900.) 3. CHARLES GOODNIGHT. 4. Grave of SAM BASS as it appeared in 1926, at Round Rock, Texas. 5. PAT GARRETT, famous sheriff, who killed Billy the Kid, 1881.

1. ROBERT FORD. 2. MRS. ZERELDA SAMUELS. Mother of Frank and Jesse James. (From photograph taken at the Samuels home near Kearney. Missouri, October, 1897, by Howard Huselton, of Kansas City, Missouri. 3. FRANK JAMES. May 18, 1898. 4. JESSE JAMES in 1875. 5. CHARLIE FORD, brother to the slayer of Jesse James. 6. DICK LIDDIL, a member of the famous Jesse James gang. (Photo 1882.)

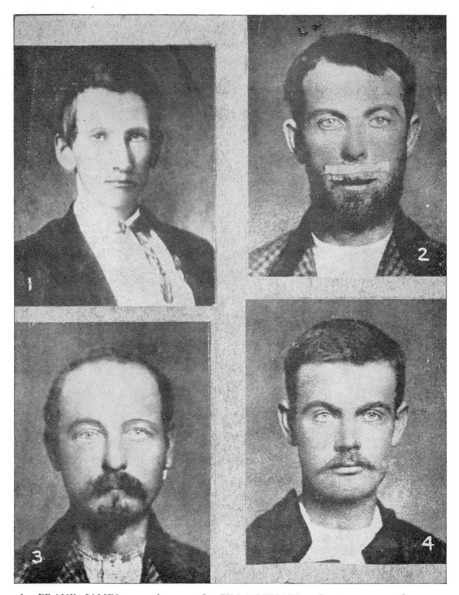

1. FRANK JAMES at early age. 2. JIM YOUNGER, who was captured near Madelia, Minn., Sept. 21, 1876, soon after the raid on Northfield bank. Photo by Stife, at the Fairbault jail. Served many years in Stillwater penitentiary. 3. COLE YOUNGER, who was captured near Madelia, Minn., Sept. 21, 1876, soon after the raid on Northfield bank. Photo by Stife, at the Fairbault jail. Served many years in Stillwater penitentiary. 4. BOB YOUNGER, who was captured near Madelia, Minn., Sept. 21, 1876, soon after the raid on Northfield bank. Photo by Stife, at the Fairbault jail. Served many years in Stillwater penitentiary.

George W. Coe   John H. Slaughter

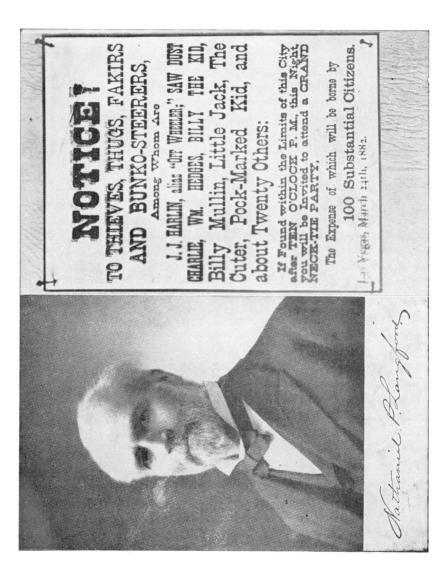

George Ives and Cherokee Bob of the Northwest and Jim Courtright of Texas either 'shook down' saloons for their 'protection' or else moved in as 'partners' notwithstanding the original owners. They were probably this country's first gangsters, in the modern sense.

The salt-water war in El Paso began over disputed rights of individuals to obtain salt from the salt hills near that city. Texas Ranger Jim Gillett tells all about this bloody affray in his memoirs, *Six Years with the Texas Rangers.*

Tiburcio Vasquez, Dallas Stoudenmire (El Paso's two-gun City Marshal), and John Wesley Hardin were (at different times and places, of course) in mortal combat arising from language differences. That is, because the Mexican bad man couldn't understand the American or vice versa, they came to blows, which might have been prevented otherwise.

John Wesley Hardin and his cousins, the Clements brothers, were driving a herd of cattle along the old Chisholm trail one time when they reached the Newton prairie somewhere in Gonzales or DeWitt County. They were closely followed by a group of Mexican vaqueros and their herd — too closely to suit the young "Wes." He rode back and told the Mexican leader to keep his cattle off the Clements' herd's tails. The Mexican stubbornly replied to each of Wes' admonitions with a loud gibberish, motioning that he was in "beeg hurry, pronto!"

The boss Mexican got mad at me for holding, as he said, his cattle back. I told him to turn to the outside of the trail, as he did not have to follow me. This made him all the madder. He fell from the front of the herd and quit leading the cattle. The result of this was that on being in front of them they rushed right into my herd, so I turned them off to the left. The boss Mexican rode back to where I was and cursed me in Mexican. He said he would kill me with a sharp shooter as quick as he could get it from the wagon. In about five minutes I saw him coming back with a gun. He rode up to within about 100 yards of me, got down off his horse, took deliberate aim at me and fired. The ball grazed my head, going through my hat and knocking it off. He tried to shoot again, but something got wrong with his gun and he changed it to his left hand and pulled his pistol with his right. He began to advance on me, shooting at the same time. He called up his crowd of six or seven Mexicans. In the meanwhile Jim Clements, hearing that I was in a row had come to my assistance. I was riding a fiery gray horse and the pistol I had was an old cap and ball, which I had worn out shooting on the trail. There was so much play between the cylinder and the barrel that I would not burst a cap or fire unless I held the cylinder with one hand and pulled the trigger with the other. I made several unsuccessful attempts to shoot the advancing Mexican from my horse, but failed. I then got down and tried to shoot and hold my horse, but failed in that, too. Jim Clements shouted at me to "turn that horse loose and hold the cylinder." I did so and fired at the Mexican, who was now only ten paces from me. I hit him in the thigh and stunned him a little. I tried to fire again, but snapped. The Mexican had evidently fired his last load so we both rushed together in a hand to hand fight.

So, the two had a tooth, toenail, and eye-gouging party. Other Mexicans rode up taking potshots at Hardin until big Jim Clements and brothers Gyp, Manning, and Joe put a stop to the whole affair. They took much besmeared Hardin to camp, dressed him up, re-armed and went back to get the Mexicans, who had meantime prepared themselves to retaliate. The Texans, being the better riders and pistol shots, killed all the Mexicans but two. Other Texas cowboys from near-by camps rode up and the two Mexicans gave up. The Texans discussed what to do, glancing and pointing at the Mexicans, until the latter became uneasy and misunderstood, thinking they were making plans for their execution, so they broke and ran. The Texans, afraid of being waylaid, ambushed, or bushwhacked later by the Mexicans, killed them on the run. This is the way the story is recounted by Thomas Ripley, Hardin's biographer.

* * * * * * *

Unusual was John Ringo's proposal that a duel be fought between him and any of the Earp faction out at Tombstone to end the feud between the rustlers and the Earp officers. No one accepted his challenge. The feud would probably have gone ahead anyway, regardless of the outcome of the hypothetical duel.

Especially in Oklahoma where frontiersmen were lined up by the thousands to get the *go* signal and to ride at breakneck speed to their claims with shotgun and forty-five ready to defend them, and in the mining districts where a difference of one foot meant thousands of dollars, there were claim jumpers and fights to the death. In Oklahoma, when the Indian Territory or other government-owned land was opened to settlement, a time was set for the go-ahead signal and a rope lined off the future settlers and claimers of land. Some of the would-be settlers jumped the gun in the dark of night before the day set for the deadline, thereby taking an unfair advantage over the other would-be claimers. These gun-jumpers were called "sooners"; that is, they got to their claims "sooner" than the rest. Hence, the name of the Oklahomer Sooners! Naturally the law-abiding claimer resented the sooner and probably showed his resentment via his six-shooter.

U. S. Deputy Marshal Fred Sutton was one of the first settlers of newly formed Perry, Oklahoma. He raced all day, killing his pony, to reach his claim and to protect it the day the land was officially opened for settlement. Said he (in an interview with A. B. MacDonald):

> I was the first man to reach Perry that day. My little pony had won the race against thousands of contestants but gave his life in doing it, and I am not ashamed to say that his head was on my lap and in my arms when he died.
>
> My familiarity with a six-shooter was of good service to me the first and second day in Perry, for without it I would have lost my one hundred and sixty acres. I had to drive off three different claim-jumpers. One drove up and started to dump a load of lumber on it. He showed fight and I was really afraid I would have to shoot him.
>
> I believe that nine-tenths of the settlers in the Cherokee Strip won their homesteads and lots with the six-shooter. It might almost be said that Oklahoma was settled by the six-shooter, for in none of the openings were there enough farms or town lots to supply all who raced, and a man who was unarmed or unwilling to fight had a slim chance to hold his land, even if he got there first. Many were killed and their land taken.
>
> I reached Perry before two o'clock that afternoon and I saw the place grow in six hours to a tented city of ten thousand people. Before dark, saloons and gambling and dancing places in tents were going. Beer sold for a dollar a bottle, ice for twenty-five cents a pound, coffee for seventy-five cents a tin cup, ham sandwiches for a dollar, and water could not be had at any price.

The weather, even, had something to do with the bad man's actions. Witness an editorial in the Monterey (California) *Sentinel* written during the year 1855 (from James B. O'Neil's *They Die But Once*):

The Killing Season: The bloody season of California generally opens about the first of May, when the country is drying up and people begin to be loaded with electricity from the attenuated atmosphere, or their stomachs become so filled with the villainously adulterated alcoholics of the San Francisco fabricator that it makes the drinkers thereof crazy . . . At the latter end of October the season closes as the air becomes cooler and the rains begin!

Emmett Dalton, whose experience qualifies him to speak for the bad man, tells what made the bad man bad, summing up the miscellaneous motives of the bad man in the words *pride, thrill, egoism, youthfulness,* and *impetuousness* (from *When the Daltons Rode*):

Observers of animal life know that the quarry as well as the pursuer responds to the high pulse of the chase. The savage lust of attack and the taut dread of escape are not so far apart in kind as they might seem, during the maneuvers of the run. Have you seen the laughing grimace of the fox when he eludes the yelping pack? Have you heard the defiant bugle of a wild stallion racing from pursuing hoofs? Even the skinny range cow, craven though she usually is, blazes with something of the deadly delight when she finally turns to face the slashing wolf. All great passions have this blend of joy and pain, forever handed on in the ancient game of life and death. And certainly the outlaw knows its terrific excitements to the full.

Soon enough he comes to know that he cannot continue successfully to pit his wits against the wits of all who spread the net for him. Soon enough he knows that he must surely be bagged or killed. Then all the more he fortifies his spirit against that inevitable day and hour, fatalist that he is.

Once a man admits himself outlaw, his ego swells enormously. What the law will do for the law-abiding he must do for himself. Self-defense is no longer a matter of proxy. The outlaw doesn't judge himself as other men. He may have regrets but no apologies. Pride rowels him. Pride, the maker of feuds, the maker of wars and of most aggressions. Reckless, gigantic, swaggering pride, ready to flout the whole world. Always the outlaw walks within the haze of this red band in the rainbow of the soul. The finest honor and dignity that men boast have sprung from this ageless arrogance. Basically it has nothing to do with ethics or morals.

This you must know to comprehend the fighting outlaw. His

vainglory is both strength and weakness. At the extreme it impels him to take senseless risks! at best it becomes a dangerous lopsidedness. More, perhaps, than any other single factor it has served to cut swaths in the legions of the lawless because it exposes the hunted man, brings him into the open. And by his own standard the outlaw has only contempt for any antagonist of less mettle. Profoundly it offends his dignity if his pursuers are impelled by money incentive. "Blood money men," he terms these with a reviling tongue . . .

If only youth were not so headlong! If only it could survey the paths ahead!

CHAPTER II

THE TECHNIQUE OF THE BAD MAN

THE CODE OF THE WEST

"WHO, me? Oh, you can call me anything from Smokey Joe to Jackass Johnny. Why, I've been called things that would peel the hide off a Gila monster," asserted the newly-arrived bad man. "Never mind about my real name. It's been copyrighted by three states where they've been advertisin' it on all the 'wanted' lists."

Indeed, many famous bad men were known only by their incognomens. For example, there were Honey Johnson, Cherokee Bob, Snakehead Thompson, Red Buck, Blue Dick, Indian Charley, Catfish Kid, Dynamite Dick (who was really Dan Clifton), Oneshot Charley, and Honest Eph (whose real name was Sam Bass, none other).

Lee Sage once applied for a job as a cowhand and didn't care to have his name known. When the foreman violated the code of the West and asked him what his name was, Lee pertly replied that he would be named anything they wanted to call him. About that time a bucking bronco cut some antics in a near-by corral and Lee casually remarked, "He's some wampus cat!" Thenceforward, Lee's name was *Wampus Cat* until he left that particular cowcamp.

Then there were Mr. Howard (Jesse James), Little Arkansas (John Wesley Hardin), Off Wheeler, Blue Pete, Shoot-'em-up-Mike, and Mr. Ben Woodson (Frank James).

Even the Rangers often went by nicknames entirely. A Texas Ranger once remarked that there wasn't much society life in a

The two huge men stood their ground, neither attempting to dodge the blows or the onslaughts of the other, each slugging as hard and as fast as he could. Finally, Coe drew back all the way and struck Bill a blow on the jaw that lifted him completely off his feet. (See page 75-76)

Ranger camp, whereupon his name changed from the one which he had been christened to *Society Jack*. Ranger Captain Jim Gillett verified this in his memoirs.

Other bad men were known only as Bull-Whack Joe, Barkeep Joe, Dirty-Face Charley and Fat Jack.

Snakehead Thompson, as we have already observed, acquired his sobriquet from the fact that he flavored his whiskey with rattlesnake heads and red pepper to make it more potent for his buffalo hunter customers. They didn't appreciate the flavor, however.

Still others went by the names of Cockeyed Frank (Frank Loving), Buckskin Frank (Frank Leslie), Wild Bill Hickok (James Butler Hickok), Dutch Henry, Shortcreek Dave, Skinny McDonald, Doc Holliday, Ground Owl, Polecat Sam, Bone Tom, Soddy O'Brien, Dugout Slim.

These names meant about as much to their owners as did Lee Sage's horse, High Power. Colonel Davey Crockett, of Texas revolutionary fame, named his rifle Old Betsy. Bigfoot Wallace, another Texas pioneer of much note, named his G. R. knife Butch and his six-shooter Sweetlips. Another unusual name was that of the Laramie, Wyoming saloon, the Bucket of Blood — probably christened more through fact than fancy.

And then there were no end of Bills — Cherokee Bill, Rattlesnake Bill, Butcher-knife Bill, Hurricane Bill, Comanche Bill, Arkansas Bill, Apache Bill, and several Wild Bills.

Probably the most famous pseudonym was Billy the Kid. He gave his real name as William H. Bonney and his birthplace as New York City, but recent evidence shows that he was born Henry McCarty in New Mexico and that he may never have been farther away from home than the Texas Panhandle.

WELCOME, STRANGER!

John Chisum owned so many acres of land in New Mexico and so many cattle that he couldn't keep track of them all. His cowboys rarely ate a meal without guests at the long dinner table. He was friendly with Billy the Kid, until the Kid started rustling his cattle. Miss Sallie Chisum, John's niece, lived at her uncle's ranch and ran the household affairs, which was a full-time job in itself. She said the Kid and his followers, before they became estranged to Uncle John, visited there often, always enjoying courteous hospitality and good cooking. Any passer-by was welcome to eat and spend the night without charge of any kind.

A traveling Englishman once insisted upon paying for his breakfast. He accosted the host, shabbily-dressed Pete Maxwell, who was lounging on the front porch of his hacienda. The Englishman mistook him for just any old cowhand, and he certainly looked the part. But in reality Pete Maxwell was owner of two million acres — one of the wealthiest citizens of New Mexico. What was money to a man like him? It was an outrageous insult for his guest to offer to pay for his breakfast — it was a violation of the code of the West.

After much insistence on the part of the Englishman, Pete finally set the price of the breakfast at twenty-five dollars. The flabbergasted Englishman gulped and remonstrated, "But hi say, old fellow, don't you think that's a rawther exorbitant fee?"

Pete then yelled to one of his cowhands to shake that "d—— Englishman" upside down till twenty-five dollars fell out. Thus threatened, the chagrined guest handed over the money in bills. Pete calmly lighted a match to them, and proceeded to light his pipe, much to the bewilderment and astonishment of the Englishman.

A FIGHTING CHANCE

The code of the West demanded that an enemy be given a fighting chance.

Out at the Payne Ranch in Utah was a pretty young girl, a relative of the owner. She had been bothered by the sinister attentions of one Matt Rash, who was suspected of being in cahoots with the Coon Hole Gang of rustlers who had stolen some eight hundred steers from the ranch. The little girl was a favorite among the two-fisted men of the ranch — and young Tom Horn, especially, swore to relieve her of the embarrassments suffered at the hand of Matt Rash, the suspected rustler. The Payne Ranch authorities hired Tom as a spy. He joined up with the Coon Hole Gang and, having agreed beforehand with the ranchmen to kill the whole gang for a fixed price per rustler, went about the gory business with special attention to Mr. Rash. But he observed the code of the West. He warned before he struck. He wrote out warnings in pencil on cigarette papers and dropped them in all the gang's beds, including his own. Each rustler suspected the others. Rash announced to the whole group that he was going to Lookout Mountain and that if anybody, friend or foe, wanted to follow him, he would shoot him on sight. He, too, would give his enemy a fighting chance. Tom followed him and, especially afraid the little ranch girl might be tempted to run off with Rash later, suave and silver-tongued that he was, shot him between the eyes while the rustler was sprucing up after breakfast one morning in a mountain cabin.

Out at Lincoln, New Mexico, Billy the Kid literally turned the cards and the tables on his jailer Bell and ordered him to precede Billy down the stairs, keeping the jailer covered with the jailer's own gun, which the Kid had taken by a clever trick to be described later. Bell took a long chance, hoping he could beat Billy's bullet around a corner of the stairs. Before Billy shot him, he yelled a warning for Bell to halt, but it was too late. Of course, Bell was killed. But the Kid had observed the code of the West in shouting the halt signal, even if there wasn't much use in it.

Then Billy sat down and calmly lighted a cigarette and waited for the other jailer, Bob Ollinger, to return. The Kid really liked Bell and hated to kill him; but he really hated Ollinger and waited to kill him, before escaping. Ollinger had just stepped across the street for a cup of coffee. But even though the Kid despised Ollinger, he would warn him before shooting him — give him a fighting chance. He called out pleasantly, "Hello, Bob." Bob looked up surprised at the Kid who he supposed was safely upstairs in bonds. In that split second he probably wished he had taken back all those taunts he had thrown at the Kid. He probably recognized his own sawed-off double-barreled shotgun, which the Kid held with both barrels pointing right at Ollinger. He probably started for his six-shooter, but of course it was too late. But the Kid had observed the code of the West in warning his arch enemy.

Practically the same thing happened between Buckskin Frank Leslie and Billy Claiborne out at Tombstone. Buckskin warned, "Hello, Billy," before the kill. It was slim but sufficient warning for Leslie later to plead "self-defense."

Wild Bill Hickock has been branded a coward for shooting Phil Coe in the back, just as any other man would have been on the Western frontier. Coe was reputedly about as fine a young man as Dodge City ever claimed. He turned about and just before expiring said, "Bill, you're a dirty yellow coward. I hope they get you." And one of them did, Jack McCall — at Deadwood, Dakota — from the back, just the same as Phil Coe got it.

Marshall Wyatt Earp never went for his pistols until his antagonist started for his own. He spared the main object of his vengeance, unarmed Ike Clanton, in the O. K. Corral fight. Another frontier deputy, Billy Breakenridge, a county sheriff at Tombstone, who was there, by the way, at the same time as was U. S. Marshal Earp, said during the forty years he served as peace officer he never shot at a man until he had already been shot at.

Uncle Billy Tilghman, peace officer in old Oklahoma until he was seventy-five, observed the same code. Not uncommonly officers would not shoot at outlaws until the outlaw had already shot first. It has been said that enough lead was slung in Uncle Billy Tilghman's direction to sink a battleship, and that's probably more fact than fiction.

Not uncommonly was extended the courtesy of sending word to one's enemy to prepare for an immediate conflict. The Cochise County rustlers sent word to Marshal Earp at Tombstone that they would be waiting in the O. K. Corral. This may have been a bluff, but the Earps called it.

In old Fort Worth, Texas, Jim Courtright, when refused "protection" money by barkeeper Luke Short, warned Luke that he "would be back tomorrow" and that he (Short) had better have that money. Jim came back "tomorrow" and got shot by little Luke, but he had observed the code of the West.

A bluff did not exist, except with the bogus bad man; but a threat was common and it usually brought about gunplay. One who killed was privileged to plead self-defense, especially if the armed combatants faced one another. And an excuse was necessary. One bad man went so far as to ply his enemy with liquor, hoping to be insulted or threatened by the adversary in the presence of witnesses so he would have an excuse to kill him.

MURDER!

The old West frowned indignantly upon shooting anyone who was unarmed. Clay Allison refused to kill his unarmed avowed enemy, Ground Owl (Bennington Du Pont). Marshal Wyatt Earp spared the main object of his vengeance, unarmed Ike Clanton, in the famous O. K. Corral fight.

A fourteen-year-old sheepherder in Colorado and a feudist cowboy exchanged shots until the latter said, "Don't shoot, I'm empty," to which the boy responded, "Well, then load up while I wait." The cowboy started to reload, but considered that one good turn deserved another and rode off saying that he had had enough.

In northwest Montana Bill Mayfield challenged a cardsharp enemy named Evans, who said, "I'm not heeled." Mayfield snarled, "Well, go heel yourself then, and come back shooting." In the ensuing fight Mayfield was killed, but he had abided by the code. In the Territory of Idaho a man named Clark shot another man named Raymond, who was unarmed. In the mob that hanged Clark as a result of the shooting, there were many respected citizens, who were enraged at the "murder." It was "murder" when the deceased was unarmed and it usually ended up with a hanging bee.

THANKS, PARD!

Gratitude had its place in the code of the West. Bill Doolin refused to let a member of his band of outlaws named Red Buck shoot Officer Billy Tilghman in the back. Uncle Billy had been a friend of Doolin's, and the outlaw leader knew the merits and quality of the fine old man. He knocked the gun out of Red Buck's hand and said, "He's too good a man for that!" Later, in Arkansas, Tilghman had traced Doolin to a Turkish bath concern with a warrant for his arrest. Uncle Billy cornered Doolin and had to fight him like a wildcat to keep from killing him. Pressing the muzzle of his forty-five in Doolin's midriff, Tilghman said, "Don't make me kill you, Bill!" At that, Bill surrendered.

Butch Cassidy saved a Pinkerton detective from death at the hands of his own gang. Later, the detective refused to prosecute Cassidy, saying one good turn deserves another.

Deputy Breakenridge "disarmed" John Ringo, having been ordered to do so; but since Ringo's pal Curly Bill had aided him in collecting Cochise County taxes, Breakenridge felt he owed them a favor. He placed Ringo's weapons in his office desk, leaving the drawer open. Of course, when Breakenridge walked out of the office, Ringo took the guns and walked away. Later a judge and the U.S. Marshals were making it pretty hot for county officers Behan and Breakenridge for not having done their duty in bringing in rustlers Ringo and Curly Bill. The judge gave the officers until twelve o'clock to procure the wanted rustlers, and at about five minutes until that time sweat was pouring down Breakenridge's face when in walked Ringo right into the middle of the courtroom!

Curly Bill, Ringo's partner, never forgot a kindness or an insult — he always returned them, regardless of who was the donor. One day a lieutenant from Fort Bowie was out hunting and accidentally bumped into Curly Bill's hideout cabin where the outlaw chieftain was nursing one of his men named Sandy King, who was severely wounded from lead poisoning. The lieutenant explained his presence while looking down Curly Bill's barrels, and Curly then put up his guns. The soldier, seeing the wounded Sandy, offered to take him to the Fort for surgical treatment, assuring Curly the man would then go free.

The outlaw recovered after the operation and went away from the army post free.

After an interim of time Curly raided an Army corral for horses and the same Samaritan lieutenant was dispatched to retrieve them. He traced down Curly and demanded him to turn over the horses. Curly nearly shot him before recognizing who he was. He then threw open the gate and shook hands with the soldier and helped him pick out the stolen animals. He further told the soldier he was welcome to anything old Curly Bill had.

THE LIMIT

Ordinarily an even-matched, fair fight, where both men were armed and facing one another, was not made a concern of such law as existed on the frontier, even if one of the antagonists was killed. And he was merely a killer, not a murderer. An old-timer, Emerson Hough, says:

"It was an even break," said the killer to himself — "an even break, him or me." But perhaps, the repetition of this did not serve to blot out a certain mental picture. I have had a bad man tell me that he killed his second man to get rid of the mental image of his first victim.

A murderer, according to the code of the West, was one who shot in the back or from ambush, who gave no warning, or who shot an unarmed man. A bushwhacker was a "murderer." Of course, if a bad man "got the drop," and the enemy, instead of going for his weapons, signified his surrender by raising his hands, it would be downright murder to shoot him; but it was self-defense if the enemy reached for his gun. To violate this code would incur the wrath of witnesses and would usually cause a hanging bee. There was a limit beyond which even the worst bad man of the West could not go with impunity.

TEN COMMANDMENTS

The "ten commandments" of the old West, summed up, were as follows:

1. Thou shalt not appear too inquisitive about one's past.
2. Thou shalt be hospitable to strangers.
3. Thou shalt give thine enemy a fighting chance.
4. Thou shalt not shoot an unarmed man.
5. Thou shalt not make a threat without expecting dire consequences.
6. Thou shalt not practice ingratitude.
7. Thou shalt defend thyself whenever self-defense is necessary.
8. Thou shalt not rob.
9. Thou shalt honor and revere all womankind; ay, shalt thou never think of harming one hair of a woman.
10. Thou shalt look out for thine own.

This was just as unwritten as the constitution of England, yet just as binding and just as effective. It was the unwritten law of the Western frontier, and the pioneers understood it quite plainly and they appreciated it — and what is more, they enforced it!

GUNS

The most popular guns used by the bad man were the Colt's forty-five caliber single-action six-shooter for close and rapid shooting, and a Winchester 45-70 rifle for long-distance accuracy. Usually one arm of each type sufficed. The bad man rarely found himself in a situation that these two could not control.

There were two types of Colt's forty-five six-guns, the single-action and the double-action. Billy the Kid was the only bad man in this entire research who is mentioned as preferring the double-action gun. All the other two hundred and fifty odd bad men apparently preferred the single-action gun. The difference is this: To shoot the double-action gun all you have to do is pull the trigger with the pointer finger, and this takes care of the hammer — the mechanism is such that the trigger is connected with the hammer so that when the trigger is pulled the hammer automatically rises up and falls, striking the percussion cap and setting off the bullet. It also revolves the cylinders of the gun so that the next bullet is in line with the barrel ready for the trigger to be pulled again.

Whereas, to shoot a single-action gun, two motions are necessary. You pull the hammer back with your thumb and then squeeze the trigger with your finger. The old-timers usually bought this type of gun and altered the mechanism so that the gun could be fired merely by pulling back the hammer with the thumb and letting it spring back, not using the trigger at all. In fact, usually the trigger was filed off. This was usually considered faster and more accurate than the single-action gun.

Professor Walter Prescott Webb has interesting accounts of the genesis and evolution of the six-gun in his *The Texas Rangers* and *The Great Plains*. It is not generally known that Samuel Colt was a sixteen-year-old sailor when he first whittled out a wooden model of the gun that was destined to play a tremendously important part in the development of the West. The story is stranger than fiction.

Other guns used by the bad men were the Sharp's 50-50 rifle for buffalo hunting and long-distance shooting; the small, pocket double-barreled derringer forty-one, most effective and accurate within ten feet; Navy, Enfield, Smith and Wesson, Remington, and Marlin rifles, six-shooters, and shotguns. Wyatt Earp used his unusual Buntline special to advantage, though its barrel was an inch or two longer that the conventional Colt's. He also placed "sawed-off" double-barrel shotguns at strategic, hidden places in his bailiwick. These held eighteen shots, which spread as they sped. Doc Holliday, however, in the famous O. K. Corral fight, disgustedly flung away such a weapon and jerked out his six-shooter. Frank Canton disposed of his derringer when its ball failed to penetrate Lon McCool's skull, merely glancing around his scalp. Tom Horn's new 30-30 rifle, accurate at very long range, was an oddity to Western folk, who curiously crowded around the gun of unbelievable accomplishments. Ordinary six-guns cost about forty dollars when new. The fancier models were, of course, more expensive. At Ben Thompson's gambling saloon at Dodge City, as the cowboys went broke, they would pawn their six-guns for twenty-two dollars for a Colt's, eighteen dollars and a half for a Remington, and sixteen dollars for other makes of six-shooters. Then they would re-enter the gambling; it was understood that they would.

Marshal Wyatt Earp preferred a well-used, second-hand six-gun to a new one which might possibly jam at the split second time that meant the difference between life and death.

Bowie or "G. R." knives were very seldom worn, but were sometimes carried on horseback for cooking or meat carving purposes — almost never for use in fighting. The Bowie knife was named after Col. James Bowie, who was the leader of the Texans in the Alamo. It was a large, hideous looking instrument. The initials "G. R." just above the hilt stood for George Rex, of England, but was commonly thought to mean "Green River." Texas pioneer Bigfoot Wallace, in relating his fight with the big Indian, said the two hugged and tugged, grunted and panted, and the Indian was about to choke him when he ripped out his old "Butch" and had to "take him up to the 'Green River' " — meaning he had to stab him up to the hilt where the "G. R." sign was.

HOLSTERS

There were several types of holsters. The most ordinary was the ammunition leather belt providing a leather holster on either hip. The traditional bowlegs of the Western cowboy have been attributed partly to the weight of this combination as well as to the contour of the sides of a horse, though this is a matter of conjecture. Usually the butt of the gun, as worn in this holster, pointed toward the rear. Indeed, so unusual was Sheriff Commodore Perry Owens, who reversed this precedent, lodging his six-guns butts-forward and cross-drawing, that the old-timers of Holbrook, Arizona, pronounced the young new long-haired sheriff a greenhorn who wouldn't last long. But Owens demonstrated his ability at the cross draw, usually considered clumsy, more than once. Several of the Graham faction, for instance, in the Pleasant Valley War found it quite efficient.

Some men merely stuck the muzzle inside their regular trousers' belt. A few carried pistols without holsters. A plate of metal with a slot was riveted onto the belt. This slot received the handmade pinhead screw replacing the regular hammer-screw of the single-action Colt's. This handmade pin was fitted into the slot and pushed down until it was caught in a niche at the slot's end, where the pistol hung in open sight swinging with each step. A pistol thus carried could be shot from the hip without being drawn. San Antonio's bad man King Fisher, Texas Ranger Captain Jim Gillett, and El Paso's Chief of Police Jenkins wore their guns thus.

Then there were shoulder holsters worn under the coat for deception, with either leather or a steel spring holding the pistol intact. John Wesley Hardin invented the Hardin holster-vest, which was made of soft calfskin, with two holster pockets on its front, slanting outward from the chest to the hips. Wes carried his six-guns in these pockets with the butts pointing inward. When he drew, his arms crossed and the muzzles of the guns also crossed as they came out. Ordinarily this would have been considered clumsy, but not for the professional pistoleer Hardin — the "World's Champion Desperado!"

Ranger Captain Gillett tried out the Hardin holster-vest and found it entirely too complicated. A friend of his said, "Jim, that's a tony rigout. The stitching of that vest is as fine as I've ever seen. And look at the six-shooters! Why, they're as good an article as Colonel Colt ever turned out. Yes, sir; they are! We'll bury you, later in the week, in that vest." (From *Triggernometry*.)

The diminutive derringer could be carried in a pocket or in a small wrist leather holster. Its bullet was small, round, and deadly dangerous at very close range, but inaccurate beyond ten or fifteen feet.

SIX-SHOOTER-OLOGY

The bad men perfected many tricks with guns. John Wesley Hardin was reputed the master gunman, knowing all the tricks. Rangers once gave him (while in jail) empty guns to watch him perform. He is said to have originated the border roll. He claimed to have used it when Sheriff Wild Bill Hickok asked for his guns at Abilene.

I spent most of my time in Abilene in the saloons and gambling houses, playing poker, faro and seven-up. One day I was playing ten pins and my best horse was hitched outside in front of the saloon. I had two six-shooters on and of course I knew the saloon people would raise a row if I did not pull them off. Several Texans were rolling ten pins and drinking. I suppose we were pretty noisy. Wild Bill came in and said we were making too much noise and told me to take off my pistols until I was ready to go out of town. I told him I was ready to go now, but did not propose to put up my pistols, go or no go. He went out and I followed him. I started up the street when some one behind me shouted:

"Set up. All down but nine."

Wild Bill whirled around and met me. He said:

"What are you howling about and what are you doing with those pistols on?"

I said: "I am just taking in the town."

He pulled his pistol and said: "Take those pistols off. I arrest you."

I said all right and pulled them out of the scabbard, but while he was reaching for them I reversed them and whirled them over on him with the muzzles in his face, springing back at the same time. I told him to put his pistol up, which he did. I cursed him for a long-haired scoundrel that would shoot a boy with his back to him (as I had been told he intended to do me). He said, "Little Arkansaw, you have been wrongly informed."

By this time a big crowd had gathered with pistols and arms. They kept urging me to kill him. Down the street a squad of policemen were coming, but Wild Bill motioned them to go back and at the same time asked me not to let the mob shoot him.

I shouted: "This is my fight and I will kill the first man that fires a gun."

Bill said: "You are the gamest and quickest boy I ever saw. Let us compromise this matter and I will be your friend. Let us go in here and take a drink, as I want to talk to you and give you some advice."

At first I though he might be trying to get the drop on me, but he finally convinced me of his good intentions and we went in and took a drink. We went in a private room and I had a long talk with him and we came out friends.

It has been said that this is the only time that Wild Bill ever backed down and permitted anyone to retain his guns, once he had commanded their surrender. Hardin is said to have employed the same gun trick once again, on a Negro officer in Texas.

Curly Bill was adept at the road agent's spin, which is performed somewhat like the border roll, but the motion is reversed. Pin-wheeling is purely a juggling act, twirling a pistol in air and catching it in firing position — to use this in actual combat is obviously foolhardy.

The border shift, pitching a six-gun from one hand to another into firing position, was used by the ambidextrous Jim Courtright when his thumb was shot by Luke Short. While the pistol was en route from one hand to another, Short fired the fatal bullet, and the border shift had failed. Everybody knew Jim Courtright was the best pistoleer in Texas. Once he was a proud city marshal of Fort Worth and later at the time of this shooting the same city's first gangster demanding "protection" money from saloons. It was a sort of accident that Luke Short's first bullet hit Jim's hammer thumb, so Jim pulled the border shift, but too late. The old-timers couldn't believe it — that somebody had beaten the redoubtable Jim Courtright in a pistol fight; said they, reported Eugene Cunningham: "Oh, yes, Short was right quick with the plow handles. But Jim Courtright — hell! he was a ringtail whizzer with red striped wheels!"

Courtright was one of the very few who could use two guns with equal speed and accuracy simultaneously. When most of the old gun-fighters were in actual combat, they used only one gun, with their shooting hand, and they aimed. It was no slap-hazard business, this shooting at a man who was shooting back at you; it was serious! Your bullets had to hit flesh to count — not a wall or ceiling.

John Young, of Texas, claimed to have been the first to discover the advantages of "fanning," when the trigger of his pistol was accidentally broken off and he was forced to alter the gun's mechanism and strike the hammer to render the gun useful. Today in the movies we see the hero dash in at the melodramatic moment fanning away at his pistol faster than we can count, mowing down villains right and left with each bullet — faster than a modern machine gun. Bunk! You take a pistol for yourself and try fanning it and see where the bullets go. There's no telling.

AW PSHAW!

Doubtless, the bad man did really possess an uncanny quickness and accuracy with firearms, since primarily his life depended upon these factors, and since many gunmen practiced constantly. But time and folklorists have made the bad men of the old West supermen. Nearly all the famous characters of the wild West have been accredited with incredible feats.

For example, one story has Al Jennings' gang galloping by at full speed emptying their revolvers at a post, all shots landing within an area the size of a man's hand. Personally, I "galloped along at full speed on a horse" once until I could hear the wind whistling in my ears and it was all I could do to stay on the animal, much less draw a pistol and still much more less shoot the darn thing and hit the side of a barn. (If I had been carrying one.)

One bad man was said to have cut a string suspending a bottle at a distance of twenty-five yards and then with a second bullet to have hit the bottle before it struck the ground. Still another is reputed as having galloped along at full speed cross firing (right hand to the left, and vice versa) twelve bullets into six consecutive posts on either side of the road.

Oklahoma's famous woman bandit, Belle Starr, was supposed to have been able to gallop along at full speed on her horse and knock off a bumble bee from a thistle at a distance of fifty paces. It seems to have been quite a fad to display one's ability to handle guns while riding at breakneck speed.

Billy the Kid is said to have shot six heads off of six little snow birds as they darted past. Wild Bill Hickok was said to have a mania for emptying his six-gun's contents into the second *O* in a "saloon" sign one hundred yards away.

Quantrill's men, all four hundred and fifty of them, have been accredited with the most astounding ability of placing twelve forty-four caliber bullets into the muzzle of a twelve-gauge gun from a distance of twenty feet, firing continually.

Wild Bill Hickok was said to have cut a rooster's throat with a derringer without breaking its neck at a distance of thirty yards. Anyone knowing about the inaccuracy of the firearms used in those frontier times and especially of the derringer will laugh at this tale.

Anyone who understands the limits of human accuracy will in all probability scoff at all of these unreasonable yarns.

TIN CANS DON'T SASS BACK

Suppose that these tales were true. Suppose that the bad man of the West were as good as Ad Toepperwein. And that would be good! Really good! In a shooting exhibition lasting ten days at the old Fair Grounds at San Antonio, Texas, using a twenty-two rifle, Toepperwein recently shot at 72,500 small wooden blocks as they were tossed into the air, missing only nine blocks out of the 72,500! Of course, that's an all-time World's record. But suppose, now, that the bad man of the old West were as good as that; it would be no definite index of his complete ability as a gun fighter. The bad man's vitally important target was not a dime, a barbed wire, or a chicken's throat from a distance of one hundred yards — but a full-sized, full-grown man usually at much closer range.

To survive, the bad man needed something beside a quick draw and accuracy. Some would call it *nerve*, others the *psychological* edge over the opponent. I don't mean to imply by the word *nerve* that the bad man was a "bundle of nerves." He was anything but that. Doc Holliday, for instance, was deceiving; ordinarily his hands and body were unsteady, since he was an invalid tubercular, until in battle, when his whole being "froze" to the intensity of steel.

Men stood before mirrors practicing the draw for hours at a time and yet found themselves greatly inferior to another, untrained man with the mental edge. Again, a potential Wild Bill Hickok or Billy the Kid was born and not made.

Another thing — a post or a tin can will not "sass back," but an angry or desperate man with a six-gun will. So, it is partly a question of mind over mind. Indeed, the victor of many a gun fight was the inferior artist-pistoleer, but the superior duelist merely by force of his nerve or personality.

TAKE YOUR TIME

Also, the fact that Henry Plummer, for instance, could draw and empty his six-gun within three seconds probably did not benefit him in real battle. Usually the sensible gun fighter gauged his timing with his ability. There was no virtue in speed without accuracy. Frequently the first to shoot was the first to fall.

Wild Bill Hickok and Dave Tutt had a mortal gun fight. Hickok, the lady's man, had stolen Tutt's sweetheart right from under his nose, eventually discarded her, and was now even courting Dave's own sister. This was entirely too much for Dave, so he avowed that he would put an end to it. But he got into too big a hurry. The two men were some seventy-five yards apart walking toward one another and each, because of preliminary warnings and so on, knew the purpose of the meeting. Tutt fired the first bullet at Hickok and the latter, walking with pistol drawn, steadied his gun hand upon his left arm and shot Tutt through the heart. Hickok had taken his time, acted coolly and wisely. Note, incidentally, that this sounds more creditable and probable than Bill's cutting the skin of a rooster's neck with a derringer bullet from a distance of thirty yards — without breaking the rooster's neck.

Had Deputy Webb not been quite so hasty, he would probably have died just the same, but he would have saved the lives of many men John Wesley Hardin killed afterwards. His bullet, the first to be fired, merely scratched Hardin's hip, but Wes's bullet, a fraction of a second afterward, struck the unfortunate Deputy square in the face.

Probably the most often cited fight to support the assertion that "haste makes waste" was related by Marshal Wyatt Earp himself. It was about the duel of Levi Richardson vs. Cockeyed Frank Loving. The motives are unimportant. Loving was a young fellow of about twenty who had never shot at a man before. Richardson had several men to his credit and was a fancy pistoleer. He had just taken up fanning and knew all the fast and fancy tricks. Loving waited nervously for Richardson to burst into the saloon, but followed Marshal Earp's advice; which was to "take your time and make your shots count":

Levi was no assassin and he yelled a warning to Frank that he was going to kill him. Loving took his gun from the drawer of the layout and stood up, waiting.

"Go to shooting! Go to shooting!" Richardson yelled.

"It's your turn," Frank told him.

With that Levi cut loose, fanning his gun and firing so fast you couldn't count the shots. Not one of his slugs hit a fair mark, his last one scratched Loving's hand. While Levi was pumping lead at him, young Loving raised his gun as cool as you please and fired three shots. Every one hit Richardson in a vital spot, and Levi was as good as dead when he hit the floor. Crack shot and courageous man that he was, Levi Richardson had tried to hurry. Frank Loving had taken his time when the split-second of deliberation took a nerve that was far beyond mere physical courage . . .

Cockeyed Frank was not locked up for killing Richardson; everyone knew he had shot in self-defense.

TRIGGERNOMETRY

The old-timers say that the proficient gun fighter had nothing but contempt for fanning. It was true, they say, that mechanisms of guns were almost invariably altered so as to enable smoother single-action shooting merely by the thumbing of the hammer — but no fanning! Wyatt Earp, frontier veteran marshal of Kansas and Arizona, should have known — he had enough experience. Said he: "The most important lesson I learned from those proficient gun-fighters was that the winner of a gunplay usually was the man who took his time. The second was that, if I hoped to live long on the frontier, I would shun flashy trick-shooting — grand stand play — as I would poison."

And bandit Emmett Dalton spoke from experience:

Never did I see a man "fan" his six-shooter.

Never did I see any shooting from the hip.

Never did I see a man waste precious ammunition by using two guns simultaneously. Bob Dalton was accounted one of the best shots in the Southwest, with rifle, pistol, or shotgun. Never once did he indulge any of the phony stunts attributed to so many "master" gunmen of the old border.

The sensible gunman did not drink — at least not enough to dull his senses. He knew that alcohol tended to "increase desire and defeat performance." He did not cram his six-gun full with six cartridges; he left the empty cylinder next to the hammer for the sake of safety. In a sudden pitched battle he usually jumped off his horse and took refuge behind it, exposing only his legs and a small portion of his head. Tombstone Marshal Wyatt Earp's last encounter with the Cochise County rustlers, led by Curly Bill, was at Iron Springs. The rustlers had been watering their horses and the Earp party, on their way out of the country (Wyatt's brother Morgan had been murdered and Virgil badly wounded), had stopped to water theirs. Both parties were surprised at the meeting.

Instantly guns started blazing from both parties. Curly Bill and his associates flung themselves behind an embankment and all but Wyatt turned tail on their horses and retreated. Wyatt dismounted, got behind his horse, exposing only his head and legs, took a few potshots over the animal's back, and gradually backed away. When he took inventory, he supposed he had gotten Curly Bill, who jumped up screaming during the battle, and maybe one or two others. It was a miracle Wyatt was not killed himself. He examined his breeches and found them nearly shot off, leaving his bare legs exposed.

In conclusion, the sensible bad man, if he may be so described, was a deliberate, nervy, calculating pistoleer with the psychological edge over an opponent.

GUNPLAY

One of the best examples of a heroic mortal gun battle was that at Blazer's Mill, in northern New Mexico. The Murphy-Riley-Dolan faction in the Lincoln County war had offered old "Buckshot" Roberts a hundred dollars for each dead McSween follower to his credit; and Billy the Kid, the leader of the Mc-

Sween faction, had heard about it. The Kid and his gang sought out "Buckshot" and found him in a small house in Blazer's Mill. Roberts acquired his cognomen because he was so crippled by ancient wounds and actually so full of real buckshot that he could not lift a rifle to his shoulder. Yet he fought like a wildcat on this memorable day. After being shot clear through the body with a rifle ball, he fought off, single-handed, the whole gang of Billy the Kid, killing Dick Brewer and wounding others, before he finally expired.

* * * * * * *

We've been talking about the Chunk Colbert vs. Clay Allison fight and I imagine you have wondered why I've saved it until now. The answer is that it was one of the most renowned, widely advertised, most spectacular gun fights of the old West — and too it was typical of the battles of guns. It was battles like these that make the old wild West so glamorous today — just as the sagas of Sigrid the Volsung and Eric the Red have been handed down from generation to generation of Norsemen to immortalize the daring deeds of their forefathers.

The avowed purpose of this fight Chunk Colbert, the challenger whose gun sported fourteen notches, widely proclaimed was merely to see who was the better man. They met at the Red River Station in Colfax County, New Mexico. First they had drinks, then they had a horse race which Allison won. Thirdly came the war of words and epic brag, each roaring to what kind of tornado specie he belonged — this ended in Clay's slapping Chunk and Chunk's apologizing. Fourth on program Chunk ordered supper for the two, consisting of coffee and pistols — and finally the climactic fight itself.

The two placed their pistols near their cups, then stirred their coffee and cream with the muzzles, making simultaneous and similar moves and sips. Finally, Chunk went for his gun, which struck the table, sending the bullet wild as Clay, foreseeing the move and waiting for it, quickly shoved the table forward and fell backward, firing his pistol before he struck the floor. The ball struck Chunk between the eyes. He died instantly — as did his reputation, which he had been seeking so desperately.

* * * * * * *

At old Tascosa, Texas, now a field of weeds in the Panhandle somewhere, a famous fight started in a quarrel over Rocking Chair Emma, a dance-hall queen, resulting in four deaths. The shooting began at midnight when Len Woodruff and Charlie Emory met Ed King and John Lang, all of whom exchanged shots, leaving King dead, Emory dying and Woodruff severely wounded. Lang ran back into the dance hall yelling to Frank Valley and Fred Chilton to come avenge King's death. Meantime Woodruff had dragged himself into an old adobe house and barricaded the door, which was presently shot through by Valley and Chilton, the bullets whizzing by Woodruff. The latter flung open the door and killed his two antagonists and was himself again wounded. Using his Winchester as a crutch he limped, crept, crawled, and finally dragged himself for three hours, crossing a creek to a ranch house a mile and a half away, thus escaping further vengeance. Blood marked every foot of his path.

* * * * * * *

The four Blevans men of the Graham faction in the Pleasant Valley war were no match for the singlehanded Sheriff Commodore Perry Owens, who approached their home knowing they had pistols or rifles trained on him. Each time he saw the muzzle of a pistol or heard one bark he fired in its immediate vicinity, killing three men and seriously wounding the fourth — without wasting any ammunition!

* * * * * * *

Dallas Stoudenmire, of the chin like a block of rough-hewn oak, and of the steel-blue eye like a riveting machine, walked into an ambush of his enemies, the Johnsons and Mannings. It occurred at El Paso while Dallas was a police officer there. What did Stoudenmire do? What would you have done had you walked into a trap and faced six or eight bad men's gun muzzles, with the bad men concealed behind barricades of boxes and corners? Evidently the thing to do is that which will most astonish the bad men — the thing they least expect. And that's what Stoudenmire did. He actually charged his would-be assassins, firing rapidly in all directions, not even aiming, and so sudden and audacious and menacing was he that the members of the ambush pocketed their guns and scampered in all directions.

* * * * * * *

Probably the most famous battle in the annals of New Mexico was the climax of the McSween-Murphy war. At Lincoln, Murphy's men surrounded McSween's home, containing his fighters, including Billy the Kid. McSween was a preacher of the gospel himself and would not carry a gun. While the McSween men were in parley with Murphy's men and Major Dudley and his miltary officials, the Murphy men had set fire to the McSween home. Dudley retired, refusing to interfere, as he should have done, and the shooting recommenced between the factions. The Murphy men surrounded the flaming house, containing McSween, the Kid, and the rest of their cohorts. Mrs. McSween left the house and walked right through the line of fire. Both sides ceased firing to let her come through. Can you imagine a modern gangster being so considerate? She was on her way to Major Dudley's army tent, where she told him a thing or two, all right.

McSween conceived the brilliant idea that if he would deliver himself, the leader of his faction, to the wolves, he might save the lives of his followers. He walked out of the burning house brushing aside the protests of the Kid and shouted, "I am McSween!" Of course, he met a hail of bullets and was killed instantly.

Enraged over the outlandish death of their beloved leader and scorched by the heat of the flames, McSween's men filed out rapidly and ran for a high fence. Some of them made an escape in this manner, but some were killed en route to the fence. Billy the Kid calmly lighted a cigarette from a burning beam, enjoyed a few good puffs while the other men left, and was the last to leave the edifice. He emptied his guns while side-stepping dead bodies, killing one enemy and wounding two others, and finally hurdling the fence untouched. A Mexican named Ygenio Salazar was hit on his way to the fence and fell, feigning death. In the lull after the battle the Murphy men examined the bodies, kicking them to see if life was extinct. Salazar, though infinitely pained, showed no signs of life, and later when the victors retired, he dragged himself to safety.

* * * * * * *

The one and only Wild Bill Hickok — what a man! It happened in a North Platte (Nebraska) restaurant. Two of his enemies (he had quite a few) came gunning for him, one from the front door and the other from the back — but Wild Bill had been warned and was ready and waiting. There was a mirror above the front door, which came in mighty handy for Wild Bill. He drew his pistols, both of them, with a movement almost quicker than the eye could perceive, and with one he killed the man in front of him, and at the same time with the other gun hand resting on the opposite shoulder he killed the man behind him, looking through the mirror. It was believed for a long time thereafter that Bill had eyes in the back of his head, or some sixth sense.

* * * * * * *

Unusual was the clasped hand duel with six-shooters. In Oregon "the famous Hank Vaughan" and a cowboy from Montana met and fought a desperate duel. The two clasped their left hands, drew their guns with their right, and emptied them. Both Hank and his assailant fell, seriously wounded, but marvelously enough, both recovered.

Of all the desperadoes or gunmen not on the side of the law ever, only one did not flee after killing or any other kind of altercation — and that was Clay Allison. Being a super-charged and perhaps over-ardent patriotic Southerner, he killed five Negro soldiers at one time and hung around for some time hoping someone would try to arrest him. No one did.

I think, too, that the famous O. K. Corral battle between the Earp officers and partner Holliday versus the Cochise County rustlers at Tombstone deserves mention again — here — as one of the most famous gun battles of the old West. I believe in this section we've about hit the most colorful of all these battles.

ROUGH AND TUMBLE

Indeed, the great majority of fights were gun fights. There are, however, a few famous rough and tumble fisticuffs in the history of the old West. The Mississippi River bullies preferred fist-fights to pistol duels.

Bill Sedley, a keelboater, thoroughly whipped a 180-pound Kentucky flatboater and, holding him by the heels, threw him fifteen feet into the water, ending up flapping his hands and crowing like a rooster. Bad man Mike Fink and Colonel Davey Crockett were veteran fighters in this style.

Most famous, probably, of all frontier fist fights was the one between Phil Coe and Wild Bill Hickok. Bill had slapped Phil's girl, since she had spurned Wild Bill and had taken up with Phil. Bill was slightly tipsy. Phil suddenly became a raging demon. Both men were over six feet and weighed over two hundred pounds. Phil knocked Bill halfway across the room. Bill rose, and witnesses said that no prize fight was ever half as intense or gruesome or brutal as that which immediately followed. The two huge men stood their ground, neither attempting to dodge the blows or the onslaughts of the other, each slugging as hard and as fast as he could. Finally, Coe drew back all the way and struck Bill a blow on the jaw that lifted him completely off his feet. Bill slumped to the floor unconscious; Coe jumped on him and began to shake his shoulders and beat his head against the floor until Jesse Hazel, the girl in question, stopped him.

Bill sobered up next day and came around to apologize to Phil for acting a heel. Phil forgave him and all looked well for a while, but Bill never forgave Phil for stealing his girl friend. One day he shot unsuspecting Phil through the back as Phil started out through the door — and that was the end of the Wild Bill Hickok-Phil Coe feud.

At New Orleans Ben Thompson, then a youth, fought an unusual duel with a Frenchman, Emil de Tour. The two were unclothed in a pitch-dark room, armed with a dagger. A romantic setting, wasn't it? Ben said, "Are you ready?" and dodged at the same time. The Frenchman did not detect the treachery and lunged at the place where the voice came from, whereupon Thompson leaped astride de Tour and gouged him to death, Ben getting a few cuts himself.

A very unusual duel, testing the wrestling strength and ability to manipulate guns under strenuous circumstances, was fought by Joe Burnette and Red Kelley, who killed Bob Ford, the slayer of Jesse James. By the way, this illustrates several "chains" of killings. For another example, these men were killed successively by one another: Webb, Hardin, Selman, Scarbrough, Carver, Bryant. This would seem to reinforce the idea that "He who taketh up the sword (or pistol) will perish by the sword." And Bill Longley said, "There never was a man so fast but what he found a man just a little faster."

But back to Joe Burnette vs. Red Kelley. The two antagonists met at very close range and each drew and grabbed the other's gun-hand wrist simultaneously. Grunting, panting, cursing, each shot three times, before they fell to the pavement with Kelley on top. At length, by superior strength and sudden effort, Burnette got into position to draw a bead on Kelley and killed him; but Burnette was so exhausted that he could not move the the body on top of him nor wriggle from under it. He had to call for help from frightened spectators.

So much for rough and tumble, catch as catch can.

HOW THEY ESCAPED

Usually escape from jail was easy for the bad man; it was simply a part of his technique. His place of confinement was usually a flimsy structure of one room, rather poorly guarded by one old man. He was allowed visitors freely. He could often bribe the keeper, whose salary was small. His wife or friends could smuggle pistols in to him, as in several cases they actually did. He could dig his way out, or set fire to the building. He had friends who would have a good horse waiting for him. Then, as is sometimes true now, he might be able to pull political wires and gain his liberty. These were the usual methods of escaping jail, although there were more complicated ones.

For example, Marshal Canton said that Bill Booth was the hardest man to keep in jail that he ever handled. Each night he would free himself from the shackles or leg-irons made by the best blacksmith in Wyoming. In Canton's own words:

> He had his back tight up against the steel cell, then com-
> menced a circular motion with his right foot until he had the
> chain badly twisted. He would then brace his back against his
> cell and straighten his right leg out with such force and strength
> that it would snap the links of the chain . . .

Canton stopped this by having a swivel put in the chain. Booth then improvised a small steel saw out of writing pens hammered out flat with a small brass crucifix, moulded into the shape of a saw by the heat of a candle and hardened by its sperm, and fastened to a sparerib. With this he sawed nearly through his shackles so that the cut was not noticeable. Only by the quick drawing of his revolver did Canton prevent his escape and save his own life.

Billy the Kid's escape from confinement under guard of officers Bell and Ollinger, at Lincoln, New Mexico, we have mentioned; and it is often cited as being one of the most phenomenal escapes by outlaws of the old wild West.

There are several versions, but the most interesting yet plausible one is that while keeper Bob Ollinger was at dinner across the street, keeper Bell and the kid were in a pleasant, casual game of seven-up. The Kid, of course, was shackled and unarmed, sitting on the table. Bell, seated in a chair, wore pistols on his hips. The Kid, sensing his opportunity, purposely dropped a card. Bell stooped over to get it, and Billy grabbed Bell's six-shooter, covering the astonished sheriff. When the two started down the stairs of the temporary jail, Bell took a long chance, leaping for the corner. Billy shouted for him to stop and, seeing Bell wouldn't, shot him. Bell fell dead. Ollinger, hearing the shot, rushed back to investigate but was met by Billy's "Hello, Bob!" and eighteen buckshot from his own gun. Billy then made the cook chop away his shackles and danced a jig while his horse was saddled. He rode away leisurely, singing a long Mexican *cancione.*

Bill Doolin effected his escape by telling a funny story. While his prison guard was convulsed with laughter, Bill reached through the bars and confiscated the guard's revolver, forced him inside the bars, unlocked the doors, and released all the prisoners. This happened at Guthrie, Oklahoma.

John Wesley Hardin was especially noted for his skill and daring in escaping from mobs and posses. Twice he rode straight into them, and so great was the befuddlement that he escaped with an easy start. Once he and Bill Taylor were pursued by two posses from opposite directions. The two charged straight into one posse, which became utterly confused, and the other was afraid to fire into the crowd, lest they shoot their allies. Taylor and Hardin rode off at a gallop and faded away into the sagebrush in the distance.

A favorite ruse of the bad man being pursued, as we have already noted, when confronted by curious strangers, was the pretension of being sheriffs or possemen ahead of the regular party in search of themselves. Sam Bass, the Jameses and the Youngers, the Daltons, Polk Wells, and little Al Jennings employed this trick successfully more than once.

HOW THEY ROBBED

The professional outlaws of the old West planned their robberies just as efficiently as a military high command plans an important campaign.

To rob a train involved three functions, usually two men to each. One duty was the mounting of the engineer's cab, covering the engineer and fireman, and throwing water into the firebox, thus "killing" the engine. Another was the covering and intimidating of passengers and train crew. The third and most important as far as proceeds and danger were concerned was the tapping of the express car, usually well guarded by shotgun agents, some of whom would fight to the death. Of course, the quicker the surprise attack, the more successful the robbery. The Daltons always gambled for these positions before each robbery, thus seeking to expel favoritism and jinxes.

Probably the most sensational bank robbery the James-Younger gang ever pulled was at a small county-seat town named Corydon. Jesse had probably planned the whole thing minutely. He chose this particular day because there was to be a big gathering on the courthouse lawn for a political speaking. Now everybody turned out to things of that kind in those days — interest and people ran riot, anything was likely to happen. Loud-mouthed orators bellowed to open-mouthed hypnotized audiences, and when the cheering started everybody went berserk.

Seven young men rode into Corydon, dressed in their Sunday-go-to-meetin' clothes with potato bags slouchily flung across their saddle pommels ostensibly to buy provisions for the week and carry back to the farm. They had dressed up for the occasion of the speaking. That was all — that was what it looked like, and no one paid any attention ot them.

When the crowd became assembled on the courthouse lawn and some candidate began bombasting away with vehement gesticulations, three of the horsemen quietly entered the bank and found the cashier all alone. They covered him from head to toe-nail with six-shooters, took his keys to the safe, extracted some $40,000 which they dumped into the "potato" bag, bound the cashier and gagged him, and calmly walked out remarking about the weather. They, too, wanted to hear the speeches, or they wouldn't have bound the poor cashier — they never did at any other of their robberies. They sat on their horses, as was common, on the outskirts of the crowd.

The fiery orator-politician was blasting away on the dark evils of black Republicanism, when Jesse started heckling him:

"Mr. Dean, I rise to a point of order, sir."
"What is it, friend and fellow-citizen?" inquired the orator. "If anything of paramount importance, I yield to the gentleman on horseback."
"Well, sir," said Jesse James, "I reckon it's important enough. The fact is, Mr. Dean, some fellows have been over to the bank and tied up the cashier, and if you-all ain't too busy you might ride over and untie him. I've got to be going." (From *The Life and Times of Jesse James*.)

The robbers with their "potato" bags bulging with greenbacks rode leisurely out of town, inciting no suspicion, and it was several minutes until the citizens of Corydon acted upon Jesse's suggestion, thinking at first it was just a gag to frustrate the speaker. Of course, by the time of the discovery of the robbery, the Jameses and Youngers were well out of town and speeding away to their hideout.

As for robbing individuals heavily laden with valuables journeying alone or in groups, in a pack train, or by stagecoach, Henry Plummer's Northwest gang of road agents was probably the most completely organized. Plummer was, for a time, sheriff at Bannack, and he or his spies knew every move of money. They worked under cover. Judge Langford once entrusted $14,000 to Henry Plummer before several witnesses, rather than meet his gang of freebooters without witnesses in some rocky ravine pass in the road where he would lose both his life and the money. As a result, the $14,000 was kept safely and delivered to its destination. Probably the completeness of detail of this organized crime group is best revealed in the confession of Red Yager, one of its members, just before being hanged. Old-timer Judge Langford tells about the event:

> On being urged by the leader to furnish their names, which he said should be taken down, "Red" told him that Henry Plummer was chief of the band; Bill Bunton, stool pigeon and second in command; George Brown, secretary; Sam Bunton, roadster; Cyrus Skinner, fence spy and roadster; George Shears, horse-thief and roadster; Frank Parrish, horse-thief and roadster; Hayes Lyons, telegraph man and roadster; Bill Hunter, telegraph man and roadster; Ned Ray, council-room keeper at Bannack; and about a dozen more roadsters.
>
> These men were bound by an oath to be true to eath other, and were required to perform such services as came within the defined meaning of their separate positions in the band. The penalty of disobedience was death. If any of them, under any circumstances, divulged any of the secrets or guilty purposes of the band, he was to be followed and shot down at sight. The same doom was prescribed for any outsider who attempted an exposure of their criminal designs, or arrested any of them for the commission of crime. Their great object was declared to be plunder, in all cases, without taking life if possible; but if murder was necessary, it was to be committed. Their pass-word was "Innocent." Their neckties were fastened with a sailor's knot, and they wore mustaches and chin whiskers.

HOW TO TREAT A BAD MAN

Suppose a bad man has got it in for you, has announced that he's gunning for you, walks in the door and there you are face to face. Or maybe you bump into him accidentally. Maybe the fellow guzzling down his roaring mountain lion at the bar is your bad man with his back right next to yours. Maybe he's already "loose as a goose" and somebody shoves you against him. He turns around scowling in your face.

You're in a mighty tough spot, partner. What are you going to do?

Well, that depends upon your presence of mind. Maybe the best thing to do is to laugh it off or smile and agree with everything he says. Texas Ranger Bill McDonald told about a Mexican bad *hombre* who had him covered and who told him to "reach for the skies." McDonald smiled agreeably and started to comply, talking amiably all the while, so as to throw the man off guard. As soon as McDonald's hands reached the elevation of his hat, he grabbed the wide brim of the sombrero and sailed it with the quickness of lightning square into the Mexican's face. In the split second of the Mexican's befuddlement, McDonald had shot him in the hand. At another time McDonald had consented to drink with a captive bad man, who, just as McDonald threw his head back to gulp down the last swig, threw his full glass of whiskey into the Ranger's face. So completely blinded and confused was the officer that his prisoner ran out the door, jumped on a horse, and escaped.

Arizona Ranger Captain Harry Wheeler, unarmed, faced two desperadoes and their pistol muzzles. The Ranger said for them to wait a minute for him to tie his boots up. On his way up from the stooping position he threw a handful of sand into their eyes, grabbed a gun and covered them.

A similar trick saved a girl named Harrington who was faced with the problem of being attacked by an evil-countenanced, large Indian. The two were alone at a lonely ranch house. She seemingly paid no attention to him, however, until to his great confusion she threw a lifting iron square into his face, thus throwing him off guard. In his surprise she ran past him and grabbed a shotgun in the corner of the room and shot him dead.

Here's another trick that might work. It did for Wild Bill Hickok. A Texas cowboy desperado was in the act of treeing the whole town of Hays City, Kansas. Bill was summoned to put a stop to the festival. He chased the cowboy into a saloon only to face two awfully big looking barrels in front of two big bleary eyes — red eyes. Bill's troubled expression slowly gave way to a sly grin as he gazed beyond the outlaw, saying, "All right, Charley, take him alive — no need to kill him. He's just a joker." The puzzled outlaw turned to see who the invisible captor could be for a mere second, but that was long enough for lightning Wild Bill to shoot the desperado's trigger finger away.

If a peace officer wanted to "down" a belligerent man without killing him, he would strike him on the head with the barrel of his heavy pistol — in other words, "buffalo" him. No experienced officer would hold the barrel and strike with the butt, as he is sometimes shown doing in the movies, for the jar would probably fire the pistol and backfire it toward the officer himself.

When men made threats against him, Wyatt Earp always said, "We'll wait till they get nervous and start something." He believed that a bad man would not ambush him among witnesses; for under the code, that would brand him a murdering coward. To establish himself as a hero or glorious victor, the bad man would have to give his opponent an even break. Usually, he would get worried, nervous, possibly scared, and probably slightly drunk, and come blustering into a room firing rapidly and inaccurately while the cool and collected marshal shot, once.

A man named Witherbee calmly walked into a barroom, unarmed, smiling, talking pleasantly in a slow voice, and staring straight into the crazed eyes of a demented bartender who was shooting pistols promiscuously. In a quiet manner Witherbee commanded the man to hand over his guns and go to bed, saying that he was a sick man. The man hesitated a moment and then, with a sheepish grin, complied.

At old wild and woolly Tascosa, in the Texas Panhandle, a cowboy named Dunn was getting a drink of water in a saloon when Ed King, drunk and maddened, came up and jabbed a pistol into his ribs. But the cowboy merely looked at him and went on drinking, as though he were a mosquito lighted on his shoulder. When Ed said, "Why don't you hold up your hands?" the cowboy replied, "Because I want another drink of water." At that the drunken man, puzzled and baffled, put away his pistol and walked out, whereupon the much relieved cowboy wiped the perspiration from his forehead.

In dealing with a whole mob of bad men, singlehanded, Wyatt

Earp always picked out the leaders, usually one or two, and worked on them. He would tell them that if one man advanced one step more, the eighteen buckshot in the double-barreled gun he held trained on the mob would go right through his belly. This always stopped the mob. This was exactly the situation out at Tombstone when Wyatt was protecting a prisoner nicknamed Johnny-behind-the-Deuce from an angry mob of some five hundred men. They came marching down the street toward the house in which Marshal Earp had jailed Johnny, about twenty abreast. Wyatt said that he had trouble picking a leader from such a motley crew, but finally centered his attention on one or two influential citizens on the front row and delivered the same ultimatum to them. They slowly, one by one, dismissed themselves and wandered on home. The next day, over the heat of the moment, these influential citizens confessed their stupidity in being with the mob.

Suppose you had to disarm a bad man, once you got the drop on him and had his hands up. How would you go about it? Without any question this is the best way to do it: walk up to him keeping your eye on his. If he's going to pull any monkey business on you, his eyes will give him away. If he does, then go ahead and shoot — to save your own hide! But if he's got any sense he'll stand still. Keep your gun trained on him all the time and with your free hand unbuckle his belt which will contain holsters, guns, and ammunition. Let the whole shebang fall to the ground and then command the bad man to step away a few yards. This will enable you to keep your eye on the bad man's every move and at the same time to keep your revolver in firing position. This technique, used by frontier citizens, officers and bad men alike, was by far the safest. Incidentally, you might feel of his clothes with your free hand to determine whether he has any concealed weapons.

Now, you should be a veteran handler of bad men. Do you reckon you would know what to do if you met him in person?

CHAPTER III

WHO WERE THE BAD MEN?

HETEROGENEOUS

"WHO *was* the bad man of the West?" you ask.

Purely arbitrarily we shall answer that he was one who acted against society for his own personal gain, and that he was one to be feared, because he was personally dangerous and took the lives of other people, innocent some of them — some not. Usually he was desperate, or soon became so, for fear of the safety of his own precious neck and hence he acquired the name of *desperado*.

And he didn't just happen accidentally, either. At no other time and at no other place could there have been a bad man of the West. Men lost their heads, figuratively and literally, over some impudent or imprudent newly freed Negro after the Civil War, or over cattle or gold or silver.

Wherever there was an American Western frontier there was also the bad man, just a few steps ahead of the establishment of law and order. At the end of the eighteenth century in Virginia, Tennessee, and Kentucky the bad man was well exemplified by the ravishing, maniacal, bloodthirsty Harpes. Wily and Micajah Harpe dragged their women, ragged and tattered, from one farm house to another, begging food and killing their benefactors, and then burning their homes to cover up the evidence. At the beginning of the twentieth century on the Western coast was Harry Tracy, a very bad man who escaped jail quite a few times with a fellow prisoner, killed him after his usefulness no longer existed, harried farm houses for food and shelter, and ran amuck for some time. Doubling back to Oklahoma, we find innumerable

Geronimo . . . was a very foxy old devil, to be sure. He raided set-
tlements and rustled cattle on both sides of the United States-
Mexico boundary. (See page 87.)

desperadoes — the Daltons, the Doolin gang and a host of others — all on the very outposts of the American white race. And there we have followed the American frontier and there we have followed the path of the "hell on wheels" set going by the bad man of the West.

Between the times and places just mentioned there's no telling how many bad men stalked the prairies of the wide-open spaces or drank their red-eye on Saturday nights at the old town bar — but accounts of one kind or another have come down about some 250 rootin', tootin', shootin', high-falutin' cyclones — who went through hell and high water, made their place in the sun and lost it.

Remember this, too, for the time being — most of them lived from 1850 to 1900, started their bloody careers at about fifteen years of age and ended them at thirty to thirty-five. And there's a reason for it all.

"Now," you patiently persist, "please tell me *who were* the bad men of the West?"

Well, they were Mexicans, Negroes, Chinamen, Indians, Americans (which means anything); they came in all sizes, shades, and shapes — in all degrees of badness, braveness, and cowardice. By far the greatest number were Americans of Caucasian race background. The American bad man seemed to have the knack of getting into scrapes all by himself without the aid of companions and to have the nerve to see the thing through by himself and in person. Probably most of us are interested more in the American bad man than in the others, so I'm going to dismiss the others by merely mentioning a few Mexicans and Indians.

INJUNS!

Take Indians, for example. They didn't fight individually, but in a tribe war; hence few of them acquired reputations as bad men. But we can't leave out the Apache Kid of Arizona. He was despised by the whites and the reds alike. He killed first for vengeance and later for diversion. He was trained by Al Seiber to be a scout for the U. S. Army and served well in that capacity for a few years until he drifted into crime. He kidnapped his squaws and mistreated them; they cordially hated him. He killed Gila County's (Ariz.) fine Sheriff Glenn Reynolds, in a phenomenal escape en route to prison. This he did by leaping on the Ranger from behind with a war whoop, striking him on the head with his handcuffs and slipping them down over his face and sides, thus pinioning his arms. Other prisoner Indians took the signal and disarmed the desperately struggling Reynolds and another officer named Holmes and promptly killed them both and escaped. They were all later recaptured; two committed suicide in jail, and the others were hanged. That is, except the wily Apache Kid. What finally became of the Apache Kid is a matter of conjecture, but it is believed that a well-known army scout at Camp Grant, Arizona, by the name of Hualpai Clarke, shot him while the renegade prowled about the scout's corral one night. At least the vicious Kid ravished no more.

Geronimo, another Apache, was a great chief and a leader of men. Perhaps he should be called a tribal hero rather than a bad man. He was a very foxy old devil, to be sure. He raided settlements and rustled cattle on both sides of the United States-Mexico boundary. Whenever he was pursued by officers of either country, he would step across the border and be out of jurisdiction of the vexed officers. General Nelson A. Miles was sent out by the War Department with orders to get the Apache chief after his last big flourish in 1885. The General found the Apache only when the Apache was quite ready to be found — in some very cleverly located ambush from which his warriors could empty Army saddles. One of Miles' old-timer scouts said, "When you see 'Pache signs, be keerful. When you don't see 'em, be still more keerful!"

Finally Lieutenant Gatewood of the U. S. Army and a famous Army scout named Tom Horn entered the picture. Horn was the one, you remember, who cleared out the Coon Hole rustlers in Arizona. He was also the one who later did wonderful work for the Army and who was still later hired by some of the big land barons to get rid of some squatters, which he did too well and for which he was hanged (for shooting a boy in cold blood).

Anyway, Horn inveigled Geronimo to surrender to General Miles. Geronimo was imprisoned in a cell (now bearing his name) in the basement of the old building now used as a museum at Fort Sill, Oklahoma. The recent movie bearing his name did not stick to the true facts of his life, but then neither do many other movies of bad men stay with the true facts.

Chief Victorio, also another Apache, was probably the greatest of them all, especially as a military tactician. He carried two hundred warriors and their families over mountain ranges, rivers, and plains and plundered, killed, raided, slaughtered, and robbed his way through Arizona, New Mexico, Texas, and far into old Mexico. He had a most effective way of drawing his pursuers into a well-regulated trap where he could exterminate them all. So strategically was his tribe situated in their mountain stronghold with sentinels properly posted that it took a formidable army consisting of Negro U. S. soldiers, Mexican infantry, Texas Rangers, and even some Apaches friendly to the whites, making five hundred or more in all, to capture his warriors. The great chief was killed in the fight and up to that time. it has been claimed, he had been a thoroughly bad Indian.

These three Indians, the Apache Kid, Geronimo, and Victorio. probably the .most famous among the bad Indians, were all Apaches. It is generally conceded that the Apaches and the Comanches were the most evil-natured of all the tribes of Indians and that the other nations were in constant fear of them.

Lawrie Tatum, the first Texas Kiowa agent, knew how to handle his bad Indians. The greatest punishment possible for an Indian, so he said, was the denial of sugar and coffee. For this rare delicacy an Indian would confess to any crime, bring in kidnapped people or even stolen horses, make any promise.

As an afterthought, ordinarily the bad Indian was sullen and dignified. However, on occasions he exhibited a most peculiar sense of humor. Chief Has-ten-de-ti-da, when sentenced to thirty years in the penitentiary, broke out in boisterous guffaws, slapping himself on the knees and pointing at the judge, saying, "Thirty year, ha! ha! Heap big joke on you, Judge. Has-ten-de-ti-da not live that long. Me die 'bout ten year! Ha! Ha! You get cheated!"

Other Indian chiefs of lesser import as bad men, yet whose crimes and thrilling experiences would fill volumes, were Satanta, Satank, Sharp Nose, Dull Knife, Two Moons, Black Hawk, Red Sleeves, Lone Wolf, and Sitting Bull (who was really more wild than bad).

The bad Indian fought for revenge; it was not in his nature to forgive nor forget. He was just like some mules — very corrupt at heart. Some mules, according to Josh Billings, are good for six months at a time, just to get an opportunity to kick somebody. The Indian would be a good Indian for twenty years, like th Apache Kid, just to get a chance to stick a knife in the back somebody who had done his father an injustice. The Indian resented the invasion of the white man into his land and the extinction of his chief food supply — the unnecessary wholesale slaughter of the buffalo.

The great General Sam Houston once said on the floor of the United States Senate that he had never known an Indian to be the first to break a treaty with the white man. Perhaps the Indian thought, not without reason, that the Indian was the better man of the two races.

But if you're one of those people who don't believe in the "brave, admirable qualities of the noble red man," then you'll enjoy Mark Twain's description of the Goshoot. He says the Goshoot and the Norwegian rat are descended from the selfsame Darwinian animal-Adam, and so on.

The Indian did not fight individually, was not generally forced to face the odds required of a desperado; hence few of them acquired reputations as bad men. According to the Indian's code, he was doubtlessly a brave man. The psychology governing his actions, resulting from his philosophy and religion, becomes readily discernible with a reading of Colonel Dodge's analysis in *The Great Hunting Grounds of the West.* I know of no better source telling what made the Indian the way he was.

Why did the Indian especially fear death by hanging or by strangulation, when he was usually fearless otherwise? Why did the Indian scalp? Why did the Indian bury his comrade with a rifle rather than with a bow and arrow? Why did he prefer being buried in a U. S. Army uniform? Why did he almost never foray or attack on a moonless night? What made the Indian remorseless? Why was the Indian not a typical bad man of the West? Colonel Dodge answers these and many other questions.

Dos Orejanas

The most famous Mexican bad man of all time was Joaquin Murrieta of California, whose career as a killer lasted from 1850 to 1863. A gang of unscrupulous white prospectors broke into his home, knocked him out, and mistreated his beautiful wife Rosita, who died as a consequence. His brother was hanged by a group of miners for stealing a horse which he probably did not steal; and Joaquin, himself, was horsewhipped.

At first he wanted revenge merely on the perpetrators of these crimes, which he hastily effected; but the gory lust of the "Robin

Hood of El Dorado" could not be abated. He raised a small army of about eighty Mexicans and declared war on the whole white race; his ultimate colossal purpose became the complete ridding the continent of the despised *gringos*.

He killed some three hundred whites, inflicting terror the state of California never knew before or since his time. He remained at large until the fearless California Ranger Harry Love and his small band killed him in a surprise attack on his camp. It took eleven balls to kill Three-Fingered Jack, one of his captains.

Joaquin's last words were, "It is enough; the work is done."

Evidently his vengeance was at last satisfied. Joaquin was decapitated and his head was placed on exhibit in San Francisco at a dollar per peep. The notoriety of Joaquin Murrieta still survives in the West — after 100 years since he first marauded. Long after his death many people of California sincerely believed that he had escaped death at the hands of Harry Love and would return to harass the state.

The Mexican bad men of fame, like the Indians, were not plentiful — and for the same reason. The Mexican bad man, like the Indian, did not fight individually, but as a rule he worked in a group which had no decisive leader. Texas Ranger Captain John R. Hughes dealt with Mexican outlaws on the Texas border for twenty-eight years and should be one of the best authorities on how to handle them. Said he:

> Lots of Texans make a big mistake and get killed by thinking that a Mexican isn't dangerous. Mexicans are just as brave in their way as any white man, but when one decides to kill a Gringo he doesn't ride right out and shoot him. They always work in gangs, four or five men, and waylay their man or lead him into some trap. A big Texas Policeman laughed at me one time when I brought in a Mexican handcuffed and admitted that he was dangerous.
>
> "I can lick a whole cowpen full of Greasers," said he.
>
> A year later he started a sheep ranch, and got killed by his Mexican herder -- with the same gun he had given him to shoot coyotes.
>
> When Mexicans rob a white man's house they always kill him first, so he won't talk. Dawn and dusk are their favorite times and I always put on my pistol as I go out to do my chores. Sergeant

Fusselman, whose place I took, always thought he could whip a hundred Mexicans. But when he rode up on six of the Bosque gang they saw him coming, lay in wait for him, and shot him dead. It was the same with Captain Jones. If you corner a Mexican he will fight like a rattlesnake, and no matter how brave a man is, a bullet will kill him. (From Coolidge's *Fighting Men of the West.*)

Burton C. Mossman was for some time the boss of the enormous Hash-Knife outfit, one of the largest cattle concerns in the old West, and later the first captain of the Arizona Rangers. He said:

> There is no such thing as a nation of cowards, for such a nation could not exist. A bad Mexican is like any ignorant man — when he starts to fight he does it through fear, and nothing will stop him. There is no use trying to get the drop on him — you have got to kill him. He fights like a cornered rat, or a cat that is shut up in a room. If he can get away, the cat will run when you throw a peanut-shell at him, but if you corner him and begin to hit him, he will charge you like a lion. It is the same with all ignorant people. (From *Fighting Men of the West.*)

But there are always exceptions. There were two Mexican bad men who *would* fight individually, who *did* gain reputations as very bad men, and who *were* leaders of men. They were Joaquin Murrieta and one other — Augustine Chacon.

Chacon killed twenty-nine Americans and approximately eighty men altogether. It was no more to him to kill a man than to kill a rattlesnake. Unlike most Mexicans, he was tall, angular, gaunt, powerful, but he moved with the stealth of a panther. He was the type of outlaw the Mexicans sing of in their long *canciones*, a man who robbed only the rich and gave to the poor peons. Nearly $12,000 in rewards was offered for his arrest. He was captured once by Sheriff Birchfield of Graham County, Arizona, but made a dramatic escape.

In a neighboring mining settlement named Morenci, Augustine had many friends and sympathizers, especially one — a very pretty Mexican señorita. She visited him while he was in jail and brought him a prayer book, inside of which he found some hacksaw blades, bound up in the cover of the book.

Chacon had been condemned to execution by hanging and his jailer stood the death watch all night. But the señorita came and vamped the keeper. She sang beautiful Spanish songs and played her guitar, while other Mexican prisoners accompanied her with a concertina and French harp. All this covered up the sound of Chacon's busily sawing his way out. The señorita finally lured the jailer away from his post and Chacon escaped in the dark of the night.

Finally, however, Chacon was caught by Captain Mossman of the Arizona Rangers and later hanged. Upon hearing his sentence, he said, "I am a man; I am not afraid to die."

Other Mexican bad men of note but not of great fame were Chavez (friend of Billy the Kid), Tiburcio Vasquez, Espinosa, the Olguin, the Carrasco, and the Baca brothers.

Like the Indians, Mexicans in their way were undoubtedly courageous.

THE WORST BAD MAN ON EARTH

And now we come to the worst bad man on earth. Reputedly he put all others in the background.. Traditionally he was more likely to uphold the code of the West. He came out in open daylight and met his foe face to face at his own proper personal peril. He was thàt rip-roarin', hell-raisin', fire-spittin' American bad man. We see him in our movies, literature, and folklore with Anglo-Saxon characteristics; but he could have been any other Caucasian or Mexican, Negro, Indian, or Chinaman.

Who was he? Well, he was likely to be anybody on the American western frontier with a gun — even you or I had we been there. It all depended upon how things fell — and how he reacted; what his motives were.

What about the law? Where did he stand? Well, bad men have been classified in two types — those on the side of the law and those on the outside of the law. Actually there were bad man of all shades of badness in either class, but the balance, of course, went to that distinctly outside the law. And the law itself was frequently merely a technicality.

A CLASS OF HIS OWN

But some of them simply cannot be classified — put into one single category. Why? Simply because they belonged to several, as we shall see — and because of their versatilities and capabilities they were unique.

Certainly there was no other one approximately the genius or of the genus of James Butler Hickok, better known as Wild Bill. He was a class to himself principally because he was a combination of many of the types of bad men we are about to decipher.

He was tall, about six-feet-one, weighed two hundred pounds, had steel-blue-gray eyes, long blond silken curls that spread down to his shoulders, sported a yellow mustache. His nose was slightly acquiline. Ordinarily he was quiet, he meant what little he said, and he was calm and collected even under fire. He was revengeful, cold-blooded, fearless — "a mad old bull outstanding among the herd." His hands and feet were small, his form was perfect, and his clothes! He was the acme of sartorial elegance. Oh yes, he was quite a "lady-killer."

He had the dauntless courage, the iron nerve — the ability both physical and mental (we will omit the moral) — to be law officer in the wildest, toughest, meanest frontier towns. No one will ever know how many men good or bad found the end of their mortal existence looking, or not looking, down the blazing barrels of Wild Bill's guns. Different accounts vary from thirty-five to eighty-five to his credit. That many of his deeds before and during his career as peace officer were questionable is doubtlessly true.

While still a youth he murdered the "vicious McCanles gang" which consisted in reality of McCanles, Woods, and Gordon. It was murder because they were unarmed. While he was sheriff in Kansas, he murdered Phil Coe in a rage of jealous hate. That he did much good in exterminating many bad men is also true. That he usurped his power in office is asserted by some and denied by others. He was accused by many, who were there and were supposed to know, of being the middle man between the small thieves and the crooked town officials of Kansas cow towns.

The Texas cowboys, especially, held him in low esteem. He is glorified by others as being an ideal American hero. Undoubtedly, at times he was a bad man, in the light of our definition — he at times went against society for his personal benefit, and no one will vouchsafe that he was not dangerous — especially when drunk, mad, angry, and/or jealous.

* * * * * * *

Dallas Stoudenmire, famous City Marshal of El Paso back in turbulent times, was somewhat like Wild Bill — he defies classification. Both men were reputed to have the figure and the face of an Adonis. They were both over six feet in height, weighed over two hundred pounds, had long blond wavy hair and blue eyes, and were handsome and fearless. He, also, usually sported a drooping yellow mustache above a chin like a rough-hewn oak block. He, also, was usually quiet in demeanor, but when he was in his cups, old Lucifer and Beelzebub combined couldn't hold a candle to him. He became boisterous and overbearing. He was an ex-Confederate, later Marshal of El Paso, and still later U. S. Marshal — but finally bad man.

Dallas is not pictured as being underhanded in any way, as was Wild Bill, but he used less discretion than Bill; he got drunk at the wrong times and treed the town when the council members were out of humor. As a consequence he lasted only a short time both as an officer and as an animate being.

* * * * * * *

I repeat — there never was another Clay Allison and never will be. He is a puzzle. He was not a rustler, nor a thief, nor a robber, nor an officer — he was merely a killer of bad men and a hell-raiser in general. At times he was probably an ordinary rancher; at least he owned a small ranch in New Mexico. Otherwise, he was employed in lighter diversions, such as drinking red-eye, treeing towns, and raising cain just for the fun of the thing. His curious sense of humor sets him off. His avowed enemy was just any and every peace officer or an enemy of the Confederacy. Yet his code of ethics was that of the West and he stuck to it. He was a killer, but by no means a murderer.

* * * * * * *

Then there was the Roy Bean class, of which there was one member — *Roy Bean*, "the Law West of the Pecos." He was probably the most singular individual among the various species of the old West. He is not ordinarily considered a bad man, not being dangerous to an ordinary pacifist. Yet according to our definition he cannot be excluded. He did, positively, use his self-made, self-maintained, and for some time extra-legal office to his own personal advantage.

He never gave change in money, whether in trading, in serving a glass of beer at his "bar" (with a twofold significance), or in receiving a fine. His pet trick was this: in between train stops at Langtry (Texas) the folks on the train would hurry down to the Judge's "bar" and have drinks. When it came about time for them to return to the train, they would pay in five or ten-dollar bills. The Judge would drop the bill on the floor and stoop over, slip it in his pocket, and pretend he couldn't find it. "By gobs, that there bill has just simply went!"

He would stoop, squat, squint, and grunt, but no bill anywhere. About that time the train would whistle and the customer would get agitated — but still no change. Finally the train would chug once or twice, and the customer would nearly break his neck in catching it — leaving his ten-dollar bill in the pocket of the smiling judge.

It was merely a question of law with the Judge to tell a recalcitrant prisoner, "No, by gobs, this here court don't give change in receiving fines. Whereupon the finee would howl in protest. Then the Judge would fine him again for disturbing the peace. If he objected to this second fine, the Judge would unlimber and spread out his two six-guns on his "bar" and the fine was always paid, without further cheep.

The town of Langtry sprang up near the meeting place of the Southern Pacific tracks when they were laid down from the East by Irishmen and from the West by Chinamen as tradition has it. It was named after William Langtry, a section foreman of the railroad. Judge Bean was quite romantic. He fell in love with a picture of Lily Langtry, a dancing and singing star on the stage in Chicago at the time. He named his "bar" after her — "The Jersey Lilly." The reason the name was misspelled was the ignorance of the sign painter — a Swede named Oscar. Oscar had gotten drunk at the Judge's bar and let it be known that he was an expert sign painter and ditchdigger. The Judge fined him promptly, giving sentence of three days hard labor, painting signs and digging ice vaults for beer storage.

Now the Judge hit upon an idea, having written and telegraphed Lily of his admiration and receiving no encouragement, not even a reply. So he telegraphed her that he had named the town *Langtry* after her, and that she was cordially invited to visit the city of Langtry. She answered that it was kind of him, and that she was indeed sorry she couldn't come — that finally she would send $25 as a donation for a drinking fountain in the city's public park. He answered that in the first place, "we ain't got no public park" and in the second place, "if it's anything these here hombres drink, it ain't water." Besides that would ruin his business.

While serving as coroner, he fined a dead Mexican $41 (found on the corpse) for carrying a gun, which he confiscated. Upon learning that a young horse thief and prospective hangee possessed $400, the Judge immediately reversed his decision of hanging. He had peeked over the fellow's shoulder as he wrote a letter to his mother, bequeathing her the $400. Now the Judge was quite sentimental, to say nothing of practical. He reversed his decision of hanging and fined the offender $300 and pronounced his sentence that he should make haste from thence with all abandon, using the customary expletives befitting the occasion — "Now get the h—— out of here."

BOGUS

Bob Ollinger was a typical bogus bad man. He pretended to be much worse than he was in reality. He looked and acted like like the dyed-in-the-wool movie or fiction villain. He was big, brawny, bleary-black-eyed with raven black hair flopping long down over his lowering forehead. He usually wore a scowl on his face; chewed tobacco, strewing it at random. He wore two six-guns and a knife similar to the Bowie knife. He would walk down the streets of Las Vegas or Santa Fe picking his teeth with it, or throwing it into a tree where it would stick with a thud and quiver, or demonstrating his quickness on the draw.

He was keeper of Billy the Kid, while the Kid was jailed at Lincoln, New Mexico — as stated before. He tossed sarcastic remarks at the Kid, ridiculed him to his face — of course, only when it was safe. Now the Kid was just the opposite — quiet, small (weighing only 130 pounds), blond, and blue-eyed, but he silently resented all of Ollinger's jibes and secretly resolved to get revenge — which he did when he broke jail.

Burt Alvord was a man of some reputation. He was elected Sheriff in a small Arizona town, he robbed a train of $10,000, and he had several men to his credit. But he had a broad streak of yellow, too, that showed up at unexpected moments. He was strawboss on a cattle drive once, and started to whip a boy named Bill for tying his horse with too long a rope. When Alvord advanced with a horsewhip, Bill whipped out his gun and shot Alvord's tip end of his finger. Bill disgustedly reported that Burt bawled like a baby and ran away, but that he had to watch Burt from then on for fear of a shot from the rear.

One large evil-countenanced Torey, formerly a rough sea

captain, who had become a foreman of a ranch near wild Tascosa in the Panhandle of Texas and had created a reputation as a rough bully, had announced to the public the fact that Billy the Kid would not pollute the ground of his domain so long as he was around. Billy cornered him in a saloon in Tascosa and got him told. Torey changed his tune and cordially and genially invited the Kid to visit just any time.

R. B. Townshend, who called himself "The Tenderfoot in New Mexico," in his book by the same name came in contact with Billy the Kid and his gang once. Of course, he was considerably frightened, thinking the Kid would confiscate his cattle and possibly remove him to prevent evidence or witnesses. However, the Kid had no such designs, even though some of his men did. At first Townshend assumed that a big, gruff, coarse-looking fellow with more of a bark and a grunt than a voice was the leader — the one who favored taking over his cattle. But Billy backed him down with the greatest of ease. The sinister-looking gentleman gave in repeatedly to the wishes of the pleasant, wise-cracking little Kid, who seemed to oppose him at every turn.

There was an old cowboy at Tombstone named Dick Lloyd, an intermittent member of Curly Bill's Cochise County rustlers. He was quite harmless until he entered a saloon and got well along in his cups, enough to imagine himself a bad man. On one of these occasions Curly Bill's gang was engaged in a serious poker game in the back of the saloon. Dick got as drunk as a skunk in a methodical way, raised a war whoop, charged into the street shooting up the town with fine abandon. He then got on Joe Hill's (one of the gang) horse and ingeniously rode into the poker game in the back of the saloon. Of course the gang could not put up with such behavior even though Dick was their old pal, so they promptly shot him off the animal. Said Joe, "But what I can't figure out is how in the hell that simple-minded pifflicated centipede ever had the cold guts to come ridin' in here on my own hoss."

Out at Langtry, a bleached young fellow from back East, a train passenger between stops, once bolted up to Judge Bean's "bar" and blated away in a couple of octaves extraordinarily low, "Gimme a drinka pizen!"

Whereupon, the much disgusted Judge about-faced and procured a fruit jar containing a concoction delicately flavored with dead scorpions, centipedes, tarantulas, and vinegarroons and poured the same into a glass right under the fellow's very eyes. "By gobs, sir, there's yer pizen! Now drink it!"

The tenderfoot's complexion changed several shades to a slightly pale pea-green, and under the menacing threat of the Judge's .45, he was actually going to drink the stuff. But Bean finally took compassion and said, "Now, young whippersnapper, let that be a lesson to you!"

Tombstone, rough as it was, tried to accept Russian Bill as a tough hombre. Especially did the ladies adore the extremely handsome young fellow. Bill gave himself away inadvertently. Instead of using the colloquial mannerism, "What the h—— did you say?" he would say, "I beg your pardon, sir?" Or Bill would inquire, "Would you gentlemen care to have a drink?" when the traditional invitation was, "Name yer pizen, you dash-blanked this-and-that son-of-a-likewise." Then, too, people occasionally suspected him of being counterfeit. For instance, he was enjoying a performance at a Tombstone bar one evening with a blonde on each knee — without a care in the world. But all of a sudden from a near-by balcony several shots rang out, a scream pierced the air, and a body fell over the railing and landed right on Bill's table. Bill dropped his two blondes, swallowed his tongue, turned pale, and took to cover. It turned out that the whole thing was a gag — the "body" was a dummy. From then on Russian Bill was scoffed at. In desperation, he joined Curly Bill's gang of rustlers and went out to steal a horse to overcome his hypocrisy — to be a "real" bad man. He was caught in the act, at Charleston, Arizona, and was hanged.

Poor Russian Bill. He had failed at acting on the artificial stage; so he became an actor on a real stage with a real setting where the audience were also actors. But it was the wrong stage for Russian Bill.

Billy Brooks, one-time deputy of Dodge City, was known as a bad man and killer, but was shooed out of town one day by a meek little fellow with a steel-gray eye that bored right through him. Brooks hid under his bed for a while, and when the coast was clear, "high-tailed" it out of town on the next freight train to nowhere and was never heard of afterwards.

A braggadocious bad man named Rayner, who professed to be the best-dressed bad man in Texas, swaggered into a barber shop in El Paso and slapped each man being worked on — that is, all who cared to remain. Of course, all activity with razors and scissors was temporarily suspended. Wyatt Earp, seated in the last chair, remained perfectly calm until Rayner approached his chair. Then a noticeable change occurred in Wyatt's demeanor. Rayner became more diplomatic suddenly when he saw Wyatt's steel-blue eye boring into his own and Wyatt's hand clenching and his whole body becoming rigid — ready to tear him to pieces. Instead of slapping Earp, Rayner showed his true color and politely invited him to have a drink.

This true anecdote illustrates another of folklore. The official town bully writes on the board, "I, Bill Jones, can lick anybody in town!" He is accosted by a soft-spoken but determined citizen, "But, Bill, I live in this town." Whereupon, Bill sheepishly amends the statement: "I, Bill Jones, can lick anybody in town — except one, that is."

The bogus bad man was most unusual. Typically he looked and acted like the dyed-in-the-wool movie or fiction villain. The real bad man looked more the part of the hero.

Usually when they saw a coarse-looking swashbuckling man wearing two six-guns and a couple of bowie knives (seldom done) striding down the middle of the street strewing tobacco juice helter-skelter, bleary-eyed, profusely blaspheming the atmosphere with vitriolic diatribes, and loudly and publicly proclaiming that he was a wild coyote and that it was his night to howl, pouring out vehement vituperation upon anyone who cared to listen, the old-time Westerners would merely look on with amusement or disgust and say to themselves, "There goes another counterfeit. Guess somebody'll maverick him, all right!"

And usually somebody with injured pride and public spirit did just that — they "dusted him on both sides" just to teach him to respect the peace and quiet of the vicinity.

In direct contrast to the genuinely bad man's, his voice was rasping and unpleasant as he boomed and thundered meaningless admonitions and ultimatums. He loved a reputation. He was idolized by adolescents, greenhorns, and tenderfeet who knew no better. His hand could have been and was frequently called by some little, quiet-spoken, blue-eyed fellow who meant what little he said.

The bogus bad man was to the genuine bad man as the yellow, sneaking, furtive, sneering, cowardly coyote* was to the re-

---

* Apologies to the coyote and to Mr. J. Frank Dobie, who maintains in *The Voice of the Coyote* that the animal has been wrongly accused of being a coward.

spected grey wolf. Both are killers and sometimes it's hard to tell them apart by their looks, but not by their actions.

This much will have to suffice for the bogus bad man, who was really small fry. He warrants no more consideration.

BEHIND THE STAR

Henry Plummer, Sheriff at Bannack, a mining town in the Territory of Idaho, was at the same time leader of the most effective band of cutthroats, literally speaking, the Northwest has ever known. He was ostensibly on the side of the law, even in his wrongdoing. He used the law merely as a convenient means to his illegal ends. We have seen how minutely organized and planned was the gang. There's one member of his gang we've neglected — Boone Helm, a cannibal reprobate. Don't forget him.

Ben Thompson was the type of bad man who would dress up in stove-pipe hat and tails and stride up and down Congress Avenue, Austin's main thoroughfare, hoping some ignorant cow-hand would insult him and start a fight, wherein he could "get him another man." He built up such a reputation as a bad man that Austin elected him City Marshal. Much to his surprise, probably, Ben, the man with the quickest draw and most itching trigger finger — which had already been used in killing — found a badge thrust upon his chest, which he elevated and expanded all the more.

Lee Sage, who called himself "The Last Rustler" in his autobiography of the same title, was by turns rustler, moonshiner, and sheriff in small communities in Montana and Canada.

Of all ironic twists of fate! Of all people ever to get behind a star! No one would ever have thought the one and only John Wesley Hardin — he of the forty-three "credits" and he of the sudden and rash temper — would ever live to see the day he would represent the law in chasing criminals. Yet it actually happened. He was deputized while incognito in Florida to arrest a criminal Negro. He was himself in hiding at the same time, being "wanted" in Texas. He was himself later captured in Florida by Texas Rangers and brought back to prison in Huntsville after lengthy trials.

Bill Longley, rival of Hardin for laurels as Texas man-killer, was protected legally under the pretense of being a deputy when he slew a man named Sawyer, who was gunning for Longley himself. Of all things! A man like Longley being a deputy sheriff!

Bass Outlaw was a Texas Ranger whose career befitted his name more than his profession. Some claim that he was killed by Rangers for murdering one of their number, but Captain Hughes claims John Selman fired the shot that killed him.

Doc Holliday, one of the coldest-blooded killers of the West, the desperado-dentist-killer from Dallas (originally from Georgia), went to Kansas and befriended Wyatt Earp and thereby became a deputy of the law in Kansas and later in Arizona.

Buckskin Frank Leslie was intermittent killer, bartender, deputy in posses after criminals, outlaw in Tombstone, and jailbird in Yuma. Indeed, he was versatile.

Johnny Behan, the little busybody sheriff of Cochise County, Arziona, who wouldn't coöperate with U. S. Marshal Wyatt Earp, appointed Curly Bill Brocius and his gang of self-acknowledged rustlers and outlaws as deputies to pursue the Earp party when the latter left the country. Here, again, the law was merely a matter of technicality. The feud between the rustlers and the Earp party had progressed for years, come to a climax, and worn out. The rustlers had foully murdered Morgan Earp and had intended to do likewise with Virgil, wounding him severely. Of course, they never got around to Wyatt. Wyatt was the leader of the triumvirate of brother-officers, and the only way to kill him was from behind. He lived to the ripe old age of eighty-one years.

Wyatt became a bad man temporarily — long enough to get revenge on the rustlers for their treatment of his brothers. He found out who the three rustlers were that did the dirty work and one, two, three picked them off, one by one. He then put the invalid Virgil on the train, gathered his belongings and a friend or two, bought a wagon and, having had enough of Tombstone, was on his way out. You remember his meeting with Curly Bill's gang at Iron Springs. Curly gave Wyatt and party a nice little farewell, at the expense of the rustler's life. County Sheriff Behan's "deputies" had failed to bring in their men.

But this is not the first nor the last instance in which officers of different units of government failed to coöperate.

* * * * * * *

Burt Alvord was simultaneously a two-gun City Marshal at Willcox, Arizona, and a train robber.

In Oklahoma, much later, the Dunn Brothers, rustlers, manhunters, stool-pigeons, and killers by turn, helped Frank Canton, much to his disgust, bring in several other outlaws. In the same state the renowned Dalton brothers, Bob, Emmett, Grat, and Bill, past masters at bank robbing and train robbing, were at one time on the side of the law. They served as U. S. deputy marshals and as chiefs of police at Fort Smith, Osage, Wichita, and in the Muskogee district.

One may be inclined to scoff at the very idea of making a bad man a deputy or sheriff. Yet in many cases, they made good. No one wants a milksop in the job of law officer. These bad men put little value on human life, including their own; they were on the side of the law only temporarily and usually to meet an emergency or a fleeting exigency. As likely as not, the week before or afterwards would find the same men looking out through barred windows or playing the part of the criminal at bay, and even their closest friends now and then found it excruciatingly painful to justify their actions, especially Ben Thompson's. Certainly they were outlaws, most of them. As I look over the list, it seems most ironical that bad men especially like Longley and Hardin should have ever served as messengers of the law.

FEUD-MADE SHERIFF

Out on the Mogollons under the Tonto Rim in the valley ironically called Pleasant Valley in Arizona raged the Graham-Tewksbury cattle-sheep war, from which survived only Edwin Tewksbury, who later served several years in the penitentiary and still later became a sheriff, and a good one. He would probably have been content to let things ride had not the Daggs sheepmen dragged him into the feud. On the other side was Tom Graham, who also would probably have been content had it not been for the Blevanses, Andy Cooper, and other cattlemen who dragged him into the feud. Tom Tucker, a Graham partisan, later became an efficient officer of the law.

George Coe, friend and co-fighter of Billy the Kid, who hid out and was pursued by the law as an aftermath of the Lincoln County War in New Mexico, was actually taken into custody by a partisan Sheriff Brady and confined in jail (only for a few days), but he later served as a deputy and got his bad man. It was a thrilling arrest, according to Coe himself:

> Our constable, John Cox, was inoffensive and inexperienced. He came up to my place one afternoon and said: "George, I need

your services. I want to deputize you to go with me to the La Platte, to take charge of that bunch of cow-thieves."

"No, I can't do it," I said. "I came up here to get away from trouble, and I have my young wife to consider now. I've never had any experience in arresting people. The only fellow I ever tried my hand on, shot my hand off, so count me out on this game."

But I let him overpersuade me, and in the end, like a darned fool, I consented to go.

We arrived between sundown and dark. A man appeared and we inquired of him if a certain party was there. The man told us that the fellow we were looking for was camped in the dugout nearby, so we rode down and found that the dugout door was open. We had gone there for business, and I had a habit of going prepared.

The constable dismounted and walked to the entrance. Instead of ordering the man to throw up his hand when he approached, he said: "I have a warrant for your arrest, sir."

The rustler lay on a cot, his six-shooter lying at his feet and his rifle standing at the foot of his bed. When Cox spoke to him, he reached for his pistol. I was standing just behind Cox, and shoved my gun around him and into the man's face.

"Drop that gun!" I yelled.

He looked up at me and hesitated.

"I mean it!" I said.

But still he waited. I got his number, and I told him, "Now, I don't want to have to kill you, but if you don't put that gun down I'll be darned if I won't."

He rolled off the cot and stood to one side. With my gun still cocked on him, I said: "John, get both of those guns, and see if he has any more on his person."

Jeff Ake, once a wealthy cattleman of central Texas, after shooting a cattle inspector, spent several nights in jail with the notorious Ben Thompson. He was, however, released, and later when the Lee-Good war was raging, he was made a Deputy Sheriff under old Mariano Barela and still later a Deputy United States Marshal.

Men like these were neither professional officers nor professional outlaws; and when the passing trouble subsided and both factions of the feud were either wiped out or satisfied, they calmly pursued their prosaic business without molesting others.

But the feud-made sheriff was merely used as a tool for legal protection of the partisans. His only purpose for being in office was to serve warrants on the enemy and give a semblance of legality to the depredations of his faction.

In the famous Lincoln County War the legal odds went to the Murphy-Riley-Dolan side. The Tunstall-McSween faction used only one sheriff, John Copeland, as its tool, and he did not last long. The Murphy faction got busy and had Governor E. B. Axtell appoint Dad Peppin in his place. President Hayes replaced the Governor by Lew Wallace (author of *Ben Hur*), because of Axtell's laxity in seeing that order was restored. Sheriff Peppin disregarded a message from President Hayes to McSween, saying that the military had no authority over the feud. The military authority in question was Col. N. A. M. Dudley of the U. S. Army, who was later recalled for his partisanship on behalf of the Murphy faction. The President's message did little good indeed. Also on the Murphy side were Sheriff Brady of Lincoln, who was shot by Billy the Kid, and Sheriff Marion Turner of Roswell.

In the Graham-Tewksbury feud, the Tewksburys had three deputies, Tom Horn, Jim Houck, and Sheriff Mulvenon, on their side; and even the great Sheriff Commodore Perry Owens, though not a partisan for the Tewksburys, served them when he shot four of the Blevans boys, who were friends of the Grahams. Sheriff Mulvenon shot John Graham and Charley Blevans. Andy Cooper, one of the Graham faction, got himself deputized and bushwhacked the Tewksburys.

You remember that in the Stevens County (Kansas) war between Woodsdale and Hugoton, their respective official town marshals, Ed Short and Robinson, were thought fit men to go after each other.

In a raging Texas feud, Jack Helms, a Sutton partisan, deputy sheriff at DeWitt, fought against the Hardin-Taylor faction. John Wesley Hardin is quoted as having said to Helms, "You have been going around killing men long enough, and I know you belong to a legalized band of murdering cowards and have hung and murdered better men than yourself." Sheriff Jack never saw the end of the feud — he was killed.

MERCENARIES

Long ago, as Sir Walter Scott tells us in *Ivanhoe*, evil Prince John hired some mercenary roughnecks to pounce upon his brother, King Richard the Lion-Hearted, who had escaped being kidnapped on the continent and was returning to merrie olde England to chastise "dear brother John" for usurping the throne. John had grabbed Richard's chair while Richard was off fighting the Saracens trying to redeem the Holy Sepulchre in the Third Crusade.

In the tale of Macbeth, from the pen of the immortal Shakespeare, we find evil Macbeth hiring mercenary murderers to run off to Macduff's castle and slaughter Lady Macduff and little son while father is away down in England. Not because Macbeth's afraid to do it himself — not the great, swashbuckling soldier Macbeth! But because he doesn't want to dirty his already filthy hands any more and add more to the one universal incarnadine of the oceans in which he would cleanse those bloody hands — he doesn't want to be bothered by still more bloody images in sleepless dreams aggravated by troubled conscience.

Wells, Fargo and Company, the Overland Stage Company, various cattlemen's associations of the West and Southwest, and the railroads of the West — notably the Union Pacific and Southern Pacific — who frequently suffered at the hands of daring robbers and rustlers, retaliated by hiring detectives, shotgun messengers, and fighters to rid the country of such thieves.

While these hired killers were by and large wholly reliable and good, they were not infrequently hard cases who either already had a reputation as bad men, and for that reason had acquired their position, or soon gained one in dispatching their official duties.

The very acme of this class was Joseph A. Slade, who "ran" one of the Overland Stage Company's stations.

Samuel Clemens tells of the incident when he first met Slade. Clemens and his older brother Orion were on their way to Virginia City via Overland stagecoach. After a long, cold, and tiresome drive the passengers filed out at a station for breakfast. Clemens wrote that the most gentlemanly-appearing, quiet, and affable officer in the service of the Overland Company that they had met along the whole journey sat at the head of the table just next to his elbow. In his own words: "Never youth stared and shivered as I did when I heard them call him SLADE!" Clemens goes on to write that this man Slade was so friendly and so gentle-spoken that he warmed to him in spite of the man's awful record of having killed twenty-six human beings up to that time.

It took steel nerve and lightning-fast trigger fingers to hold down such a job, but Slade the Terrible was not found lacking. Later he was hanged by a vigilance committee for excessive drunkenness and indiscriminate and promiscuous shooting.

Another mercenary bad man was Black Bart, who robbed twenty-eight stagecoaches in California between 1873-1883 and left poetry in Wells Fargo consignment boxes that won't do to print. He was perhaps the only robber of stages who preferred not to use a horse. He has been called a mild and romantic introvert, resembling more a Charlie Chaplin rather than a John Wayne (or Dan Duryea, who played the part of Black Bart). He dropped a silk handkerchief and a linen cuff with his laundry mark on one of them. He was traced in San Francisco by the same mark, served a term in jail, was released and hired by Wells, Fargo and Company — the very company he formerly robbed.

Still another was Tom Horn, who was cattle detective, scout, manhunter, and deputy, but who was accused of murdering a fourteen-year-old boy named Willie Nichols, a son of a land squatter — and therefor hanged.

The hired killer bad man was frequently in the employ of unscrupulous big cattlemen, who would obtain warrants for their men to carry in case they were asked by what right they professed jurisdiction. One New Mexico land baron, who owned more cattle than he could count, carried a bill of sale for cattle he "confiscated" in his saddlecloth wrapped in an iron pipe.

Some of the dealings of cattle and land barons of the West and Southwest cannot be justified by a right-thinking society. Some of these barons succeeded by chicanery in acquiring plots of land containing millions of acres; some patronized rustlers like Billy the Kid; and some intentionally absorbed or appropriated smaller cattlemen's herds.

Nor does it seem excusable for them either to oust the land squatter or buy him out for a mere song at the point of a Winchester. The exception is Colonel Charles Goodnight of Texas, whose honesty and integrity were unquestionable, though even he did not like squatters. These men were, of course, not directly dangerous as man to man (the land barons), but they were indirectly dangerous through their hired detectives and fighters.

It's true that the class of hired bad man is the smallest and least known, because many of them were under-cover men and never revealed their identity or purpose.

* * * * * * *

Ridiculously enough, these bad men knew how it felt to wear a badge and to represent the law. How did they look upon it? Probably the great majority looked upon the act of representing justice as a mere incident, a great joke, a crafty undertaking, or even as an ironical perversion of fate. However, some did well in that capacity; a few were conscientious.

THE BULK

Most of the bad men in the West were strictly, technically, and actually illegal in their questionable acts.

Probably William H. Bonney, better known as Billy the Kid, and his associates are the most famous. Most of them never were clothed with lawful authority. Among them were Jesse Evans, Tom O'Folliard, Fred Wait, Charley Bowdre, Tom Hill, Dick Brewer, Jim French, and Doc Scurlock.

From down in Texas emerged into immortal fame and ballad one illiterate Sam Bass, among whose companions in crime were Frank Jackson, Jim Berry, Henry Underwood, Arkansas Johnson, the Collins brothers — Henry, Joel, and Billy — Seaborne Barnes, and Jim Murphy.

Others of import were the Harrold brothers of Lampasas, the Marlow brothers of Young County, the Dixon brothers, relatives of Hardin, Alfred Y. Allee of Goliad County, Texas, and the redoubtable Tumlinson of South Texas — all expert pistoleers.

From the far Northwest were members of Plummer's gang — Boone 'Helm, Cherokee Bob, Charley Harper, Hayes Lyons, George Ives, Clubfoot George Lane, and a host of others. Then there was Teton Jackson, the Destroying Angel, messenger of Brigham Young — Frank Canton, intrepid sleuth, captured him in Montana.

Birds of a feather flock together. Gangs leaving their indelible mark on the crime-stained history of outlawry were those of Butch Cassidy, Bill Doolin, Quantrill, the Jameses and Youngers. Away back before the nineteenth century existed Micajah and Wiley Harpe and Sam Mason, river pirates and fiendish assassins.

Among the thoroughly illegal outlaws of Oklahoma were Bert Casey, Ben Cravens, Ezell, Welty, and Henry Starr. These men operated independently or drifted from one gang and place to another.

Of the Cochise County, Arizona, outlaws who faced the sheriff's star were Billy Claiborne, John Ringo, Old Man Clanton and his sons, Frank Stilwell, Joe Hill, Pete Spencer, Zwing Hunt, Billy Grounds, Jim Crane, Harry Head, and Bill Leonard. The last three mentioned were road agents, also.

All of these men and myriads of others of the same ilk were never appointed or elected officers of the law for any purpose whatever. They fought against the good of society technically and actually — they were impediments to progress, even though they couldn't help it in some cases.

The reader may ask why certain other "bad men" were not included in this account. It is true that I have learned of many others but they have been omitted for very good reasons, among which are: (1) lack of adequate and willing testimonial authentication, (2) objections of living relatives, and (3) the fact that many were of local notoriety only.

IN MEMORIAM

All the foregoing bad men were at one time or another, if indeed not all the time, a menace to society, and the plodding honest and peaceful pioneers of the old West would probably have been better off without them. Nearly all met a sudden and violent end. Crime did not pay even then.

> But once a tougher hombre beat him to the draw,
> For that was the way of the Wild West law.
> The roar of the six-gun was loud and bad,
> And now he's in Boot Hill and we ain't sad.

Equivalent to the modern, efficient and thoroughly disinterested "G-men" and yet hesitant to use deadly means of quelling crime were many humane peace officers who were entirely without fear in the pursuit of their somewhat unappreciated efforts. They built the foundation for the West. It has been said the Anglo-Saxon race is a lover of law and order.

There is no term of praise of sufficient magnitude to describe the good frontier marshal who neither looked for nor evaded trouble, who conscientiously did all his work, who constantly abstained from indulging in the ever-tempting, ever-present vice accompanying a frontier, who risked his life rather than take another, no matter how degraded, and who used his guns sparingly. One man of this caliber was worth ten ordinary citizens and frequently counteracted many times that number of bad men.

But since we are concerned primarily with the bad man, the

valiant deeds of the peace officer will be omitted except when necessary in telling the story of the bad man and the names of only a few of them will be mentioned.

The highest tribute is due men like Harry Love of California, Billy Tilghman of Oklahoma, Billy Breakenridge of Arizona, Bat Masterson of Kansas, Commodore Perry Owens of Arizona, Burton Mossman, the first captain of Arizona Rangers; Wyatt Earp of Kansas and Arizona, Charley Bassett of Kansas, Pat Garrett and José R. Lucero of New Mexico, Frank Canton of Oklahoma and Alaska and Montana, Harry C. Wheeler of Arizona, Tom Smith of Kansas, John Slaughter of Arizona, Neil Howie of Montana, "Bucky" O'Neil of Arizona, Kosterlitzky of the Mexican Rurales, Captains Hughes, McDonald, Reynolds, Baker, Hayes, McCullough, Ranger Jim Gillett, Jeff Milton, and many other Texas Rangers.

We owe them our sincerest thanks.

CHAPTER IV

THE DESCRIPTION OF THE BAD MAN OF THE WEST

HIS EYES

 HE eyes are the most expressive feature about a person, and it was mainly through them that the bad man showed his nature.

John Ringo, for example, did. He was an associate of Curly Bill and his rustlers at Tombstone. His blue eyes emitted a pathetic expression and he wore a sad, morose, almost tragic look on his darkly handsome, lean, saturnine face. If you had met him, you would have said, "Poor fellow, he must have some mighty weighty problems on his mind. He would make an excellent Hamlet."

He was loyal to his friends, moody, quiet, quarrelsome when drunk, brave, mysterious, given to melancholy — as we have seen in his suicide. He was well educated, having read extensively, and this was an unusual characteristic according to frontier standards. His was a sculpturesque physique. He presented a handsome but unfortunate spectacle.

It was through his cold, steel-blue-gray eyes that the typical bad man gave vent to all his pent-up wrath as his eyes stared frigidly, riveted upon his foe, *setting* him just as snakes do their prey, throwing him off guard by a hypnotic gleam.

Doc Holliday could do it. When somebody tried to shift a card on him, the Doc would slam his fist on the table and the opponent would look up in surprise at a couple of the coldest gray eyes he had ever seen — boring right through him — and there seemed to be nothing he could do but sit there and look. These cold gray eyes well befitted Doc's cold-blooded character. He

In battle . . . he (Quantrill) became a malicious, cold-blooded, degenerate who laughed, shouted, and shrieked over the din of his guerrillamen's battle guns. (See pages 119-120.)

could shoot a man without flickering an eyelash. He was ash-blond, about five feet eleven, was frail, weighing only 130 pounds. Remember that he was consumptive. It showed up in his haggard, well-proportioned, lean, pox-marked face into which were set a fine nose, heavy eyebrows, and a trimmed mustache. You can see by the picture that his face was of a handsome contour.

The cold glare of the eyes, coupled with the spring-like alertness of mind and body, was usually sufficient to make the prey cringe — if the odds were even. If the odds were against the bad man, then his eyes usually dispensed with their glare and became jovial to throw the adversary off guard, but at the same time remained extremely vigilant to find a means to turn the tables. The eyes of Jesse James, John Wesley Hardin, and Billy the Kid are described as being restless, shifty, "foxy," never remaining fixed on an object, constantly roving about as if to take in the whole situation and leave no gap through which harm might come. Wild Bill, for instance, would side into a saloon so as to keep the wall to his back, squinting his eyes around the room and keeping the situation under control. Only once did he get careless and let someone get behind his back while he played poker — and that was enough.

In the Appendix of this book is a group of descriptions of the most notorious bad men of the old West — fifty-seven to be exact. Only nine are known to have had brown or black eyes, whereas a clear majority of thirty-eight were known to have blue or gray eyes.

HIS FACE

In all phases of his personal appearance — his eyes, face, dress, size, physique, and demeanor — the typical bad man was indeed deceiving, especially in comparison with the movie bad man or fiction villain or the bogus bad man. The genuine product was the exact opposite. I repeat, he looked more the part of the hero than the villain.

Take Jesse James, for example. He wore a disarming smile on his roundish, full, innocent face with its fair complexion and stubby little turned-up nose. Very seldom did he let his dark brown whiskers cover it — only for disguise, it is said. His short, brownish hair was always well combed and his steel-blue, shifty, snappy eyes wore an intelligent expression. His five-feet-ten carried 165 pounds with lightning-like movements. Except when robbing, he usually wore a business suit of cashmere dark brown. He was usually spruced up in spotless white shirt with collar and cravat, and he wore gloves. His finger tip had been shot off and he perhaps feared detection because of it. He was religious, knew the Bible well, and his language around women and children was quite circumspect. He had small, woman-like hands. He was usually good natured, except when excited and then pretty hot tempered — usually carefree but at once watchful. He was more outlaw than criminal.

The typical Western bad man's face was not infrequently handsome or it was at least good-looking. He was usually quite sun-tanned, because he spent a considerable time in the open. It was a custom of the frontier times for men to wear a handle-bar mustache and long sideburns. Nearly all of them, bad men included, conformed to this precedent at one time or another. Too, many of them added a goatee or chin whiskers to the mustache, as many of their pictures show. A square jaw and a chin like a rough-hewn oak block are usually considered evidences of determination and fierceness. Clay Allison, Burt Alvord, the Daltons, John Wesley Hardin, Edwin Tewksbury, Ben Thompson, Bill Longley, and Al Jennings had these features, while Bass Outlaw is the only *orejana* with a receding chin.

Sam Bass was noted for his square jaw and chin. He wore a brown mustache usually. He liked to joke and show off in front of his companions, and every time he laughed he showed his teeth. Even when he talked, they were nearly all visible. He had black eyes, brown hair, was about five feet seven. He was usually very quiet natured, slovenly dressed, happy-go-lucky, not given to drink. He was not cold-blooded — not a killer until cornered.

I can make no conclusion about the bad men's necks, noses, foreheads, mouths, ears, or fullness or thinness of the face. The anthropologist will tell you that the man with the lofty, shapely forehead is the further advanced in the evolution of the specie, and that the man with the low, receding forehead hearkens back to the brutal prehistoric progenitors. Yet there is only one bad man whose forehead fits this description — Henry Plummer.

His forehead was low, brutish, sinister — frequently termed a sure sign of the murderer. It is said that Plummer's only discourtesy was that he seldom doffed his hat; he practically never removed it, for he knew his forehead would give him away. His eyes were cold, expressionless, fishy, as they frequently stared away into space with his preoccupied thought. His face, too, was expressionless, immovable; and his complexion was colorless. You could tell by looking at him that he was a cold-blooded sort of person — a quiet, intelligent, cold killing machine. He was quiet even when drinking — no bravado nor swagger. He was usually polite, had a monotonous voice; and his strong nervous system stood with him well until just before he was hanged and then went to pieces. He fell on his knees crying like a baby imploring forgiveness of his executioners and begging for his life.

So much for foreheads. About noses, Wild Bill had an acquiline nose, but Hardin's nose was short and Jesse James' was stubby. Otherwise there isn't much to be said.

From the bad man's countenance one, as a rule, would think him incapable of emotion. He practically never scowled, as did the bogus bad man. About the only expression visible on his face was a smile, which was frequently there during his carefree moments among friends. Billy the Kid nearly always smiled, laughed, joked, or wisecracked among his associates. It's only natural to deduce that the bad man's poker face was acquired in playing poker — or monte or faro or seven-up, which were the most popular gambling games on the frontier. However, it may have been an inborn characteristic for the killer to be void of facial expression, especially if he was cold-blooded.

Billy the Kid, Henry Plummer, John Wesley Hardin, and many others of the same ilk were said not to have flickered an eyelash while in the act of killing a man; and the bad man was almost universally remorseless, as tradition has it — I believe he felt himself thoroughly justified in his homicides. Arkansas Tom, an acquaintance of U. S. Marshal Frank Canton and member of the Doolin gang, was the sole sufferer from remorse I have come across. He always promised to reform and lead a good life upon leaving prison. But he always came back. Finally he gave up. He buried his face on his arm and beat his hands on the walls of his cell and wailed, "I just cain't be good any more."

People could hardly believe their ears when informed of the identity of Billy the Kid, Polk Wells, John Wesley Hardin, or Jesse James. They would answer, "Oh surely that nice-looking young fellow couldn't be such a vile desperado — why he's only an innocent youth!"

That's the way William H. Bonney got his monicker. He was simply just "the Kid" since he started on his bloody career at the tender age of twelve and was slain by Sheriff Pat Garrett at the age of twenty-one, having killed twenty-one men himself. Some record! — an average of a man for each year! Merely a youth was this little left-handed desperado whose asymmetrical wolfish-tan thin face nearly always wore a light-hearted, wisecracking, devilish grin — just a kid. Why, he was only five-feet-seven and a half and he weighed only 135 pounds. His hands were unusually small, as were his feet. He was not given to drink, and his shifty, foxy blue eyes vibrated with his quick catlike movements. In that little body of his was the concentrated strength and agility of a wildcat. Despite the asymmetry of his face and the protrusion of his buck teeth, he was quite a lady's man. With his long, light brown hair, and with his voice that sang like a bird, and with his dandy clothes, he was quite an attraction. It is lamentable that his only picture was taken in ranch clothes.

They *were* youths — the bad men — during their prime. A man's nerves and fighting ability are at their best when he is a youth, usually considered at the ages fourteen to twenty-five years. Invariably the bad man's career seemed most prominent during his youthful age and seemed to terminate a few years afterward. When a man passes this period of life, his actions usually become retarded, he gains superfluous avoirdupois, his eyes, nerves, muscles fail to coordinate perfectly. The bad man was no exception.

HIS HAIR

According to the Appendix, the bad man was probably just as likely to be blond as brunette (fourteen and nineteen respectively), but not a red-head (two). Tradition has it that the typical bad man was blond — the traditionary idea may have been juxtaposed with blue eyes.

Much has been made of Curly Bill Brocius' luscious black curly hair. Excepting Curly Bill's fairly good looks, he might have been made into a movie villain — but that's a matter of doubt, too. He was rather portentiously black-eyed, heavy-set, burly. His face was round, dimpled, swarthy, and freckled — set up on a short bull-neck buried almost in his big shoulders. It was strictly business and no romance with him, though he was usually good-natured and amiable. He was panther-like in his movements. I doubt that he was a cold-blooded killer though — merely a rustler.

ON THE RANGE

How did the bad man dress? Of course, his dress varied with

the occasion. He was usually a rustler, a robber, a cardsharp, or a combination of any two or all three. As a rustler or a robber his attire was usually that of an ordinary cowpuncher. This consisted of high-heel leather boots with spurs, usually with rowels about the size of a quarter, hairless leather chaps *(chapaderos)*, sometimes a leather jacket, jeans, a colored shirt, a bandanna around his throat, and a large wide-brimmed ten-gallon hat.

Although the cattle rustler probably wanted to look just like an ordinary cowboy, his costume was designed more for its usefulness than for effect. The leather boots and chaps and buckskin jacket afforded adequate protection against beating grass, brush, thorns, or limbs as the desperado rode away from a robbery or after stolen cattle. Without the protection of leather, his clothes would have been torn from the body and his skin completely lacerated as he galloped away at breakneck speed through the dense river bottoms, uncultivated woods, or chaparral country.

The large hat served as a sort of umbrella to ward off rain, sun, snow, or sleet. The bandanna could be used to conceal the man's identity or more likely to keep the dust of the prairies from his nostrils — or at least sift it. In freezing weather the handkerchief often prevented a frost-bitten nose. The high heels prevented his feet from slipping in the stirrups and aided him in keeping a stubborn steer under control just before the branding act.

The long hair, fashionable in the latter half of the nineteenth century, was worn partly through egotism, partly through fear or superstition, and partly for utility. It was believed that the Indian thought a man with long hair was more dangerous and that the Indian would be less likely to attack him than if his hair were trimmed. Too, the long hair served as a sort of mat and protection against the weather. Of course, the most useful and most indispensable article about the person of the bad man was his six-shooter.

DUDE

If and when the bad man came to town to throw away his money (and he usually did) or to make a killing, either of money or of a human being, he was likely to dress as the traditional dandy. Again, he looked the part of the hero instead of the villain. Almost invariably he was clothed entirely in immaculate

116

white and black garments. Just look in the back of this book at the descriptions of Ben Thompson, King Fisher, Jim Courtright, Doc Holliday, Wild Bill Hickok, and John Wesley Hardin and you will see that the typical gambling bad man of the West was flashingly over-dressed.

Take Wes Hardin, for instance. He was a dandy! He appeared in town in a $25 hat, a bright black overcoat costing $100, polished boots, black broadcloth suit, with a plush sash around his waist. On his boots he sported silver spurs the size of a dollar. On his horse was highly ornamented saddlery. Wes liked to show off. He was not usually given to drink. In his demeanor he was talkative, boastful, restless, ordinarily mild-mannered, but when aroused, cold-blooded and easily angered — he shot before he thought. His eyes were sharp, unsteady blue, his hair was light, he was five-feet-ten, and he weighed only about 150 pounds. On his face he usually wore a devilish, reckless grin. It was light-complexioned, babyish, innocent, mild-featured, but his large chin and determined mouth showed that he was not one to be trifled with.

The bad man usually spared no expense in clothing himself in the most elegant foppery — a black broadcloth suit, cutaway long-tailed coat, trousers pulled down over fine black patent leather boots with fancy designs in myriads, a snow-white pleated shirt with collar and black cravat, a fancy vest with numerous designs, and a spotless white or black hat — exemplified by Butch Cassidy's derby, Ben Thompson's stove-pipe hat, or King Fisher's big white sombrero. This was also the style of the Mississippi River gambler.

It is said that Hickok spent $60 for a pair of boots, Hardin $100 for a pair of boots, Thompson $1,500 for a silver-studded saddle. Yes, they liked to show off — especially before the ladies.

And further speaking of a dude — there was Ben Thompson. He would dress up just hoping for a quarrel, if for no other reason. He was stocky, thickset, square-jawed. His bulldog face wore a swarthy complexion and a black mustache. He was blue-eyed and black-haired. He was about five-feet-nine inches. In his demeanor he was something like an English bulldog. His friend and champion, lawyer Buck Walton, vouched that he was kind-hearted and chivalrous — a protector of women and children, a fair fighter — "fair" in the sense that he would pick a fight, but would always wait for the other fellow to make the first move. Ben was the champion of the Texas cowboys in the Kansas cow towns.

He was a friend of Phil Coe, but he didn't like Wild Bill Hickok, who was Yankee in sentiment. He made a good, loyal husband and father — but he was a bad man.

HIS HEIGHT AND WEIGHT

Again, the bad man looked the part of the hero — he was the exact opposite of the traditional movie or fiction villain or bogus bad man, who always seems to be tall, huge, lumbering, brutal, and malevolent-looking. The typical and genuine bad man of the West was deceiving in his size. He was not as tall nor as large as you might imagine.

His average height was five feet, nine and one-half inches, ranging from barely over five feet (Al Jennings) to six-feet-two (Johnny Ringo and Clay Allison).

Nor was he so heavy. The average was 169 pounds, varying from 120 (Al Jennings) to 200 (Hickok, Cole Younger, Longley). It is interesting to note that a few of the worst bad men were small: John Wesley Hardin, 150 pounds; Doc Holliday, 130; Billy the Kid, 135; and Luke Short, 150 pounds.

HIS PHYSIQUE

The bad man was usually well built physically and very healthy. The open range and frontier atmosphere, free from the contaminated dirt, dust, and smoke of the crowded city, was conducive to the well-being of any frontiersman. Lee Sage once went to the windy city of Chicago to cut up and have a good time. But he confessed he didn't. He couldn't stand the stifling atmosphere. He said he took in two whiffs of that secondhand stale air and wished he were back out on the prairie.

The bad man's bodily movements have been so frequently described as being furtive, stealthy, panther-like, soft and sure-footed, lightning quick, agile — that it seems more than coincidence. His body and muscles are usually described as being hard as a brick and quick as a steel spring to act when action was demanded, as it frequently was. The quickness of that action, the split part of a second, frequently saved the bad man's blood and spilled another's.

Of course, the hands were a vital part of the desperado's mechanism. Traditionally the bad man's hands were small, slim, supple, and nimble. Wild Bill, Wes Hardin, and Billy the Kid, reputedly the three quickest-on-the-draw pistoleers in the old West, with the greatest number of dead bad men to their credit, had such hands. Wild Bill constantly exercised his fingers and massaged his hands to keep them supple and in tip-top condition. These men also had small feet — almost the size of a woman's.

Clay Allison's right foot was lamed in an accident, while Club-foot George Lane was naturally clubfooted (he belonged to Plummer's gang).

Now Clay was a character, and he presented an eye-filling spectacle. He was handsome as Apollo. On his large, hard, bronzed, handsome face he sometimes wore a mustache and whiskers, and heavy black eyebrows. His high forehead showed intelligence; it was covered by fine black hair. His eyes were a clear, keen, cold, dancing blue. He was six-feet-two and weighed 175 pounds. He was polite but dominant in his conversation. He seldom laughed but usually smiled pleasantly, except when angry. He, too, had small, woman-like hands. He raised cain and played tricks on his friends when he was in his cups. He was a killer but not a murderer, and he wasn't afraid of fish, fowl, or flesh.

HIS DEMEANOR

The typical bad man was usually quiet, soft-spoken, mild-mannered, and his voice was low, well-modulated, even in danger. Bob Dalton was. When you describe him, you have the Daltons, all of them — Bill, Emmett, Grat, and Bob. They all came from the same mold. They were all pugnacious, well-built, square-jawed. But Bob was the leader. His pugnacity was well directed; he was cool, deliberate, tenacious, fearless. He was fairly handsome. Like all his brothers, he was tall, blue-eyed, and blond.

While conducting business or meeting a foe, the bad man talked very little, and that to the point — and he meant every word he said. He was not, as many would think after seeing a Western movie, the swaggering, blustering, or bragging kind. He was intelligent but usually uneducated. In his lighter moments he was jovial and carefree — an excellent companion "in fair weather." However, frequently he was given to violent anger, which showed especially in his eyes; but if he was cold-blooded, tradition asserts that he went about his "routine" of killing as calmly as if he were shuffling a pack of cards — he was without remorse.

Quantrill was. I have saved him for last on purpose, because he

119

was, in my estimation, the worst of our bad men — at least he caused the most havoc, the most deaths. He was just an ordinary looking man of the vanilla flavor. In his blue eyes a dull, sad feeling resided, betraying the morbid recollections in his brain or lurid visions in his conscience. He weighed 171 pounds. His face, too, was deceiving — it was ordinary, gaunt, lean, expressionless. He was usually quiet and lazy except when in battle. You would not ever suspect him of being the rascal that he was unless you had seen him in battle. It was then, and only then, that he became the malicious, cold-blooded, degenerate who laughed, shouted and shrieked over the din of his guerrillamen's battle guns.

THE COMPOSITE BAD MAN

Suppose, now, that we do a bit of magic by making a hypothetical composite bad man. That is, let's take the features many of the bad men had in common and put them together and thereby conjure up a vision of the typical bad man of the West.

There he stands before you. He isn't so bad to look at. He's sun-tanned; a cold steel-blue-gray eye seems to read your mind. He's blond, square-jawed, mustachioed, rough-chinned. He wears a pleasant expression or even a smile on his face. He's five feet, nine and a half inches, and he weighs 169 pounds. His hands and feet are small. His body is compact, muscular. He walks quietly and he talks quietly. He's well dressed, except when on the range. He's a youth, possibly between twenty and twenty-five.

Now don't think for one minute, however, that the next fellow you see walking down the street with those dimensions and looking the part is a bad man.

THE OFFICER

Noteworthy and interesting is the fact that the good frontier officer looked and acted much like the bad man, as the Appendix of this book shows. He, also, had blue eyes, quick, catlike movements, a soft voice, quiet demeanor, an airy sense of humor while off duty, a square jaw, a firm chin, and a flair for dress. The chief difference between the two types of men was that their actions were instigated by motives entirely different.

CHAPTER V

INHERITANCE OR ENVIRONMENT

THE BROW OF CAIN

THE bad man of the old West was a product of both environment and inheritance. Bad man Polk Wells once said:

> I was born like all other children with a latent germ of savagery in my little breast, consequently the loss of a mother's care and love, and a father's pleasant greeting and protection on the one hand, and cruel treatment and opposition on the other (by his stepmother and older step-brothers) caused the beastly in my nature to rapidly develop.

There is usually something inherently wrong with a man who is cold-blooded and remorseless. A fundamentally good man may be driven to act against society because of unyielding circumstances, but he regrets it and usually sooner or later rights his wrongs. The inherently bad man, if there ever was one, could not go straight.

The criminologist would revel in the story of John Wesley Hardin and his family. He had a host of relatives throughout Texas who were bad men themselves and constantly on the dodge. One reason why they could continue their depredations so long was their system of hideouts, espionage, and clan loyalty. Among his relatives were the Taylors — Jim, Bill, Charles, and Buck; the Clementses — Gyp, Joe, and Manning; the Dixons — Simp, Bud, Tom, and Charley; the Mannings, and even Jeff Ake. Nearly all of these had "killed their man."

Too, the Jameses, Youngers, Daltons, and even John Ringo were all related.

121

Old Man Clanton begot Billy, Ike, and Finn, all four of whom were among Arizona's worst rustlers.

The Harrold brothers of Lampasas, the Marlow brothers of Young County, and the Horrell brothers, all of Texas, and the Reno brothers of Wisconsin, and a host of other families of outlaws are to be found in the annals of Western outlawry.

"Like father, like son" is a phrase of significance.

The geneologist would probably cite by way of contrast to these families of outlaws the Earp family. Brothers Wyatt, Virgil, and Morgan Earp formed the most striking and formidable triumvirate of frontier officers. They were the sixth generation of Earps on American soil — of Scotch descent. Their forebears were famous soldiers, lawyers, and officers. They fought for the United States in the Colonial Army and in the War with Mexico.

Likewise, Arizona Ranger Captain Harry Wheeler was born a soldier. His father was a Colonel in the Regular Army, coming from a line of distinguished officers himself. Harry would have entered West Point himself, had he not fallen half an inch short of the minimum requirements for registration. But he felt he should serve his country in some warlike way, so he became by turn a Government Scout, a soldier in Cuba, a day laborer, a Ranger, a border sheriff. Again, "like father, like son."

Several of the bad men's forebears were also fierce fighting men. Louis Dalton, father of the Dalton boys, was in the Mexican War under Zachary Taylor. Campbell Longley, Bill's father, was a veteran of General Sam Houston's army. Barney Wells, an uncle of Polk Wells, was a major in the Mexican War, and another relative, Benjamin Wells, was a lieutenant under General Scott in the War of 1812. Fighting blood ran through the old soldiers' veins and was tranfused into the offsprings'.

Some of the bad men's characteristics were probably hereditary. For example, the pugnacious expression on their faces and somewhat belligerent attitude of the Daltons was probably an inherent trait. Al Jennings admitted that he had a consuming and at times uncontrollable temper. Bass Outlaw, who slew an innocent fellow Texas Ranger, was continually quarrelsome; trouble followed him as steel does the lodestone — it was simply his nature.

Judge Isaac C. Parker, probably the greatest American authority of all time on the frontier criminal often said that he believed the criminal baby came into the world with the mark of Cain upon his brow. You will remember that he was judge of the

Boone sliced off the other leg, put it in a burlap bag, and hiked off toward the nearest settlement. (See page 125.)

first court of justice with jurisdiction over Oklahoma and Indian Territory, a refuge for Southwestern criminals of all types. The Judge certainly should have known, from experience. Again, during his twenty-one years as judge, he sentenced more murderers to death than any other American judge.

Old-time Emerson Hough wrote:

> Practice assisted in proficiency, but a Wild Bill or a Slade or a Billy the Kid was born and not made.

Along with Henry Plummer of Idaho, probably the most thoroughly degraded villain throughout the West was the all-time champion guerrilla chieftain William Clarke Quantrill. His father was a captain in the War of 1812, Captain Thomas Quantrill. The father had one fairly decent son, Thomas Henry Quantrill — but it is said that all the others, including William Clarke Quantrill, inherited the "seed-ground for tears which kindled a conflagration on the border and drenched a land in blood."

The father (Captain Thomas Quantrill) was said to have been an embezzler, and his mother has been described as a diabolical creature. Quantrill's brothers became thieves and low scoundrels. It is said that an uncle of his was one of the most outstanding criminals for a decade or so before the Civil War, being a forger and confidence man and having served sentences in quite a few state prisons. This same uncle married and deserted six women and attempted to murder his first wife; he defrauded people coming and going, and for offenses serious or petty he was incarcerated in jails in New Orleans, St. Louis, Cincinnati, and in other cities. Quantrill's grandfather on his father's side was supposed to have been a sharpster in trading horses and was a professional gambler. His great uncle was a pirate. But all his criminal forebears rolled into one couldn't have held a candle to William Clarke Quantrill, the leader of the border guerrilla men in Missouri. He shed blood like water. He burned and looted whole towns. He held mass executions. Apparently there was no excuse for his actions, unless it was his hereditary inclinations. He suffered no remorse, and his deeds were indescribably cruel. He was bad all the way through. Every man is a sort of modified sum total of his ancestors.

Boone Helm was another naturally depraved murderer — accused even of cannibalism. He was a member of Plummer's gang of freebooters and road agents. About his cannibalism — he and a friend were on a hunting trip in the dead of winter in the frozen Northwest. A big storm came up and they had to take shelter in a rough log cabin. They stayed there for about a week after they had eaten all their provisions and there was no way to get help. The cabin was snowed under about fifteen feet and the nearest settlement was miles away. So Boone shot his companion, sliced off his leg, cooked it, and ate it. The storm subsided and the snow hardened sufficiently on top to support a man on snowshoes. Boone sliced off the other leg, put it in a burlap bag, threw it over his shoulder, and hiked off toward the nearest settlement. He stopped on his way and spent the night with a trapper and his family. The trapper asked him what he carried, to which Boone answered casually, "Just a ham." The trapper was suspicious, however, and the next day, after Boone had left, he traced his steps back to the cabin, opened the door, and in frozen horror viewed the ghastly sight of the bloody torso.

Boone escaped temporarily into Canada, but was captured on Frazer River in the fall of 1862. A report of the incident was given in a British Columbia paper:

> The man, Boone Helm, to whom we referred some weeks since, has at last been taken. He was brought into this city last night strongly ironed . . . He made no resistance to the arrest — in fact, he was too weak to do so — and acknowledged without equivocation or attempt at evasion that he was Boone Helm. Upon being asked what had become of his companion, he replied with the utmost *sang froid*:
>
> "Why, do you suppose that I'm a——fool enough to starve to death when I can help it? I ate him up, of course."
>
> The man who accompanied him has not been seen or heard of since, and from what we have been told of this case-hardened villian's antecedents, we are inclined to believe he told the truth. It is said this is not the first time he has been guilty of cannibalism.

Boone was probably mentally unbalanced. His is not the only instance of cannibalism on the frontier. Some of the Donner emigrant party in the 1840's became demented from privation and ate of the flesh. Professor George R. Stewart tells their stirring plight in his book *Ordeal By Hunger*.

Old-timer Judge Langford, who knew Boone Helm, said:

Some men are villains by nature, other become so by circumstances.

The wretch I am now about to introduce [Boone Helm] was one of those hideous monsters of depravity whom neither precept nor example could have saved from a life of crime.

"VICTIM OF CIRCUMSTANCE"

But there are two sides to this question. There are many who believe that no one is born bad — that he becomes that way because of environment. Many of the Western bad men came from fine, respected families.

John Wesley Hardin's mother was accounted a good woman and his father a minister of the gospel. John Wesley himself was a schoolteacher for three months in Navarro County, Texas. For that matter, the degraded William Clarke Quantrill was a schoolteacher before his more lurid career.

Lawyer Buck Walton, Ben Thompson's champion and biographer, insisted that the bad man Thompson's English parents were good people.

From Sam Bass' gang Seaborne Barnes' father was a respected man — a sheriff and tax collector of Cass County, Texas. A couple of youthful recruits were picked up by Bass in Dallas County — farm youths from highly respectable homes and families. And Billy, Joel, and Henry Collins, also of Sam Bass' gang, were outlaw sons of highly respectable citizens. Picture, if you can, the tragic countenances of Pioneer Albert Collins and his wife in tears, standing on the railroad station platform waving goodbye to their son Billy at Tyler, Texas. Billy had been captured by Texas Rangers and was being taken to Austin — he cried like a baby to see his poor old parents so brokenhearted. Albert G. Collins and wife Pamelia had come from Kentucky to settle in Dallas County in 1846. They were exemplary members of the Christian Church and had tried to bring up their seven sons and three daughters in good Christian faith to be good upright citizens. All but three of them were. But Joel had died an inglorious death of an outlaw in Kansas, here was Billy being taken away in handcuffs, and somewhere off in hiding right then was their youngest son Henry. Woeful and sorrowful it must have been to Mr. and Mrs. Collins.

Even Sam Bass came from a line of good people. "He was born in Indiana," as the old song goes, in Mitchell, in Lawrence County of that state. His parents were staunch citizens of Marion Township, where they moved when Sam was still little. It was true that they were hard workers — they died while Sam was yet young, but their consciences were probably clear — they had set before their children the examples of honesty, industry, and respectability. Both his mother and father were descended from families of pioneer settlers coming from North Carolina — English-Dutch stock on his father's side and Dutch-German on his mother's.

Even Henry Plummer, whom I have called thoroughly degraded, had a respectable brother and sister in New York, who knew nothing of his underhandedness. Upon learning of his depredations, they were greatly chagrined at what seemed to be the incredible. They severely lamented the career of the black-sheep brother. Also among Plummer's henchmen, George Ives and Buck Stinson were black sheep of respectable families. Even the depraved cannibal Boone Helm, whom nothing could induce to lead a straight life, had a good, hard-working, honest brother named "Old Tex" Helm, who would invariably help his brother out of many difficulties and send him forth on a path of temporary righteousness.

Tom Horn had numerous brothers and sisters who were all well-behaved, industrious, and who led exemplary lives. Wild Bill Hickok's father was an inoffensive, quiet little storekeeper with a family of six children, only one of whom became renowned.

Joe Hill, notorious member of Curly Bill's rustlers in Cochise County, Arizona, and the same man who shot poor old Dick Lloyd off his horse for riding it into his poker game, was reputed to be a scion of a fine old aristocratic family.

The redoubtable Doc Holliday, born and reared at Valdosta, Georgia, came from a line of aristocratic Southern cotton planters and slaveholders; his father was a Major in the Confederate Army.

Jesse James' father was a preacher and his forebears are said to have come from the blue-grass region of Kentucky. Jesse himself was supposed to have been quite religious.

Al Jennings came from the stock of proud, belligerent, Southern slaveholders — "the best blood of Virginia." Oklahoma settlers accounted his father, Judge Jennings, the perfect type of the ancient Southern colonel. Judge Jennings was successively schoolmaster, physician, Methodist preacher, lawyer, editor, and lawyer again. Al himself practiced law with his brother-partner. Another brother was also a lawyer.

Oklahoma's half-breed, part-Indian, master bank robber was

127

Henry Starr. He spoke his sentiments to Fred Sutton on what made the bad man bad:

Criminology? Where do you get that stuff? There is no such thing as criminology, a science of crime. There is no such thing as a confirmed criminal mind. There is no such thing as a criminologist, a man learned in the science of crime. There is no such thing as a born criminal, as hereditary badness, unless the person is insane. I think I ought to know criminals. They have been my companions for forty years, in prison and out. I have eaten and slept with them, helped them plan crimes, led them into crimes, knelt beside them when they died. I have known their innermost thoughts, their strivings, their sufferings, their failures and their successes.

If the bad criminal mind is hereditary, then the good honest mind is hereditary, too; and all the sons of preachers and doctors and deacons and honest bankers would be good, like their parents, –but nearly all the bandits and outlaws and criminals I have ever known were sons of good fathers and mothers. In all my life I never knew a criminal who had a bad mother. I never knew a criminal who didn't love his mother. I've heard the last word on the lips of several outlaws and it was always: "Mother." And the most of the hundreds of criminals I have known had good, honest fathers. One of the worst outlaws I ever knew was the son of a preacher.

If the criminal tendency was hereditary the sons of every criminal would be criminals, too. I never knew the son of an outlaw to be a criminal. Some of the best men I ever knew were the sons of outlaws. The sons of criminals usually turn out well, just as the sons of drunkards are nearly all prohibitionists. As an example, look at the children and grandchildren of Frank and Jesse James, the two worst outlaws the West ever knew. Frank's only son, Robert, was born when Frank was in hiding, an outlaw with a price on his head. If there is anything in hereditary badness Robert James should be a humdinger for wickedness, but he is a farmer in Clay County, Missouri, married and highly respected by all his neighbors. Why, they talked about running him for a high county office recently. They don't make 'em any better than Robert James.

Jesse James had two children, Jesse, Junior, and Mary. Jesse is a lawyer here in Kansas City. His four daughters were graduated with honors from high school. They are all members of the church and one went nine years to Sunday School without missing a day and was the gold-medal student in a Sunday-school with a thousand pupils. Mary James, only daughter of Jesse, the bandit, married Henry Barr, a farmer of Clay County, and her three sons are leaders in the Methodist church in Excelsior Springs. One of them is studying to be a preacher and he graduated at the head of his class in a Baptist College. How is that for heredity?

So, criminals are made by environment and circumstance. Crime is simply misdirected energy. Emerson said a weed was a plant out of its place. A criminal is a man out of his place. Maybe he never had a chance to be honest.

There is no more a science of criminology than there is a science of eatology or drinkology or lawyerology. You say a criminal has certain wheels in his head that lead him to be always a criminal in spite of all efforts to reform. You might as well say a lawyer has certain cogs in his brain and bumps on his nut that makes him follow the law in spite of all efforts to get away from it. Bunk! We all know a lawyer can quit that game any time he wants to. So can a criminal quit, and they do. There are millions of former criminals in honest occupations in this country. Any criminal may take a notion any time to be an honest man. The best inducement to hold out to criminals to reform is square, honest, kind treatment. The worst thing you can do to a criminal is to put him in a class by himself, to treat him as if he were a creature set apart. He is just an average man who has gone wrong, that's all.

There was never a criminal in my ancestry as far back as I can trace it. I am the first, and I was forced into it.

SO WHAT?

It is charitable to believe that the criminal is made and not born — that he is a victim of circumstances and that given an opportunity to right himself with society he will do so. This is a test which Henry Starr himself could not meet. Several times he promised Uncle Billy Tilghman that he would "go straight" and his prison record seemed to indicate that he would. He kept thinking that he would retire after the next bank robbery with enough to live comfortably — but the next robbery was always next. He met his death while robbing a bank.

Now, what does all this mean? What conclusions can you draw from all this information? Was it inheritance or was it environment or was it both that made the bad man bad? There isn't any definite formula that will give the answer as to which made the bad man bad, inheritance or environment.

Each influence, no doubt, played its part in directing his actions and reactions in somewhat the same way that the influence plays its part in directing the lives of other men. Some of the bad men were black sheep from the very best of families and apparently were victims of circumstances, others appeared to have been born bad and remained so, and still others were from the very best of immediate families but had near kin who were not so good — John Wesley Hardin, for example.

So what?

CHAPTER VI

THE PHILOSOPHY OF THE BAD MAN
OF THE WEST

HIS RELIGION

 *LL day long on the prairie I ride,*
Not even a dog to trot by my side,
My fire I kindle with chips gathered
round,
And I boil my coffee without being
ground.
My bread like unleaven, I bake in a pot,
I sleep on the ground for want of a cot,
I wash in a puddle, wipe on a sack,
And carry my wardrobe all on my back,
The skies are my ceiling, my carpet the grass,
My music the lowing herds as they pass,
My books are the brook, and my sermons the stones,
My parson a wolf on a pulpit of bones.
But now if my cooking ain't complete,
Hygienists can't blame me for living to eat,
And where is the man who sleeps more profound
Than a puncher who stretches himself on the ground?
My books teach me consistency ever to prize,
My sermons that small things I should not despise,
My parson remarks from his pulpit of bones,
The lord favors those who look out for their own.

Of all the 250 or so bad men I have read about, only a handful
ever said or wrote anything about their religion. George Coe
said:

> My religion [had been, while a bad man with Billy the Kid]:
> 'Right between man and man, and the practice of the Golden
> Rule.'

But somehow, it wouldn't stand the searchlight of Phoebe's [his wife's] faith and prayers [after he reformed]. I realized that my religion was of the head and not of the heart. I was baptized one morning in November — the snow falling on us during the services. From that day forward, I never doubted the faith I claimed, and have been a member of the church and an ordained deacon for thirty-five years.

Before his trial during which he was sentenced to death by hanging, the depraved Boone Helm sacrilegiously kissed the Bible and ostentatiously swore false testimony before a group of miners, much to their disgust.

Jeff Ake, of Texas, said:

I used to read the Testaments until I got convinced that there was too many men a-writin' the Bible and too many contradictions, till you couldn't depend on nothin'. When they talk about Jesus Christ bein' holy, I always ask myself, "Who was his father?" And I figger that he was a smart man — a mighty smart man born of a woman. They talk about visions. Anybody can see visions.

Jesse James carried a Bible with him everywhere, and he refused to curse. He attended church regularly. He was baptized in Muddy Fork, in 1868, when he joined the Kearney Baptist Church. His membership was later nullified.

Jesse James, John Wesley Hardin, and Al Jennings were all sons of ministers, but little is known of the religion of the latter two. Polk Wells' father knew the Bible by heart, but his own training in religion was obtained only in an Ohio penitentiary. Sam Bass refused to talk about religion on his deathbed, explaining, "What's the use? I am going to hell anyhow." Black Bart, the California stage robber and poet, limited his education to the reading of the classics and the Bible. These men were fairly representative of the Western bad men, and their religious views vary.

The typical bad man's thoughts were probably more terrestial than celestial. He followed the maxim of an eye for an eye and a tooth for a tooth. Interesting, though, is the fact that most bad men feared a death of disgrace, such as hanging by law, by vigilantes, or by a mob, more than they feared death in battle. Furthermore, they were superstitious about dying with their boots on, supposedly an evil omen to a bad man. There is a tradition, too, that the bad man was either quiet or spoke the truth when dying.

This practice of "mavericking" continued in Texas up to and even after the Civil War. (See page 137.)

Now, don't these facts seem to indicate some sort of semblance of a fear of or a belief in an after life?

HIS EDUCATION

Likewise, little is usually said about the bad man's education. Frontier conditions at best provided only a rudimentary education. Cherokee Bob, a member of Plummer's gang, was known as an uneducated Southerner. Wild Bill Hickok's education was termed "rudimentary." His favorite book was the story of Kit Carson. Emmett Dalton vouched that he remained in the country schoolhouse, built by his father, until only eleven years of age. Sam Bass never found enough time to spend on the rough log benches of the Woodville (Indiana) school to learn to write a clear hand. His signature once closely resembled "Sam B. Ass." Also, Burt Alvord, who wrote his name as "Burt Alvoid" several times, was accused of not being able to spell his own name. Jeff Ake's education consisted in the reading of the *New York Herald's* love stories.

There were, on the other hand, Western bad men who were well educated according to frontier standards. Henry Plummer, by his polished tongue and intellectual resources, inveigled the miners of Bannack, Idaho, to elect him as sheriff. Judging by their demeanor, their language, and the books they liked to read, John Ringo, Jesse Evans, and Black Bart were well educated. Jesse Evans was first pal, later enemy of Billy the Kid.

Doc Holliday had a college education in dentistry, which he practiced in Dallas until tuberculosis set in. Al Jennings attended the University of West Virginia for two years, where he studied law, which he practiced before and after his penitentiary term. Little Bill, a renegade college graduate from Pennsylvania, joined the Doolin gang in Oklahoma. Polk Wells studied the Bible and the classics, became well versed in both while in an Ohio penitentiary, and wrote his autobiography. George Coe, Lee Sage, and John Wesley Hardin were well enough educated to write their autobiographies, also. Hardin studied law under the tutorship of a Huntsville (Texas) lawyer, and practiced that profession after his release from prison.

Frank James was well educated, and was a student of the Shakespearean drama; Coleman Younger, his cousin, was well informed on the Bible and the Elizabethan drama.

Whatever education the other bad men had was apparently

self-acquired and utilitarian. They majored in equestrianism, "Six-shooterology," in crime, in the science of scouting, and in their own peculiar indelicate vernacular — but they had, as a rule, little "book-larnin'."

Lee Sage, in speaking of his bandit-father, said:

> The horse he couldn't ride never looked between two sand-hills. He could handle a rope like double-geared lightning. When it come to tracks, he could foller a wood tick on solid sandrock in the dark of the moon. He wasn't much for size, but he could stir up more dust in five minutes than Noah's flood could settle in forty years.

Such an education was adequate requisite for the frontier bad man. Bernard De Voto has perhaps best summarized such an education in *Across the Wide Missouri,* on page 158, to be exact.

HIS SUPERSTITIONS

The bad man was often superstitious. It was a distinction for a peace officer to die with his boots on — "in line of duty" so to speak. But such a death was an evil omen to the bad man — "they caught him in the act" so to speak. Many a bad man's last request was to take his boots off.

Some of them believed in fate and many of the famous characters of the old West came to believe sincerely that they were invincible. George Coe, in commenting upon his recovery from serious wounds, said that Providence had watched over his life. Jeff Ake, who shot a cattle inspector and spent a night in jail with the notorious Ben Thompson, said, "I believe that what is to be is a-goin' to be, no matter what comes." Through long impunity Plummer and his gang conceived that they were invulnerable. They found out that they were considerably mistaken, however, when nearly all of them were hanged simultaneously.

Henry Starr thought himself bullet proof, having his clothes literally torn from his body by bullets on his various raids and never being touched by a bullet until his Stroud (Oklahoma) affair.

Belief in premonitions was also common among Western bad men. Judge Roy Bean swore that his pet cinnamon beer-drinking bear had a premonition that his master was about to be assasinated while in bed, and so shook the bed that Roy moved it. Uncannily enough, there was an attempt. Thus, the bear probably did save his life.

135

Marshal John Slaughter of Arizona was firmly convinced that a guardian angel watched his every move. For no other reason except for a strange "presentiment" he would suddenly spur his horse to a gallop or jump up from his chair to look out for an unseen source of danger. Uncannily enough, several times these strange presentiments did save his life.

Desperado Polk Wells, commenting upon similar experiences, said:

> When I allow my mind to dwell upon this affair, I become more thoroughly convinced of the practicability and utility of presentiments, or of the visitations of disembodied spirits.

Gambler Soapy Smith was superstitious. He picked up a collar button off the corpse of Bob Ford and wore it as a luck piece. Ford, Jesse James' assassin, had just been killed by Red Kelley. The charm had little effect for Smith, however, because he was killed in Alaska the following year.

HE COULDN'T SETTLE DOWN

As a rule, the bad man could not reform. Frequently, however, he was tired of being chased and became temporarily law abiding. Bill Longley, tired of being hunted in Texas, went to Salt Lake City. Frank James left Missouri for California for the same reason. Hardin left Texas for Florida from the same motive. All three soon returned to their old haunts and sooner or later renewed their old habits (except Frank).

George Coe, used to the free and wild New Mexico, when back on a Missouri farm with a wife felt like a "bird in a cage." He moved to the West to become a reliable rancher. Henry Plummer's, Boone Helm's, and Ben Thompson's good wives and children could not turn them from their wayward careers.

Henry Starr tried to quit robbing banks, but could not. Frank Jackson stopped his career temporarily at Sam Bass' death and was not heard of for a long time, until, posing as a Mr. Downing in Arizona, he got drunk and was shot by a Ranger named Speed. As we have seen, Arkansas Tom, one of the very few remorseful killers, after several attempts at reformation, finally wailed, "I don't know what's the matter with me!"

No doubt, some of the bad men were sincere in their attempts at reformation, but because of their past record, society was prejudiced against them.

John Wesley Hardin actually tried to reform, but society would not accept him with his lurid background and prison record. At the very least quarrel he got into as lawyer and as a candidate for public office, charges were made that he was back in his old boots again.

Society would not let the bad man reform nor the good officer retire, because of their past records. People feared the former and wanted the latter for the protection he afforded.

They demanded, for instance, that intrepid Wyatt Earp continue as Marshal even after the work became distasteful to him. Everywhere he went he was met by a petition to represent the law. Restless Marshal Frank Canton could not settled down to a normal, peaceful life. He was officer of the law wherever he went — be it Oklahoma, Montana, or Alaska. And he had some real experiences in the frozen wilds of frontier Alaska during the Klondike gold rush of '98. He tells about them in his autobiography, *Frontier Trails.*

HE EXCUSED HIMSELF

The bad man probably felt justified in appropriating cattle or minerals or other wealth for his own sustenance.

Charlie Taylor, a cousin of John Wesley Hardin and an ex-Confederate soldier, was arrested on a cattle charge in 1886 at Bastrop, Texas. The officers said it was plain stealing, but not so according to Charlie. He claimed he took only unbranded mavericks, which were free to take for anyone who could catch them. On the strength of his argument, he considered himself justified in breaking jail and escaping. This was the initial firecracker of the Sutton-Taylor feud. Charlie may have been using the branding of mavericks, young unbranded cattle, as an excuse.

According to an old Spanish law, when Texas was under the Spanish flag, this branding of stray mavericks was not illegal, provided the brander paid a small tax to the Spanish government. This practice of "mavericking" continued in Texas up to and even after the Civil War, during which time many unbranded Texas cattle strayed, rendering their exact ownership unknown upon the return of the ex-Confederates to their ranches.

As for the bad man's relations with other men, he probably excused himself by the use of such terms as "self-defense" or "victim of circumstances." Even when Jack McCall shot Wild Bill Hickok in the back, and when he was asked to give an excuse, he replied, "I didn't want suicide."

George Coe claims to have been an unwilling victim of a vendetta, and states that his leader, Billy the Kid, was merely an accessory to many of the killings accredited to him. He further stated that the Kid was made "the goat" of his side of the war, being the only one ever to appear in court for trial.

The bad man, like other human beings, usually craved sympathy and understanding. Jesse James, incognito as Mr. Howard in Tennessee, discussed his real self to a friend, saying, "Oh, the Jameses aren't so bad as all that, do you think?" The friend belittled them considerably, but "Mr. Howard" merely laughed. Imagine the friend's consternation when he found he had been running the James boys down to Jesse himself!

Likewise, Sam Bass, pretending to an old farmer to be a Ranger, after himself, said Bass must have some good traits, since he had a great many friends. The farmer responded that he had a pretty good opinion of Bass himself. But he didn't go ahead to explain his opinion, and Sam let it drop there, being satisfied.

Clay Allison said he never killed "nary a feller what didn't need it." Likewise, Bill Longley considered he had done the country a favor in ridding it of many pests and varmints.

Judge Langford, who knew Plummer personally, said that this leader of renegades excused himself:

> So true it is that the worst men are the last to admit to themselves the magnitude of their offences, that even Plummer, stained with the guilt of repeated murders and seductions, a very monster of iniquity, believed that his restoration to the pursuits and honors of virtuous association could be established.

But Henry Starr said the Bandit deserved no sympathy even though he craved it. He himself had instructed his men to spare life whenever possible, but to shoot to kill if necessary and not to waste ammunition. In his own words,

> Of course that's murder. Every bandit is a potential murderer. No man ever robbed at the heel of a gun without murder in his heart, and he deserves no pity nor sympathy.

ROBIN HOOD

Many bandits felt it wrong to rob individuals but were not bothered by conscience when robbing the more impersonal Wells Fargo Express Company, banks, or other corporations. For that matter many of them, bad men and others, considered big business concerns as robbers.

Death Valley Scotty made the rather intimate acquaintance of both robbers and millionaires. He claimed to have discovered a fabulously rich gold mine and with the proceeds built a palatial mansion on the edge of the valley. But being just a hobo, he lived in a wooden shack near the place — he felt more at home there. His money may have been given him or furnished him in some way by a millionaire pal of his from Chicago, who, for his vacation, would come out each year and visit Death Valley Scotty. The two would get up an outfit and strike off somewhere in the desert for their "gold mine." The millionaire was probably one of those fellows you read about who never grew up.

At any rate, Death Valley Scotty played host to millionaires and train robbers alike — some of either unasked but not unwelcome. Scotty said he found no material difference between the two classes of men. Both, according to him, were out for the jack and took it via the easiest means — either by robbing trains or by wrecking a bank from the inside. Incidentally, Scotty said that he had trouble with a few millionaires, whereas the hold-ups always treated him respectfully. But Death Valley Scotty was by no means by himself in his opinions about robbers and big business men.

"Easy come, easy go" applied to the bandit's money. He threw it away in a prodigal fashion, for the sake of magnaminity or of making friends to establish a system of espionage and hideouts. His generosity was partly sentimental and partly mercenary. He was plutocrat and pauper all within a very short duration of time — gambling, spending, or giving away the proceeds of his daring. Said Jeff Ake:

> I've been worth $50,000 twenty times, I reckon, but it would go — gambling and giving it away and helping other people. Now I have nothing . . . but I don't owe any man in the world anything.

Sam Bass' share of the $60,000 Union-Pacific Big Springs robbery was gone in a short time. It was the only really big and successful robbery Sam was ever connected with. But he gave it away and spent the rest just like a grasshopper, probably thinking that much more would come, just as easily:

Jim, there goes the last piece of '77 gold. It hasn't done me the least bit of good; but that's all right — I'll get some more in a few days. So let it gush. It all goes in a lifetime.

Many are the tales about the generosity of the bad man. They vary from the buying of circus tickets for poor children (Polk Wells) to the forcing of marriages (Mexican Rurale leader Kosterlitzky). Cherokee Bob, Henry Plummer, Langford Peel, Joseph A. Slade, Billy the Kid, Jeff Ake, Bill Doolin, Curly Bill, Al Jennings, Jesse James, Sam Bass, John Wesley Hardin, and Joaquin Murrieta all figure in these tales — all have been cited as modern Robin Hoods. Joaquin Murrieta was even named the "Robin Hood of El Dorado."

Little Al Jennings and his gang hadn't eaten for some time. They rode up to a farmhouse and asked the lady for some food. She caught her last chicken and fed them in a hospitable sort of way. During the meal she complained that her cruel husband mistreated her and her son (his stepson). Upon ascertaining that the woman did not care to have the husband around, the gang of robbers reached in their potato bag and pulled out a pile of greenbacks for her. Then the fun began. They unlimbered their pistols and shot at the husband's feet as he scampered down the road with high steps.

Sam Bass once took compassion on a one-armed man while robbing a train, "H——, have you got only one arm?"

The passenger meekly replied, "Only one, sir," as he held up the stub of an arm.

"Well, take back your stuff," said Sam as he handed back the man's watch, wallet, and ring. "We don't want it. Sit down and keep still."

John Wesley Hardin wrote about one of his experiences quite befitting of a Robin Hood:

A man named O'Connor, returning from Louisiana, was going back to Austin, and stayed one night in Hemphill (Texas). A state policeman arrested him because he had on a pistol and brought him into Hemphill, where on the policeman's bare statement the magistrate fined him $25 and costs, besides confiscating his pistol. I heard of the outrage and explained the case to the justice, who granted O'Connor a new trial and acquitted him. In the meantime the policeman had taken possession of O'Connor's horse and saddle and was trying to sell them to pay the fine and costs, O'Connor being broke. I was in front of the courthouse talking

140

matters over with O'Connor and some others when a small boy about ten years old began abusing Spites for arresting O'Connor at his father's house. Spites came up and listened to him and finally told the boy that if he did not shut up he would arrest him. The boy ridiculed him and defied him to do it, telling him that no one but a coward would arrest a poor traveler. Spites told him if he did not shut up he would whip him. The boy told him he was not afraid, just go ahead and whip and arrest him. Spites got up and slapped the boy, then I told him to hold on, that if he was in earnest to slap a man. He told me he would arrest me for interfering with him in the discharge of his duty. I told him he could not arrest one side of me, and the boy laughed. Spites started to draw a pistol. I pulled a derringer with my left and my six-shooter with my right and instantly fired the derringer. The dauntless policeman ran to the courthouse and asked the judge to protect him.

Down in old Mexico in the fastnesses of the Sierra Madres lived a whole village of outlaws who smuggled Bacanora Mezcal into New Mexico. They defied the Mexican Rurales of Kosterlitzky and even Zorro's legions, who dared not enter the region of the village for fear of an ambush. Oh yes, there really was a Zorro — a Mexican officer who perfected the art of disguise and who would by clever spying subterfuges and valiant gestures capture Mexican criminals and turn them over to the government.

Anyway, these smugglers, whose best market was Silver City, New Mexico, were headed by one Don Jorge. Jorge was a Robin Hood. The Mexicans of Silver City regarded him as an honest, hospitable soul. He would sell his liquor and set up an outfit for carrying smuggled drygoods back into Sonora. But before leaving he would give a big *baile*, a Mexican dance, where he would serve Bacanora Mezcal free. Thus, he had many friends and few enemies, mainly officers.

Road agents Bill Mayfield and Cherokee Bob, Plummer's gang of road agents in Idaho, were pals and buddies until a woman came between them. Her name was Cynthia, and report had it that she was quite a beauty. She liked both Bob and Bill, and of course they were crazy about her. Now, which should she take as husband? She eany-meany-miny-moed and picked Cherokee Bob, the more prosperous of the two at the time. Both men proved themselves Robin Hoods. Bill, the spurned, cleared out and told Bob that he fell heir to all their belongings, including the girl. But Cherokee Bob insisted on paying Bill for half the value of their traps and other property Bill left behind. Bob finally forced the money on Bill, who left with the parting injunction to be sure to take good care of the girl.

Judge Langford heard two men talking of a strange incident. Bill Graves was telling Tom Caldwell that he knew too much about the Plummer gang for his own good — that he wouldn't testify against them for fear of the after effects. Bill said, further, that he was reminded of an occurrence in California. He said that he was robbed of two thousand dollars by a road agent, whom he distinctly recognized. He asked the robber at the time of the robbery whether it wasn't pretty hard on him to take all he had in the world. The robber then gave him back forty dollars. The truly surprising part was that later the robber walked up to the same Bill Graves in a saloon and asked whether Graves recognized him. Of course, he did, knowing that he was the robber for certain, but he dared not say so, for fear the robber would kill him to prevent a witness at a possible trial. He replied to the robber that he had never seen him before. The generous robber, being a grateful sort of Robin Hood, gave Graves four thousand dollars "just for keeping his mouth shut."

Langford Peel called himself "chief" of a band of somewhat gentlemanly ruffians in old Salt Lake City. Peel befriended all the gentle peace officers, but he stoutly boasted that he would sooner die than submit to some of the bully officers of the region. One day Peel got very intoxicated and strode up and down the streets yelling that no one who ever wore a star in Salt Lake could arrest him. Now there was a highly respected citizen, a peaceable law-abiding man named Patrick Lannan, who had just been elected as policeman. He had had nothing to do with the roughs on the force. But he heard that someone was causing a disturbance and rushed to the scene. He saw it was Langford Peel and would have reasoned with him, but out in public it was too late — he had to make an arrest or immediately start off as a "weakling" officer. Peel once more growled, "No man that ever packed a star in this city can arrest me."

But the next man he saw was the respected Patrick Lannan, and he added hastily, "I'll take that back. You can arrest me, Pat, for you're no fighting man. You're a gentleman."

Peel surrendered his guns, bowed low in a chivalrous manner, and Pat led him off to jail quietly.

Again, Jesse James and his gang were eating at an old farm-lady's home, which she said was mortgaged and which would have to be evacuated as soon as a miser-shyster came to collect. Jesse reached in a potato bag and produced, much to her amazement, the required $1,400 and gave it to her. The miser called, collected, and on his way back to town was relieved of the same $1,400 by the same James gang.

WHAT DID THEY THINK OF HIM?

To the public, the bad men were too often either Robin Hoods or arch-fiends, and nothing in between.

For an example of fabricated hyperbolic gruesomeness, a story had Cole Younger lining up fifteen men like dominoes killing them all with one bullet through their heads, just to see them fall in regular cadence. Incredible!

An erratic newspaper had Polk Wells' notches as thirty-two, whereas he swore that his killings were limited to two. He had killed his uncle in self-defense and had been an accessory in the death of a jailer.

On the other hand, some bad men became such romantic heroes that those who brought them to justice were denounced by the sentimental public.

Jim Murphy was called "a dirty skunk" for aiding the Texas Rangers in capturing Sam Bass. Pat Garrett was blamed for doing his duty in killing his former friend, Billy the Kid. In his next election race after he had killed Billy, the two-gun, two-fisted sheriff was defeated by the "bloodless" sheriff José R. Lucero, who used no guns. José, strange as it may seem, used no guns in arresting his desperadoes, yet lived to be seventy-three. He died recently, on July 30, 1940, having served with his brother Felipe as officer for Dona Ana County, New Mexico, for more than thirty years during the bloodiest and most hectic years of the county.

A mob hanged Jack McCall for shooting Wild Bill Hickok in the back.

The whole country uprose in violent protest against the State of Missouri for "sponsoring" the Ford brothers in their "foul" murder of Jesse James. Newspapers in the largest cities carried scorching editorials saying that the hero Jesse died a royal death and reprimanding Bob Ford as the vilest of villains. The *New York Sun* said, "To make a new murderer in the process of getting rid of an old one cannot be justified."

The ballads written about these men indicate the maudlin public sentiment:

Sam Bass was born in Indiana, it was his native home,
And at the age of seventeen young Sam began to roam.
He came out to old Texas a cowboy for to be —
A kinder-hearted feller you'll seldom ever see . . .

Jim (Murphy) had borrowed Sam's good gold and didn't want
to pay,
The only shot he saw was to give poor Sam away.
He sold out Sam and Barnes and left their friends to mourn —
Oh, what a scorching Jim will get when Gabriel blows his horn!

* * * * * * *

Poor Jesse (James) had a wife to mourn for his life,
Three children, they were brave.
But that dirty little coward that shot Mister Howard (James, in-
cognito)
Has laid poor Jesse in his grave.

* * * * * * *

Now this is how Billy the Kid met his fate:
The bright moon was shining, the hour was late,
Shot down by Pat Garrett, who once was his friend,
The young outlaw's life had now come to its end.

Chapter VII

THE CHIVALRY OF THE WESTERN BAD MAN—WHEREIN HE DIFFERED FROM THE MODERN BAD MAN

DELICATE FLOWER

ROBIN HOOD was chivalrous as well as generous.

Jesse James' language was said to be as circumspect as that of a Sunday-school superintendent in the presence of women and children. Of several surrounding men, Jesse, only, came to the aid of a young lady annoyed by a masher in a train day coach. He said to the offender, "You dirty loafer, get out of this coach, or I'll kick you out, right through this window!" Needless to say, the man got out.

Billy the Kid was the essence of politeness. The señoritas were crazy about him. Miss Sallie Chisum, niece of land baron John Chisum, was acquainted with the Kid and his followers and many of their enemies. She said that they were all very nice and polite around ladies. They all sought her attentions.

On the Western frontier women were highly prized articles. This was due in part to their paucity or fewness and probably in part to their demeanor. The disproportionate number of males in the old West made it natural for a woman to command more attention and even more respect, although she might be degraded at times. The immortal wit Mark Twain tells about the first woman ever to come to a mining camp he was in at the time of her arrival. Everybody quit work to see what the critter looked like. The miners all got in line to take a peep at her through a knothole in her kitchen wall while she prepared supper. It came

Clemens' turn and he looked through, and sure enough, there she was — a hundred and sixty-five years old, and turning flapjacks. When he overcame the heat of the moment, Samuel deducted a hundred years or so from her age. But this little incident just goes to show how women were prized as a rare delicacy on the frontier.

Too, the pioneer woman "kept the place" of a woman. She seldom if ever went into business or entered a profession. Lee Sage, "The Last Rustler," upon visiting a place of questionable reputation in Chicago "back East," was greatly disillusioned about women. He thought the place was an innocent barroom, but when he got in and sat down he looked up and found a blonde on each knee and one around his neck, and he said they hung on to him worse than a stupid range steer he once roped. Said he:

> I always held a woman as a pretty high article. This made them drop in my estimation. They was cheaper than dirt and harder to get shed of. I wonder how they lived in such a mob, what they wanted and what was going to become of them. I sucked in a breath or two of that stiff stale air. It made me hanker for the clean West.

The pioneer woman was more likely regarded as a "delicate flower" to be protected and cherished. Perhaps this was due in part of the Southern influence, where the aristocratic old "Suhth-uhn gen'leman" was supposedly a real "gentleman." The Appendix of this book shows that about two-thirds of the bad men of the old West (whose birth places are recorded) originated in the deep South, steeped in the chivalrous traditions of the English lord-and-lady aristocracy.

Indeed, it is not an accident that this disproportionate number of bad men came from the old South, as the appendix information proves. The median date of the birth of the bad men was 1851 the median date of their deaths was between 1880 and 1885. Again, youth begins at about fifteen and ends at about twenty-four. For the next ten years a man should be at his physical prime; but at thirty-five his eyes, muscles, reflexes, nerves become retarded. This would make the typical bad man of the West fifteen years old at the end of the Civil War and thirty or thirty-five years old at his death. The youthful Southerner, resenting the defeat and invasion of his beloved South and the evil effects of the reconstruction period with impudent newly-freed Negroes, carpet-

Jealous Edgar Watson . . . was reputed to have ambushed and murdered the notorious Belle Starr. (See page 149.)

Note: The picture has Watson using a pistol, as has been reported. Some old timers maintain that he used a rifle.

baggers, and scalawags, became a potential bad man and went West. He was the same typical Southern youth who had been taught to revere all womankind, to be courteous, gentle, polite. No, it was not an accident. At no other time and at no other place could there ever have been another typical bad man like that of the West.

Typically, the bad man of the West was a product of the Civil War moved to a new Western frontier from the old South. Joseph G. Baldwin shows in *The Flush Times of Alabama and Mississippi* that the old South was a proper breeding ground for a bad man of the later West.

Oklahoma bandit Al Jennings had something relevant to say in this respect:

> The historians of the Old West have, it seems to me, ignored the part which the Southerner played in making that curious, manly half-civilization which grew up in the West and Southwest during the fifty years after the War. Burning with chagrin of defeat, convinced of the justice in their lost cause, stripped of their slaves and property, born or reared among the hideous disorders of a devastating war, they brought West not only their courage, their chivalry, their sentiments, but also their belief in the *duello* as a corrective of social disorder, and their resentment against the transition from a feudal state to an industrial one.

Today we find self-supporting women in all walks of life. Subways and elevators are too crowded for gentlemen to offer a seat or even remove a hat. The cowboy frequently rode the trail for a month at a time without seeing a female of his specie.

Haven't you heard people say, "The age of chivalry is dead"?

DON'T HARM THE LADY!

You remember the ninth commandment in the code of the west (*see* page 62):

9. Thou shalt honor and revere all womankind; ay, shalt thou never think of harming one hair of a woman!

Hold-up men often exhibited chivalry in their robberies. Henry Plummer did. He refused to rob a lady. Judge Langford, who personally knew of the incident, told about it:

148

Mrs. Davenport surrendered the three purses containing the money, together with her gold watch, remarking as she did so, that two of the purses and the watch belonged to her. With much gallantry of manner the robber restored them to her immediately, retaining only the single purse belonging to her husband.

Polk Wells would not take $12,000 from a locked safe, when he saw a Mrs. McCarthy slip the key to the safe into the bosom of her blouse.

To do bodily harm to a woman, any kind of woman, was unthinkable and usually brought swift retribution, frequently in form of capital punishment. Charley Harper, incensed to madness by his inamorata's refusal to dance with him at a New Year's Eve celebration in Colville on the Upper Columbia, knocked her down, beat, and kicked her in a most inhuman manner. Bystanders immediately escorted him to the nearest elm tree and hanged him.

One will recall that Wild Bill Hickok, drunk and jealous of Phil Coe, slapped Jesse Hazel while she drank wine with Coe. Thereupon Coe nearly killed Hickok in a memorable fist fight.

It is said there were no tears shed in Willcox, Arizona, when Ranger Billy Speed killed Bob Downing (formerly Frank Jackson of Sam Bass' gang), who had been beating up his woman companion and reeling from saloon to saloon.

Some cowhands showed this same attitude when attending a dance in New Mexico; they shot a roughneck called Old King for "goosing" a girl in the ribs.

Buckskin Frank Leslie's wife divorced him because of his playful antics, such as shooting her profile on the wall while she posed. She evidently didn't appreciate her husband's artistic talents. The same Buckskin, while drunk, shot a woman caretaker of his ranch near Tombstone, for which act he was imprisoned at Yuma, Arizona, for twelve years.

These cases show that the Western man, bad or otherwise, was very chivalrous to women — any kind of woman — or if he wasn't, he immediately and dearly paid for his discourtesy — either with his blood or his life.

To kill a woman, *any kind of woman,* under any circumstances, was downright murder. Jealous Edgar Watson, who was reputed to have ambushed and murdered the notorious Belle Starr, was killed by an avenger soon afterwards. Polk Wells and his friend named White ambushed an enemy who rode in a wagon with his wife. Polk struck White's gun just in time to save her life. When a report that the woman was slain by the "murderer" Polk Wells reached Atchison, an influential citizen named Mark Taylor, who knew Polk, said, "I'll never believe Polk guilty of shooting a woman."

Beautiful and favorite, though shady, Dora Hand of Dodge City was murdered while asleep in bed, by a Mr. Kennedy, who thought that he was assassinating Mayor Dog Kelley. A posse caught him after Bat Masterson had shot him in the chase (right in the middle). Wyatt Earp was also a member of the posse. He told the prisoner that his bullet had killed Dora Hand instead of the Mayor. Now, Kennedy appreciated Dora as much as did the officers or anyone else; and perceiving that it was Bat who had shot him, he turned in rage on Masterson: "You blank-dash so-and-so of a this-and-that," he growled, "you ought to have made a better shot than you did."

"Well," the astounded Bat managed to reply, "you blank-blanked murdering son-of-a-likewise, I did the best I could."

FIGHT FOR HER!

Defense of the honor of a woman, even though she sometimes had very little, was occasionally the cause of combat.

Cherokee Bob and his friend Bill Willoughby planned to avenge the humiliation which Bob's inamorata, Cynthia, had suffered at an elite ball. All the other ladies present had snubbed her and wouldn't speak to her. Their first victim was to be Jakey Williams, who had planned the ball and sent out the invitations, omitting Cynthia at the request of the other ladies of the community. They went gunning for Jakey, but Jakey was prepared. Some one had warned him and he sat with his legs forked over a chair and a six-shooter in each hand resting over the top of the chair to steady his aim. Bob and Bill blazed into the room throwing lead in all directions, while Jakey fired his two guns simultaneously — that sufficed.

Interesting is the love triangle between Cynthia, Cherokee Bob, and his friend Bill Mayfield, before mentioned. She chose the more prosperous Cherokee, but returned to Mayfield after the death of Cherokee Bob and remained with him until he was killed in a duel with a man named Evans. It was said of her that she had been the cause of more personal collisions and estrangements than any other woman in the Rocky Mountains.

An interesting "love quadrilateral" is that in which Polk Wells left Nora to marry her cousin Mattie. The two lived and loved happily for two years until her death. Mattie's last request was for Polk to marry Nora, which he did. They, also, were happily married, having one daughter, who died while a child. But Nora married G. A. Warnica, believing Polk to be dead as had been reported. Polk, however, returned, and Warnica and Polk left the choice to Nora, who could not decide which to go with. Polk then took the initiative, leaving the two with a gift of $300 and a shotgun. Warnica was the publisher of Polk's memoirs.

Matt Bledsoe and a friend were drinking in an oyster saloon in Portland, Oregon, each with a courtesan by his side. Some angry words between the women soon involved the men in a quarrel, terminated by Bledsoe's fatal blow upon his antagonist's cranium.

No doubt there were many duels fought because of jealousy over a woman.

Young Roy Bean killed a jealous California Frenchman in a dramatic duel on horseback in the public square. The two rode into town from opposite directions, met in the square, and exchanged shots. Of course, Roy killed the Frenchman. The señoritas favored Roy so much that the *muchachos* hanged him and left him for dead. But Roy's neck was tough and the señoritas cut him down. However, ever after that memorable event, Bean's neck was slightly crooked. Years later when he was "The Law West of the Pecos" customers at his "bar" would ask the Judge how come his neck twisted, and the Judge would delight in telling how it took place.

Doubtless, many of Wild Bill's "eighty-five men" or John Wesley-Hardin's "forty-three" were jealous rivals for some "fair Cyprian." It has been shown that the handsome bad man appeared in the most elegant clothes the frontier afforded, probably to attract some fair lady and incidentally arouse the wrath of her intimate.

"I'LL MEET YOU BY MOONLIGHT
THO' HELL SHOULD BAR THE WAY"

Many bad men were captured because of their connection with a woman.

Bill Longley confessed his identity to his sweetheart, whose father was a sheriff. His would-be father-in-law threw down on Bill and captured him.

John Wesley Hardin, incognito, would probably never have been detected in Florida had it not been for a letter in which his wife "Jane" was mentioned. By means of this slight clue, Texas Rangers traced him to Florida.

Billy the Kid would have been safe in Mexico had he not gone to see a girl in Fort Sumner, where Pat Garrett found him.

Doc Holliday's inamorata, Big Nosed Kate Elder, while drunk, betrayed him by procuring his arrest at the request of his enemies, thus aggravating the Earp-Clanton feud.

But for Bill Doolin's return to get his wife and child he would have escaped death from a posse composed of "The Three Guardsmen" and other officers. "The Three Guardsmen" were Chris Madsen, Heck Thomas, and Billy Tilghman. They worked together frequently and effectively.

"The Three Guardsmen" were instrumental in rounding up most of the Doolin gang, freebooters and bank robbers of Arkansas and Oklahoma frontiers. Uncle Billy Tilghman had already captured Bill Doolin once and had taken him to jail, where he reprimanded Bill for leading the life he did, saying that Bill's wife and babe deserved something finer in life than constantly being hunted like animals at bay. And Bill ultimately planned something better for them. He escaped jail, as has been stated before, by telling his guard a funny tale and surreptitiously swiping his guns.

Heck Thomas and Chris Madsen were sent out again for Bill and they found him where they expected. Outside his home in the moonlight he was packing provisions in a wagon in which he meant to skip the country with his family and start life anew. Heck Thomas, about fifty feet away, said, "Hands up, Bill!"

But Bill didn't hands up. He yanked out his gun and fired twice at Thomas, missing both times. The officer fumbled his shotgun to his shoulder and pulled the trigger. Bill stopped all twenty-one of the buckshot before he measured his length on the ground beside the wagon.

You may be touched by sentimental pity at this bandit's sad demise, when he meant to lead life anew with his loving wife and child; but you must remember that Bill Doolin, although he was quite admirable in some ways, had run up a debt to society for which he had to account, a debt of about twenty lives for the loss of which he was either directly or indirectly responsible.

"The Three Guardsmen" continued their hunt for Doolin's men. For instance, they surprised Red Buck in a dugout. He was a blood-lusty murderer who rode with Doolin for a while and with the Daltons. He was the same one whom Bill Doolin once prevented from shooting Uncle Billy Tilghman in the back, and he was also the one who always wanted to kill somebody on each raid in order to add another notch in his gun. He came up firing at Madsen, Thomas, and Tilghman, only to meet a face full of six-gun slugs — and he pitched headlong into a ditch on his face.

Little Dick, another of Doolin's gang, jumped to Al Jennings' group until it was broken up by officers. Little Dick, however, remained on the wanted list. On April 7, 1898, Little Dick was currying his horse when Heck Thomas and Billy Tilghman said, "Hands up!"

But Little Dick dropped the currycomb and went for his guns, whirling around and blazing away. It would have been a sheer accident if he had hit either officer. Thomas carefully aimed and shot just once. The bullet went through the outlaw from hip to shoulder.

SHE STAYED BY HIM

Among the women who "stuck" with bad men through thick and thin was Mrs. Slade, who saved her bad man husband, Joseph A. Slade, doomed to hang, by riding at breakneck speed to smuggle pistols concealed in her clothing to him. They both came out firing and thus escaped.

Similar escapes were made or attempted by Bitter Creek, helped by the Rose of Cimarron; Blue Dick, aided by Belle Starr; the Shelley brothers, aided by Mrs. Shelley; Polk Wells, aided by his wife Nora; Chacon, aided by his little señorita.

Among the more notorious wild women of the West were Belle Starr, known as the "Outlaw Queen," Pearl Black, Rose of Cimarron, Cattle Annie, Little Breeches — all of Oklahoma; Bronco Moll of Ogallala, Doña Gertrudis of Santa Fé, Madame Mustache of Deadwood, Virginia Slade (Joseph A. Slade's wife), and the ubiquitous Calamity Jane.

"HORSE TIED BUT SKIRT FREE"

The marital status of the bad man was varied.

Among those who were happily married, never divorced, and

had families were Henry Plummer (his wife did not know of his depredations until his death), Joseph A. Slade, Wild Bill Hickok, Jesse and Frank James, Cole Younger, Frank and Al Jennings, Tom Graham, George Coe, Wiley Harpe, and Ben Thompson. Ben, according to his lawyer pal Buck Walton, at the birth of his first child. said, "Oh, how sweet is rest! Wife, mother, and a new-born child to call me father."

Among those who were separated from their wives, by bigamous remarriage, or by desertion, were Bill Mayfield, Boone Helm, Polk Wells, John Wesley Hardin, Micajah Harpe, Lee Sage, and Henry Starr. Hardin's first wife was very happy with him. She died while he was at the Huntsville penitentiary. His second marriage resulted in divorce.

Bad man Dick Liddil and Doc Holliday were among those who had common-law wives.

Clay Allison was reputedly a woman-hater and left all women alone, but he finally broke down and got skirt tied and raised a family.

Among those bad men who had Indian or Mexican wives were Charley Reeves, old man John D. Tewksbury, Charley Bowdre, Fred Wait, and Billy Stiles.

Probably the typical bad man or cowboy sentiment about marrying is summed up by Lee Sage, "The Last Rustler":

> I was horse-tied but skirt-free! Up to this time none of that disease called Love had ever crept into me. I figured you could reason with an old horse or else flog it out of him. You couldn't do neither with a woman. Women was mighty nice things but they was better free than captured.

MOTHER!

> *Go write a letter to my gray-haired mother,*
> *And carry the same to my sisters so dear;*
> *But not a word of this shall you mention*
> *When a crowd gathers 'round you my story to hear.*
>
> —*From* Cowboy Lore.

Bandit Henry Starr said that he knelt beside many a dying confederate bank or train robber, and that almost invariably the dying bad man's last word was "Mother!"

As a rule, the bad man was quite devoted to his mother, who

was usually one of the few people kind to him. Traditionally he responded favorably to kindness and sympathy.

Lee Sage consistently sided with his mother against his father.

Billy the Kid once said to his friend, George Coe, "George, I wish I had a home like this (Dick Brewer's ranch — Dick was also a member of their gang). I'd send for my mother and be the happiest kid alive."

Wild Bill Hickok has been portrayed as once shedding tears at the mention of the word *mother*.

Just before hanging, Dutch John wrote his mother bequeathing all he had to her and begging her forgiveness for his life of avarice. He was one of Plummer's gang.

Confined, Cherokee Bill, raging and shooting off a smuggled pistol, was quieted by his fellow-prisoner, Henry Starr. All he did was to say soothingly, "Now, now, Bill, you know your dear old mother wouldn't want her boy to act like that and probably kill somebody, would she?" With that, Cherokee Bill gave his guns to Starr, who turned them over to prison officials. Starr was rewarded for his efforts.

Of all the 250 or so bad men whose records I have encountered the one Western bad man to deceive his own mother was William Clarke Quantrill, the leader of the Missouri Border Ruffians. He claimed to have sent his mother money, but he gave it instead to his mistress to start a house of ill fame in St. Louis. He is accused of many other similar deceptions.

Henry Plummer and John Ringo sincerely hoped that their sisters would never find out their infamous careers. Ringo's real name may have been Ringgold.

HOLD YOUR FIRE!

That womankind was revered in the old West was often shown by courtesies to them in battles.

As before mentioned, Mrs. McSween came and went freely to and from her burning home which housed her husband and his fighters, including Billy the Kid — traversing the line of fire of the McSween-Murphy antagonists. Whenever this happened, firing from both factions would immediately cease.

Likewise, in a raging battle between the Tewksburys and the Grahams out in Pleasant Valley, Mrs. John Tewksbury came out of hiding to bury two of her dead compatriots whose bodies were menaced by hogs. As she spaded directly in the line of fire, both sides halted their shooting.

Marshal Canton and his men surrounded the cabin in which the Shelley brothers and Mrs. Shelley had taken refuge. Canton sent word for the lady to come out, promising that she would not be molested. She did so, bringing her pet great dane. Both Shelleys were shot during the battle and there was hardly a square foot of their cabin without a bullet hole after the fight.

It was a custom for peace officers to rake up enough money to pay the widows of the desperadoes they killed for their burial.

NO COMPARISON!

Today, when we say "gunman," we usually think of a gangster — and our stomachs turn. We visualize an arch-fiend villain, who puts innocent, helpless men, women, or children on the spot or takes them for a ride or throws them into the river with a lead weight around their necks. We think of a gang of six against one, of time bombs, tommy guns, armored bullet-proof cars, steel vests — of baby-killers — of cowards.

To compare the modern gangster with the typical bad man of the old West is absurd. There is no comparison. The typical Western bad man set no dynamite to the ignition of his enemy's automobile. He came out in open daylight to meet his foe face to face at his own proper and personal danger. And typically it was a gun fight of one armed man with another, both dangerous — not of six armed thugs to one helpless unarmed victim. And it may here occur to you that the F. B. I. could use a Bat Masterson or a Billy Tilghman or a Wyatt Earp or a Frank Canton, or even a Wild Bill Hickok, to great advantage in places like Chicago or New York.

Billy Breakenridge, who served as an officer for twenty years in Arizona and who ought to know, depicted Tombstone, Arizona, not as the place that had a man for breakfast every morning, but as a quiet place where killing were done only among the toughs. He claimed it was perfectly safe for men, women, and children to walk the streets of the town at all hours, unmolested by anyone. He said he never heard of anyone being held up in Tombstone.

Robertus Love, Jesse James' biographer, said to compare Jesse James himself with a modern gangster would be an outrage.

Another difference between the gangster and the old Western bad man is, of course, in their settings in time and place. Emmett Dalton was one of the few desperado-outlaws who lived long enough to compare his way of crime with the modern:

One of the inducements to crime in the West was the presumed ease of escape into untrammeled lands. This supposed easy refuge was a fallacy, for in a sparsely settled land every stranger was a bid for curiosity. The color of his horse was noted, the cut of his beard was marked, the directions he asked were remembered. A thousand-mile ride for the Western outlaw might harbor more pitfalls than a city block for the modern gangster.

Today the country-bred outlaw is practically extinct. Crowded places, city canyons, night clubs, and public amusement places, are his cradle and his habitat. Naturally he clings to his environment. He takes his spoils close to where he spends it. And amid the millions of justling but incurious strangers in a Chicago, New York, or Detroit he is as safe or safer than was the plains outlaw in his remote brush camp.

The safe and shameless!

Symbolic of the passing of the bad man are the ghost towns he once tread — Towash, Tascosa, and Indianola in Texas; old Fort Sumner in New Mexico; and Galeyville and Charleston in Arizona. Nothing but weeds now mark the spots where men were once shot down on Main Street.

Indeed, there are but few similarities of the old with the new bad man. Probably the outstanding ones are found in their motives and influences — the desire for easy money, lack of correct early training, desire for freedom, drink, and a reputation. The bad man is still affected by these influences and probably always will be. The gangster, like the Western bad man, makes friends to protect himself. Only in that way has he the faintest resemblance to the bad man of the Western tradition.

But the modern gangster could no more have fitted into the code of the old West than he could have flown to the moon.

Chapter VIII

THE WESTERN BAD MAN AND MOB VIOLENCE

FEW FEARS OF FAUNA

 HAT did the bad man of the old West most fear? Mob violence and a rope.

The desperado was not afraid of tarantulas, centipedes, or rattlesnakes, but he was in common with many other Westerners, in constant fear of hydrophobia skunks at night, while sleeping on the ground. Fatalities from the bite of such an animal were certain and not uncommon among cowboys, and there was no known anecdote for the infection.

Jeff Ake said:

> Now, here's a funny thing: I never saw a man I was afraid of, no matter whether he was drunk and shooting or cold sober and ready to kill. But I did fear fire, high water, earthquakes, and cyclones. It was cyclones that drove me out of Oklahoma. They was too much for me . . . so I sold out for only $3,500 and left.
>
> The one other thing I was afraid of was rope. I have been mobbed twice, and the idea of dying by a rope is one I never liked to think about.

Notable peace officers were daring and faithful in protecting their bad-man captives from mobs. Texas Ranger Captain Jim Gillett could find no leader in the mob threatening to lynch his prisoner, Enofore Baca. The mob seemed to act as an individual when it overcame Gillett and hanged Baca.

As before mentioned, Wyatt Earp could find no apparent

The next morning a mob of about thirty men from Bisbee and Tombstone came to the jail, took Heath out, and hanged him to a telegraph pole. (See page 161.)

leader in the mob of five hundred angry Tombstone miners coming after Johnny-Behind-the-Deuce, in Earp's custody. But Wyatt invented a leader, as he oscillated the muzzle of his Wells-Fargo shotgun across the first twenty mobsters. He picked out a wealthy owner of one of the mines at Tombstone, who was in front, and told him he would be the first to "get it" if the mob advanced. At that, the mine owner retired and the mob dispersed slowly, one by one.

Sheriff Pat Garrett faced an angry mob which closed in his railway coach and which threatened to lynch Billy the Kid, in Pat's custody. Pat yelled at the top of his voice that if they made a rush, he would give the Kid two six-shooters and they would both open up on the crowd. The mob lost its enthusiasm immediately, and the train finally pulled out. Billy the Kid was one of the very few exceptions among bad men who seemed not to fear mob violence. He looked out his coach window at the crowd with a smiling, calmly interested expression.

Similarly, Texas Ranger Captain N. S. Reynolds, holding John Wesley Hardin in his custody, threatened a surging mob that he would hand over two full six-shooters to the desperado if they did not disperse. They dispersed.

THE VIGILANCE COMMITTEE

On the Western frontier evolved the vigilance committee, which became one of the most effective instruments for combating crime. It was composed of people who were unable to act against outlaws individually. Group action gave them a feeling of security partly because of the submergence of their individuality and partly because they assumed that the outlaw would not resist a group.

It's a peculiar fact that a vigilance committee is successful only among Anglo-Saxons, who are known as lovers of law and order; elsewhere it becomes overbearing and tyrannical. It served its purpose admirably in the lawless Northwestern frontier and in California. It became necessary for the honest citizens to organize themselves as a law-enforcing agency as a matter of self-preservation against organized crime. It would have been suicide for an individual to resist organized gangs.

Trials by jury were often a farce, or tragedy, depending upon the point of view. Judge N. P. Langford, altruistically argued against a vigilance miner-committee's methods, being a stickler by the literal word of the law, and finally induced them to have a trial by a legal jury of twelve to determine the fate of two murderers. Everyone knew they were guilty and deserved hanging, but of course how could twelve men later (individually) combat a whole gang of thugs? They had their own hides and families to consider, after all. Of course, the thugs supported the conviction that there should be a lawful and "just" trial and nominated Judge Langford himself as a juryman (thinking he was on their side):

> After much conversation of this sort [on the danger of retaliation], which only served to intensify the fears of the jurymen, a vote was taken which resulted as follows: not guilty, 11; guilty, 1; myself, the supposed friend of the roughs, being the only one in favor of the death penalty . . .
> [Upon the verdict's being read aloud] an expression of blank astonishment sat upon the face of every person in the room, which was followed by open demonstrations of general dissatisfaction, by all but the roughs, who, accustomed to outrages and long immunity, hailed it as a fresh concession to their bloody and lawless authority. [Later the vigilance committee was organized and revised this verdict.]

At Bisbee, Arizona, the Heath gang killed four men, robbed them of $2,500, were captured, and were tried by a jury of twelve men. William Breakenridge, who was law officer at Tombstone at the time, told about the incident:

> All six were indicted by the grand jury, and Heath was the first one brought to trial. The other five were tried together. In the case of Heath the jury brought in a verdict of murder in the second degree. The next morning a mob of about thirty men from Bisbee and Tombstone came to the jail, took Heath out, and hanged him to a telegraph pole, and threatened to hang the jury if they brought in any more such verdicts.

How did the vigilance committee go about its business? How did it try criminals? Judge Langford, who was there and who personally witnessed many of them, said,

> This form of tribunal grew out of the necessities of mining life in the mountains. It originated in the early days and still exists in inchoate mining communities as a witness to the fairness and honesty of American character. (The property holders of a camp) elect a president or judge, who is to act as the judicial

161

officer of the district. He has both civil and criminal jurisdiction. All questions affecting the rights of property, and all infractions of the peace, are tried before him. When complaint is made to him, it is his duty to appoint the time and place of trial in written notices which contain a brief statement of the matter in controversy, and are posted in conspicuous places throughout the camp. The miners assemble in force to attend the trial. The witnesses are examined, either by attorneys or by the parties interested, and when the evidence is closed the judge states the questions at issue, desiring all in favor of the plaintiff to separate or to signify by a vote of "aye" their approval of his criminal case. The decision is announced by the judge and entered upon his record. Where the punishment is death, the criminal is generally allowed one hour to arrange his business and prepare for death; when it is banishment, a few hours are given him to leave the camp. If he neglects to comply with the sentence he is in danger of being summarily executed. Where the rights of parties are settled by the court, and the defeated party shows any resistance to the decision, it is the duty of the court, if necessary, with the strong hand to enforce it. The court is composed of the entire population. To guard against mistakes, the party in defeat, in all cases, has the right to demand a second vote.

The progress of the trial in one of these courts is entirely practical. Often the miners announce at the commencement that the court must close at a certain hour. Cross-examinations are generally prohibited, and if lawyers are employed, it is with the understanding that they shall make no long arguments. Each party and their respective witnesses give their evidence in a plain, straightforward manner, and if any of the listeners desire information on a given point in the testimony they request the person acting as attorney to ask such questions as are necessary to obtain it. The decisions of these tribunals are seldom wrong, and are always enforced in good faith. They have many advantages in mining regions over courts of law. None of the tedious incidents of pleading, adjournment, amendment, demurrer, etc., which at law so often consumes the time of litigants and put them to unnecessary expense, belong to a miners' court.

The miners themselves have little time to spare, and hence these courts are held on Sunday in all cases where the exigency is not immediate. They are held in the open air. Whenever, from any seemingly unnecessary cause, their investigations are prolonged, as by argumentative display, there are always those present who, by the command "Dry up," "No spread-eagle talk," force them to a close.

The criminal seldom feared law itself. His one great fear was that of being hanged by a body of citizens. Vigilance committees were not confined to the Northwest and the far West; they were to be found wherever there was a bad man — on the Western frontier.

So great was his fear of being mobbed by lynchers that John Wesley Hardin dragged himself out of bed, almost unconscious with fever and the pain from several buckshot lodged in his intestines, and rode over fifty miles at full speed on horseback. He said that he was not afraid of the law or of any Texas Ranger, to whom he would surrender for protection against mobs.

THEY BROKE DOWN AND WEPT

Outlaws whose courage and bravery had never before been questioned, such as Henry Plummer, Hayes Lyons, Dutch John, Cherokee Bob, and Joseph A. Slade, broke down completely and wept, crawling on their knees begging vigilantes to spare their lives. Even while they were fitting the rope around Slade's neck, he repeatedly exclaimed, "My God! My God! Must I die? Oh, my dear wife!"

Sam Bass lay dying beneath a live oak when Deputy Sheriff Tucker found him:

I have seen you twice before. I'm not afraid of you or the Rangers, but I don't want to be mobbed.

With that, Sam handed Tucker his gun. Sam had seen Tucker at Georgetown.

Nearly all the real desperadoes of the old West said that they feared only mob violence and a rope.

CHAPTER IX

THE PASSING OF THE BAD MAN OF THE WEST

A FEW REFORMED

HAT became of the bad men of the old West? Very infrequently they reformed and became good citizens. They had a hard time turning good. Either their depredations had become habituated or society would not give them a chance to reform.

However, occasionally there were "mildly" bad men who changed from a life of crime to one of good citizenship. George Coe, a fighter of Billy the Kid, married and became a peaceful New Mexico rancher.

Al Jennings reformed, married Miss Nellie Bunyan, the society editor of *The Guthrie Leader,* and practiced law with his brother-partner in Oklahoma City. Al lacked only five hundred out of twelve thousand votes being elected County Attorney.

Emmett Dalton, after serving out his prison term, married, settled down, wrote his autobiography, led an exemplary life.

Dutch Henry, leader of Texas Panhandle rustlers, reformed and often visited in the homes of sheriffs who formerly had ridden in posses after him.

Frank James walked into Missouri's Governor Crittenden's office. No one paid him any attention. About ten or fifteen clerks and stenographers were busy filing reports, typing, milling about the office. Finally, he walked up to the desk of one young lady. She asked him what she could do for him. He answered that he wished to have a conference with the Governor. She asked what

Harry Head, Billy Leonard, and Jim Crane had tried to rob a Tomb-stone stagecoach laden with a Wells Fargo consignment box. (See page 196.)

was his name, so she could tell the Governor who it was that wanted to see him. He quietly replied, "Frank James." Promptly every one of the clerks and stenographers dived for cover, and immediately the room was evacuated.

Eventually, however, Frank got to see the Governor and surrendered his gun for the first time after twenty years of banditry. He and Coleman Younger, his cousin-outlaw, made excellent citizens thereafter. Sanger Brothers, a large department store in Dallas, Texas, hired Frank to be a shoe salesman, principally as an advertising trick. But so many people came just to see what the notorious Frank James, brother of Jesse James, looked like that they fairly cluttered up the store and wrecked the place, and eventually Sanger Brothers had to let Frank go.

They tell this story about Frank, and I don't doubt it. A big gruff bully once came into the shoe department of Sanger Brothers. A mild, slim, pleasant fellow waited on him — a pacifist-looking, soft-spoken, blue-eyed blond.

"Gimme a pair o' boots, you," the bully roared.

The salesman procured some black patent-leather fancy numbers and slipped them on the bully's feet.

"I don't like 'em, see? Git me down some more!"

After about twelve more pairs of boots, the salesman's patience was slowly wearing out.

"I don't like these neither. Haven't you got no good boots? What kind of store is this?"

"Oh, those you have on are pretty nice, I think."

"What? Are you disputin' my word? Are you tryin' to say I don't know good boots? Why, I've a good mind to bash you one in the head! Do you know who I am?"

"No."

"Why, I'm the notorious Bill Duggans!"

"Glad to know you. Do you know who I am?"

"No. Just who are you, anyway?"

"I'm Frank James."

"Gulp! I like the boots and I'll take them. Here's the money. Good-bye!"

And they do say that Frank and several of his close neighbors were bothered continually by youngsters who persisted in ringing doorbells and hiding. Frank put a stop to this nuisance merely by placing a small note, "This is Frank James' doorbell," above the button. It is steadfastly maintained that these are the only two occasions on which Frank James ever made use of his reputation.

* * * * * * *

My own grandfather, after whom I was named, once collected bad accounts for this same Sanger Brothers, during the late '70's, long before the time Frank James worked for the company. This work carried Grandfather into the farthest corners of Texas and brought him into contact with all sorts of people.

He collected on a single trip as much as $1,500, which was a whole lot of money in those days, and he carried a six-shooter and a shotgun on his rounds for protection against holdup men. On one such trip a debtor had paid his bill with a horse and saddle, not having any cash — and Grandfather led the saddled animal away, riding on his own. While making camp the next night, he was suddenly confronted with a holdup man who said in a staccato accent, "Reach for the stars! I've got you covered."

Luckily for Grandfather, about that time the extra saddle horse pawed the ground somewhat behind the robber. Grandfather took the cue, and he knew what to do. He raised his hands and smiled. His eyes slowly wandered beyond the robber toward the extra horse, as he drawled, "No need to shoot him, Johnny. We'll just take him in and collect a reward."

The puzzled freebooter turned his head slightly to see whoever might be Grandfather's imaginary companion. When he looked back, Grandfather was gone — had jumped like a wildcat behind his own horse a few feet away and drawn his six-shooter. At his quick and unexpected warning, "Now, you drop that gun or I'll shoot!" the outlaw obeyed.

When adventures like this actually happened to a man as gentle, just, and kind as my grandfather was, I don't doubt for a minute some of the things they tell about men like Jesse or Frank James, whose lurid careers befit the tales.

FATALIST

The cards were stacked against the Western bad man, and he knew it. He expected a sudden and violent death. There was the element of chance. Many times his clothes had been literally torn from his body by flying missiles.

It is maintained, for example, that Cole Younger carried seventeen bullets encysted in his body, which bore the scars of twenty-six serious wounds. He must have been mighty tough, but it was just by chance that any one of those seventeen bullets didn't finish Cole Younger.

167

Many were the miraculous escapes from death, which seemed certain as a result of bullet wounds clear through the chest, neck, or other vital parts of the body.

Lee Christmas, "one-man army corps" and at the time of this incident a peace officer in a Mexican town named Tegucigalpa, was sitting calmly outside his headquarters when a Mexican enemy shot at him from his side, taking off his coat lapel and burning his arm. Lee started to rise from the chair when a second shot took off his hat. But let Lee himself tell the rest:

Well! I got up, pulling the one automatic I had on. I started shooting, walking toward the man as I shot. My first bullet knocked him down. I kept on shooting — seven or eight shots in all — till I got right up against him. He was shooting, too, but his bullets were going wide. I put the muzzle of the automatic against his head and pulled the trigger. But it didn't go off. I didn't realize until I had pulled the trigger a half-dozen times that I had shot it empty.

There was a big Colt .45 hanging up inside headquarters. I ran in after that. When I got back with it the police had that fellow like a pack of hounds on a coon. You know — that fellow wasn't dead — didn't die at all! He had all my bullets in him, too! In his lungs, in his thigh, in his ankle. A bullet entered his breast and ranged down and came out below his kidney. When they undressed him in the hospital, this bullet fell out on the floor. It was lodged between his undershirt and his skin . . .

Burton Mossman, once the first captain of the Arizona Rangers, was at another time made manager of the enormous Hash-Knife outfit, formally known as the Aztec Land and Cattle Company, with herds of 40,000 cattle along the head of the little Colorado in the Territory of Arizona. Finn Clanton, one of the tribe of Cochise County rustlers, had been run out of Tombstone by the Earp brother officers. In spite of his reputation, however, he was given a job as a Hash-Knife cowpuncher by Mossman, to whom he became quite attached. Of course, Mossman had trouble with rustlers and contrary bosses and possibly crooked superintendents. Finn came in handy for Mossman in quelling these rustlers and ejecting one superintendent who started trouble. He unlimbered his six-gun and asked the big boss: "Say, do you want me to tell you what you are?"

The superintendent knew precisely Finn's opinion and didn't hang around to hear it — and furthermore didn't come back.

But to illustrate my point, one night a man knocked on Finn's door; he opened it, and the enemy shot a pistol bullet right through Finn's open mouth, knocking out four front teeth. The assassin considered Finn dead and went away; but Finn, with great presence of mind, rolled to a barrel of flour and stuffed it in his mouth, thus checking the flow of blood and saving his life.

Death Valley Scotty (Walter Scott) could show the scars where he had been shot through the arm, lungs, and leg — where rattlesnakes had bitten him and even where a hydrophobia skunk had nipped his ear. The time he was shot through the lungs, he was alone, prospecting. He fell to the ground feigning death. Later, he slapped his horse and told him to go home to their camp eighty-five miles away. He got out his complete set of first-aid instruments and surgical kit and operated upon himself, tying ends of broken arteries and draining his wound with medicated tubes — bleeding profusely all the while. His Indian, Bob Black, was aroused by the horse with Death Valley's blood still on the saddle as it arrived back at the camp. The Indian immediately set out after his master and brought him back to safety where he recovered, by little less than a miracle.

Charley Duchet, the French bodyguard of cattle partisan Tom Graham, met enemy-feudster Edwin Tewksbury on his mule and shot him in the head. The sheepherder fell from the mule; and Charley, supposing he was dead, rode away leaving him there. This was another small incident in the famous Graham-Tewksbury cattle-sheep Pleasant Valley war. A week later, Duchet met the same Ed Tewksbury riding on the same mule. The two kept their gun hands close to their holsters, but neither drew. They kept their eyes glued on one another until out of sight. How Tewksbury escaped death was miraculous. The bullet probably just grazed his head, producing a temporary concussion of the brain.

But the bad man knew that some day, somewhere, one more bullet would hit the vital spot — that his good luck would not hold out forever. And that made him all the more desperate.

Then, too, the cards were stacked against him. He was fighting a hopeless fight, one against a whole society of many law-abiding citizens — he knew he could not live long against such odds.

In addition, as he approached middle age, the bad man's nerves, muscles, eyes, and reflexes were considerably retarded. Again, the median and the average age at death of the 250 or so bad men about which we know was from thirty to thirty-five years. Most of them lived from the middle of the last century to about 1885. When they reached the age of about thirty-five years, they felt their time was near.

As they approached middle age, John Wesley Hardin, Henry Starr, Jesse James, Doc Holliday, and Wild Bill Hickok were known to complain about lack of agility in themselves. They seemed to feel themselves cracking under the strain.

When they told him he was to hang, George Shears (of Plummer's gang) said, "I knew I should have to come to this some time, but I thought I could run another season."

Henry Starr started robbing banks in Arkansas when a youth and he robbed his last bank in the same state. For thirty-five years he had been intermittent bandit, outlaw, and jailbird. He had spent about two-thirds of this time in various penitentiaries. He died, as most other desperadoes who wanted to get-rich-quick did, without a cent. But he had foreseen his death and had, several years before it happened, gone to a Tulsa undertaker and paid his burial expenses in full. Said he to the undertaker, "Some day you will read in the paper that Henry Starr was killed while holding up a bank. Then you see to it that I am buried decently, with my boots off."

And that's the way it happened. He walked into a little bank at Harrison, Arkansas, and backed two clerks into a vault. Now one of these clerks was plenty smart. He had hidden a loaded gun on a shelf just about the level of his upraised hands; and while Starr was busily grabbing money bags he craftily, inch by inch, obtained the gun and shot the unsuspecting robber, killing him instantly.

Shortly before being shot in the back by Jack McCall, Wild Bill Hickok said, "I won't leave Deadwood [Dakota] alive." As evidence of the fact that age sets in, Wild Bill became careless and for the first and last time in his life permitted someone to stand behind him while he played poker. Although McCall's bullet fatally wounded Hickok and knocked him clear out of his chair, Wild Bill's reflexes worked so fast that by the time his body struck the floor he had drawn both his six-shooters and cocked them ready for shooting. But, of course, he was a dead man by the time the floor flew up in his face.

Billy the Kid at twenty-one years of age said that he had killed twenty-one men and that all he wanted then in the world was just to make it two more before he, himself, met death. The two men he wanted were Pat Garrett, who he knew was gunning for him, and Lew Wallace. Lew Wallace was the Territorial Governor of New Mexico, who had promised to pardon the Kid if he ever got in jail and who failed to keep that promise. Wallace was also, incidentally, the author of *Ben Hur*. It is strange that such a splendid, beautiful tale of the goodness and righteousness of the Saviour with all its moral teaching should have come from that lurid and bloody background — the outposts of the flaming, lusty American Western frontier! Of course, Garrett nipped in the bud the Kid's plans for his two more "credits."

Jesse James was once supposed to have said, "They may get me some time, prob'ly will, but I'll stir 'em up a couple of times or so before they do."

Old man John Tewksbury, the father of his warring clan in the Pleasant Valley feud, said that he expected every one in the vendetta to be killed, and warned his visiting friends to leave at once for their own safety. His premonition came true — "to the last man."

Indeed, some of the bad men, realizing there was practically no alternative and tired of being hunted, probably shared the sentiments of Charley Bryant, a member of the Dalton gang, "Me, I want to get killed — in one hell-firin' minute of smoking action!"

William Clarke Quantrill was another superstitious bad man who saw the handwriting on the wall. At the battle of Independence (Missouri) he secured a magnificent horse from a man named Buel, a Confederate officer. He named the horse Charley. The animal acquired his master's vicious, untamed nature and soon became so wild that no one could handle him but Quantrill. He even acquired the guerrilla instinct; he would neigh a warning at the approach of enemies and in this manner actually saved the border ruffians from capture or destruction several times.

However, once when a blacksmith named Jack Graham was shoeing the horse and using a buttress, the horse became so unruly that he was hamstrung by this instrument and thus disabled himself — was useless thereafter. When news of this reached Quantrill, it is said that he jumped as if he had been shot and actually turned pale. It seemed as though he had suddenly lost his own feet. Said he, "That means that my work is done. My career is run. Death is coming, and my end is near."

From then on Quantrill was a changed man. When he lost his horse, he lost his confidence. No longer was he the fearless, dashing, carefree bandit that he had formerly been. His band of once four hundred and fifty ruffians had diminished to a mere score. It looked as though he sat back and waited for death — and he didn't have to wait long.

Toward the end of the Civil War, of which he was a very unofficial part, Quantrill was quartered at the residence of James H. Wakefield on the Salt River in Spencer County, Kentucky, with his disintegrated band of about twenty-five. His intentions were to proceed to Virginia for fresh recruits. But Federal guerrilla captain Edwin Terrill intended otherwise. So one morning bright and early he swooped down on the peaceful Wakefield abode with his thirty men, surprised Quantrill and company, and sent them fleeing in all directions. At the time of the charge Quantrill was asleep in a hayloft. His premonition about losing his war horse Charley and his life simultaneously was about to come true. He had borrowed a horse from Miss Betty Russell. Now this was a good horse, but not a war horse. Scared by all the excitement and gunshots, it bucked and reared so that Quantrill could not mount it. He then tried to mount on the run behind one of his men named Hockensmith, who had sounded the alarm, both of whom shot at the Federal guerrillas, checking their onslaught. Just as he leap-frogged up behind Hockensmith, a bullet struck Quantrill, entering at his left shoulder blade, ranging down to the spine, paralyzing him below his arms. He was shot again after he fell, the slug knocking off the index finger of his right hand.

On Friday morning, May 12, 1865, Captain Terrill loaded Quantrill into a wagon and carried him to a Louisville military prison hospital, where he lived for twenty-five days, dying at 4 p. m., June 6, 1865. Thus ended the career of probably the worst bad man these United States ever knew — William Clarke Quantrill. Frank James upon hearing of Quantrill's condition came to his deathbed, and along with others of the band surrendered to Terrill. (This was several years prior to Frank James' final surrender, related on page 166.)

THEY CHECKED IN THEIR CHIPS

How did the 250 bad men of the West about whom we have accounts die? In a variety of ways. We've already accounted for the departure to realms beyond of about sixty bad men.

Typically they were killed in an apparently evenly matched gun fight by a citizen in self-defense. At least the slain had a fighting chance, be it ever so small in some cases.

For example, a semi-bad man in San Antonio named Jack Harris ran a combination gambling house, saloon, and variety theatre of low quality. He incurred the enmity of Ben Thompson, who went straight to Harris' place to have it out. At the door Ben peeped through a slit in a Venetian blind and saw Harris poised behind the barrels of a rifle pointing at the door. The gun rested across Harris' crippled left hand and the trigger finger on his right had resumed its position. Thompson yelled in, asking Jack what he was doing with that gun. Harris replied, "To get you."

Ben jerked out his pistol and thumbed its hammer three times so fast that it almost sounded like once. The first bullet hit Harris square in the forehead. The other two, according to Ben, were to frighten the customers and friends of Harris. And Harris had friends, too, who later showed their resentment of his death.

Billy Sims was among them. He, too, owned a variety theatre named the White Elephant — in San Antonio. Several months after Harris' death, Thompson and his friend big King Fisher of the enormous white sombrero entered the place. Why they came probably no one will ever truthfully know. Possibly it was to bury the hatchet, possibly to raise it again. At any rate there they were, Thompson and Fisher, Billy Sims, and a big Mexican policeman named Coy, all together talking about Harris' death. Then King Fisher suggested they change the conversation and adjourn to the bar for a friendly drink. Thompson saw Joe Foster and asked him to join them. Foster refused to have anything to do with the man who had killed his ardent friend Jack Harris. He would not drink with him nor would he even shake hands with him, saying he wanted no trouble with him but just to be let alone by him. This was the firecracker.

With that Thompson, as goes the testimony, slapped Joe in the face with his gloves in his left hand and drew his pistol with his right. Policeman Coy grabbed the gun by its cylinder and struggled with Thompson. Then King Fisher piled on the two and all three fell in a heap as a bullet sizzled by Coy's ear. Sims said almost everybody started shooting instantaneously and it is hard to tell who shot whom. But when the smoke rose, Ben Thompson and King Fisher lay together on the floor, dead, and Joe Foster was crawling away with a fatal wound in his leg. The coroner judged that Thompson had three bullets in his head and that Coy and Foster had killed Fisher and Thompson in self-defense. Of course, there were those who loudly complained that it was plain unadulterated murder, that Thompson had been ambushed, that bullets entered his body from all directions. But it had to happen to Ben Thompson and King Fisher sooner or later. It was merely a question of who would get them or how many more they would get before they checked in.

* * * * * * *

That hell-roarin' Bill Longley, as he called himself, in November of 1875 worked at a cotton gin near Waco under the name of Jim Patterson. He got into a quarrel there with a hard case named George Thomas and they had a rough fist fight. Nobody had ever heard of "Jim Patterson" but George Thomas was known as a pretty tough customer in McLennan County. Everybody expected Thomas to riddle "Patterson" with bullets and they knew it would have to be settled in some such manner. Thomas announced publicly that the next time the two met, he would settle his account with "Patterson." Longley was duly informed and rode right up to Thomas in front of a small store. Thomas started to draw but by the time he pulled the trigger he had already been shot and had fallen halfway off his horse. The old-timers who saw it couldn't understand what happened, and their heads whirled in blank amazement as unheralded "Patterson" quietly rode off into the night out of the vicinity.

At another time a bad man named Sawyer took up with Bill and decided to capture him to collect a reward. Longley suspected Sawyer, however, and the two shot it out in a fierce duel through the cedar brakes. Bill threw four bullets into Sawyer, who must have been mighty tough, because he kept right on fighting, killing Bill's horse. Longley kept up his chase, however, having to reload his six-guns as the two men darted and dashed among the brush. Finally Sawyer gave up and died, but it was only after Longley had pumped thirteen bullets into his leather-like body.

* * * * * * *

In 1867 at Helena, Montana, Langford Peel met his death. He was a pretty good bad man, as bad men went. That is, he always observed the code of the West. He always gave his antagonist a fighting chance, and this time it cost him his life. He had struck up a mining partnership with a John Bull. But they quarreled, dissolved, reunited, and quarreled again. Peel accused Bull of misrepresentation and falsehood about a prospect of theirs. They met in front of Hurley and Chase's saloon, exchanged compliments, and Peel started for the draw.

"I'm not heeled," said Bull, on discovering his design.

"Go, then and heel yourself," said Peel, slapping him in the face.

Bull stared, saying as he went, "Peel, I'll come back sure."

"When you come," replied Peel, "come fighting."

Bull went out and armed himself, informed a friend of his named William Knowlden what to do with his property in case of his death, and returned, meeting Peel as the latter emerged from the saloon. He fired three shots before Peel could draw; each one would have done the job. They hit Peel in the neck, face, and left breast. He died where he fell without uttering a word. Bull was acquitted, but he knew Peel had many friends and so moved on to greener pastures. And thus ended the life of Langford Peel, who was a good man in many respects — but when drunk a bully, a braggart, and a dangerous character.

In the same frontier town a newly arrived hard case was James Daniels, who had previously murdered one man in Tuolumne County, California, and had tried to kill another. Daniels got into an argument over a trivial card game with a citizen of Helena named Gartley. Daniels jumped on him, pulled a knife, and instantly stabbed him to death. Daniels was jailed, pardoned, caught by the vigilantes, and finally hanged.

* * * * * * *

Mike Fink, the Mississippi River keelboater bully, and a friend of his named Carpenter got into an argument over a squaw. Both being fairly well lubricated with bacchanalian oil, they decided to have a William Tell duel. They drew straws and Fink was to shoot first, Carpenter second — at the black spot on a tin cup placed on the forehead of the other from a distance of thirty paces. Such are the games inebriates play.

When the smoke cleared away from Mike's gun, the black spot on the cup was still there, but a new one was to be seen on the forehead of Carpenter, who fell dead. At first Mike said the gun's barrel was warped, but later bragged that it wasn't. So Carpenter's friend, named Talbot, took Carpenter's own gun, went out and found the river bully and shot him for revenge. Talbot was drowned in Mad River, South Dakota, a year later.

* * * * * * *

Do you remember Bill Rayner? He's the one who called himself the best dressed bad man in Texas — a resident of El Paso. A series of killings occurred there, in which he figured.

The same bad man Bill Rayner who the same night had tried to intimidate Wyatt Earp at the same place, later on imbibed too many potations of liquor for his own good. When he got that way, he had to fight. But he fought no more after that memorable night.

A young fellow named Bob Cahill was dealing at faro in Rickabaugh's gambling house, not far from the very barber shop where Rayner backed down from Earp. Cowboy Bob Rennick was playing at Cahill's table. Drunken Rayner swaggered in and started bothering Rennick, merely trying to cause a fight. Finally Rennick told Rayner to get away and stop his foolishness, whereupon Rayner went out some swinging doors saying he would be back soon and for Rennick to get ready. Cowboy Bob vacated his seat and waited for Rayner's return with his six-guns drawn. Rayner burst through the doors like a streak of greased lightning with both six-guns drawn and blazing away at the empty chair, only to receive two of Rennick's well-aimed shots, one in the stomach and the other in the chest. They took Rayner home where he died shortly. An erroneous report had reached a friend of Rayner's named Buck Linn to the effect that the young faro dealer Bob Cahill had caused Rayner's death. So Linn came gunning for Cahill, who was warned. Now Cahill had never shot a gun at a man in his life, let alone been shot at. He asked the veteran officer Wyatt Earp what to do, and again Wyatt's advice was the same he had once given to young Cockeyed Frank Loving, who killed the notorious Levi Richardson — *TAKE YOUR TIME, AIM, AND HIT!*

No sooner had Earp counseled Cahill than Linn pounced into the middle of the gambling house throwing hot lead that sounded like a tommy gun. Bob Cahill waited until Linn's third shot and from a distance of only ten feet fired the decisive bullet, which struck Linn squarely in the abdomen and splintered his spine. Cahill's second shot hit Linn in the heart and Linn was dead before his body struck the floor with a dull thud. Of course, both Rennick and Cahill were subsequently acquitted on the grounds of self-defense. Just like Ben Thompson and King Fisher, Bill Rayner and Buck Linn had to get their dose sometime, and it was just a question of who gave it to them.

ROUND-UP TIME

We have seen what became of Henry Plummer's gang, the

Coon Hole gang of Utah, the Daltons, Doolin's gang, Al Jennings' group, Quantrill's guerrillas, Joaquin Murrieta's band, and one or two other bands of Western outlaws. Invariably the answer was the same: crime did not pay, even then, even on the lawless Western frontier. There remain but a few gangs of Western outlaws to dispense with.

* * * * * * *

Sam Bass had only two faithful members of his gang left with him at Round Rock, where the Texas Rangers killed Sam and Seaborne Barnes. Jim Murphy had double-crossed him and Frank Jackson escaped to Arizona, only to be killed by Officer Speed for indiscriminate drunkenness and subsequent conduct, as we have seen. Now, what became of the rest of the Sam Bass gang?

Arkansas Johnson, one of Sam's best men, was killed in a surprise attack on the outlaws' camp on Salt Creek in Wise County, Texas, by Ranger Captain June Peak's men. After that event, Henry Underwood fairly and simply quit, wisely seeing no more profit in the game. It wasn't a question of being yellow; Underwood was probably the nerviest one of Sam's gang. He was just one very unusual outlaw who knew when to quit. He took his family and left Texas for parts unknown.

The Collins brothers all three came to bad ends. Joel had died a bandit's death in Kansas, after the big $60,000 Union Pacific robbery had been pulled in Nebraska in 1877. And about a month after Sam's death, Henry, the youngest of the Collinses, met death. Deputy Sheriff H. H. Haley of Grayson County and his posse found him hiding at a cousin's country home a few miles south of Sherman, Texas. Henry caught sight of them and made a dash for some thickets, exchanging shots on the way. Posseman Bond's second bullet hit Henry in the leg; he fell, lost his gun, begged for mercy. The officers took Henry to Sherman where his leg had to be amputated. His parents arrived shortly before his death.

Billy Collins had been captured by Rangers at Tyler and sent to Austin for trial, where he had broken bail and roamed all over the United States, lodging somewhere in North Dakota. U. S. Marshal William Anderson of Dallas, who knew Billy, was sent after him and went alone for his man. He accidentally found him in the post office at Pembina, walked up to him with gun drawn, and ordered his hands up. Billy jerked his hands up so quickly that his overcoat buttons popped off, leaving his shoulder-holstered gun accessible. He slowly lowered his arms, laughingly "giving in" to Anderson. The officer told him to keep his hands up if he didn't want to be killed. A third person grabbed Collins by the arm and Billy went for his gun. Anderson fired, the bullet going through Collins' shoulder and neck, and jumped behind a stove. Billy jerked in a convulsion as though greatly pained. Anderson perceived the outlaw was near death and foolishly exposed his body. Then with a dying effort Billy pulled the trigger of his gun and shot Anderson clear through the heart. Both men died within two minutes.

Sam Pipes and Albert Herndon were pardoned by President Grover Cleveland for volunteer nursing aboard a ship quarantined in New York harbor. And that's what became of Sam Bass' gang.

* * * * * * *

Only a part of Curly Bill's rustlers were wiped out by the Earps in the O. K. Corral at Tombstone. Wyatt judged that he killed Curly Bill and one or two others as he backed away from their last encounter at Iron Springs, but some of the old-timers claim that he did not — at least Curly Bill discontinued his rustling after the fight. Finn Clanton served ten years in Yuma for cattle rustling and was later hired by Captain Burton Mossman as a Hash-Knife cowboy. Still later Finn retired to a ranch of his own near Miami, where, strange to relate, he died a natural death in his own soft bed. Brother Ike Clanton was killed in 1887 on Bonita Creek twenty miles west of Montmorenci by Deputy Sheriffs J. V. Brighton and George Powell. They yelled "Hands up!" as he emerged from his cabin and Ike made a break for it, getting two bullets on the run between his shoulder blades. John Ringo committed suicide and Billy Claiborne was killed by Buckskin Frank Leslie. We've seen most of all this. But what happened to the rest of the rustlers is another tale.

Once Curly Bill and company attacked a wagon train of Mexicans carrying gold and killed nearly all of them. A Mexican youth who had three dead brothers as a result of the fight determined to avenge their murder. So, one day at the break of dawn during a slow, drizzling rain, five of the rustlers were preparing for breakfast at their camp. They didn't see the canyon walls alive with Mexicans getting set for the kill. A shot rang out from the rocky cavern and the rustlers reached for their irons, but one by one they were all picked off, except one named Ernshaw. Old man Clanton fell out of his wagon where he had slept, with face buried in the mud and a bullet through his chest. Bud Snow was pierced by a hot missile just as he awoke, wondering what it was all about. He may have thought it was just a dream, but it was everlasting. Dick Gray reached out for his gun across the campfire but never quite got there. He plopped squarely across the fire, extinguishing it with his corpse. Billy Lang took refuge behind big boulders and barked back at the unseen enemies, revealed only by flashes of gunfire. But the wily Mexicans knew what to do. They circled behind him and shot him from behind.

Only Ernshaw escaped. He forked his bronco and mixed with the milling herd the rustlers had stolen and which the Mexicans were now stampeding. Holding on for dear life, Ernshaw rode low and fast. Once out of range, he jumped off and crouched under sagebrush near the wall of the canyon. He held his breath when later the Mexicans rode by only a few feet away. Next day Ernshaw staggered into the Cloverdale Ranch with news of the fight. John Ringo headed the group which retrieved the bodies but not the cattle, which the Mexicans had driven across the border. Within two months five dead Mexicans were found in the San Pedro Valley near the Clanton Ranch south of old Charleston, Arizona. It was generally conceded that they were atonement killings, executed by the Clanton boys and John Ringo and Curly Bill. All told, there were nineteen deaths in this feud. Thus ended the bloody saga of the Cochise County rustlers. And may that section never see another similar group!

* * * * * * *

The demise of Butch Cassidy's gang deserves mention because it was typical and it, too, proved that crime did not pay on the Western frontier. They were brave men but on the wrong track. They fearlessly robbed Union Pacific trains, mining settlement paymasters, and express companies. They were "gentlemen" crooks, few of them being cold-blooded killers, robbers of individuals or cowards. Cassidy himself never killed a man — and that is a most singular fact. And they were patriotic. News came to their section of the sinking of the *Maine* and the Spanish-American War, and the *buscaderos,* knowing they could not enlist in the U. S. Army, actually considered organizing a separate unit of their own to combat the enemy, whom they personally held in indignant apathy. They even convened at Steamboat Springs to discuss the move. Sheriffs were informed of the meeting and thought another raid was in the making. Governors of Utah, Colorado, Idaho, and Wyoming conferred. Posses were gathered and struck at various gangs in Wyoming, Utah, and Colorado.

The outlaws decided it was no use — they had forfeited their

179

right to serve their country. And what finally became of Butch's wild riders? Eugene Cunningham calls the roll in about as precise a manner as possible:

> Bob Lee, lieutenant of Cassidy at Castlegate, of Logan at Will-cox — in Laramie for ten years. Eliza Lay, as dangerous as any rider of the "high lines" — "doing the book" in Santa Fe. Flat-nosed George Curry — dead with boots on in Green River neighborhood. Will Carver, whimsical and deadly, cowboy troubadour brooding through the years over a faithless wife — dead in Sonora, Texas. Camella Hanks, veteran outlaw and boon companion of Cassidy and Logan — on the dodge, with death waiting in San Antonio. Ben Kilpatrick "The Tall Texan" — Atlanta penitentiary, fated to die under Express Messenger Trousdale's ice mallet near Sanderson, in 1912. Cassidy and Longabaugh and Logan (the leaders) — all were to make South America.

It is believed that Harvey Logan was last seen on an Andean slope, starting out on a climb from which he never returned. Cassidy and Harry Longabaugh attempted to become peaceful *rancheros* but incurred the enmity of the authorities, who made a raid on their ranch house. They killed Longabaugh in his sleep, but Butch fought a day-long battle like a wildcat from a rocky corral. With his last bullet he shot his brains out with his unnotched gun, as the *soldados* made a rush at his shelter.

George Le Roy Parker and company had faded away before the march of civilization. That was his real name, but posterity will be more likely to remember him as Butch Cassidy, boss of the wild riders.

* * * * * * *

And what became of the James-Younger gang? Bill Stiles (not the Billy Stiles train robber of Arizona) and Clell Miller had fallen at the Northfield (Minnesota) bank robbery, and Cole, Jim, and Robert Younger had been wounded, captured, and taken prisoner as a result of this failure to loot the Northfield bank.

It's a peculiar fact that up to their eighth year of bank and train robbing not a James and not a Younger had ever been wounded. But there would come the inevitable day. Allan Pinkerton had founded his famous detective agency before the Civil War and from his headquarters at Chicago he sent countless men out to get the James-Younger gang.

In 1874 the band of outlaws looted a train on the Iron Mountain Railroad (a part of the Missouri Pacific) in the foothills of the Missouri Ozarks. Pinkerton sent Captain J. W. Allen of Chicago and James Wright of St. Louis after the robbers. They deputized Edwin B. Daniels, former county sheriff at Osceola, and the three posed as cattlemen. On March 16, in search of the gang, they stopped at farmer Theodoric Snuffer's house (he was a relative of the Youngers) near Monegaw Springs, asking him the direction to Widow Simm's house where they expected to find Jesse and company. John and James Younger were in hiding in Snuffer's house and followed Allen and Wright when they suspiciously took the wrong road.

They caught up with the detectives, threw down on them, and disarmed them except for a hidden revolver in Allen's coat. After much questioning by the outlaws, Allen decided they meant to kill him and Daniels, so he whipped out his hidden gun and shot John Younger through the head; but almost as quickly John had already fired back, dealing Allen a death wound. Daniels had broken and run, but James Younger took aim and shot him dead. Allen's frightened horse leaped away through the thickets and brushed against a tree, unsaddling Allen. James rode away and escaped. Allen lingered several weeks before dying in Chicago, where he had been taken. John Younger was twenty-four at his death, which he had earned if for no other reason than resisting arrest by Sheriff S. W. Nichols of Dallas several years before and killing the Sheriff. Very little about John Younger was known to be praiseworthy.

Mark off two more of the James-Younger gang — Wood Hite and Dick Liddil. Dick, because he had quarreled with Jesse and was afraid of being killed by him, surrendered himself to Sheriff James R. Timberlake of Clay County, Missouri, and just five days before Jesse's death signed a confession which further broke up the gang. Robert Woodson Hite was Jesse Woodson James' cousin and intermittent member of his gang. He was shot by another member, Dick Liddil, whom he accused of stealing $100 when the band divided up the spoils of the Blue Cut train holdup. The two, with Bob Ford, were hiding out at the home of Mrs. Bolton, sister of Bob and Charley Ford at the time Hite was killed. Liddil's confession to Sheriff Timberlake illuminates what took place:

> When Wood Hite first came in he spoke to me, and I told him I did not want him to speak to me, as he had accused me of

stealing $100 at the divide in the Blue Cut robbery. I told him he lied; he said he could prove it (his accusation) by Mrs. Bolton, and I wanted him to prove it. He then denied ever saying anything of the kind. I told him he did say it, and we both commenced drawing our pistols.

We fired about the same time. He shot me through the right leg between the knee and the hip, and I shot him through the right arm. He fired four times at me and I five times at him, and then I snapped another barrel at him. I drew my other pistol when he commenced falling.

Bob Ford fired one shot at him. I did not know this until afterward, when he, (Bob) exhibited the empty chamber. The wound that killed Hite was through the head. It struck him about two inches above the right eye and came out in front of and a little above the left ear.

Bob claimed that his shot was the fatal one. Hite lived 15 or 20 minutes, but did not speak. We carried him upstairs, and that night of Dec. 4, Cap and Bob dug a grave in the woods about half a mile from the house and buried him. My leg was too sore to help. We did not use a coffin.

Jesse James himself was next to check in. The St. Joseph (Missouri) *Evening News* of April 3, 1882, was the first to carry the story:

JUDGMENT FOR JESSE

The Notorious Bandit at Last Meets His Fate and

Dies With His Boots On

There is little doubt that the killing was the result of a premeditated plan formed by Robert and Charles Ford several months ago. Charles had been an accomplice of Jesse James since the 3d of last November, and entirely possessed his confidence. Robert Ford, his brother, joined Jesse near Mrs. Samuel's (the mother of the James boys) last Friday a week ago, and accompanied Jesse and Charles to this city Sunday, March 23.

Jesse, his wife and two children (Jesse and Mary), removed from Kansas City — where they had lived several months, until they feared their whereabouts would be suspected — to this city, arriving here Nov. 8, 1881, coming in a wagon and accompanied by Charles Ford. They rented a house on the corner of Lafayette and Twenty-first streets, where they stayed two months, when they secured the house No. 1381 on Lafayette street, formerly the property of Councilman Aylesbury, paying $14 a month for it, and giving the name of Thomas Howard.

The house is a one-story cottage, painted white, with green shutters, and is romantically situated on the brow of a lofty eminence east of the city, commanding a fine view of the principal portion of the city, river and railroads, and adapted by nature for the perilous and desperate calling of Jesse James. Just east of the house is a deep, gulchlike ravine, and beyond that a broad expanse of open country backed by a belt of timber. The house, except from the west side, can be seen for several miles. There is a large yard attached to the cottage and a stable where Jesse had been keeping two horses, which were found there this morning.

Charles and Robert Ford have been occupying one of the rooms in the rear of the dwelling, and have secretly had an understanding to kill Jesse ever since last fall (to get the supposed $10,000 reward offered by Missouri — actually it was only $5,000 for assistance in his capture, not 'dead or alive'). Ever since the boys have been with Jesse they have watched for an opportunity to shoot him, but he was always so heavily armed that it was impossible to draw a weapon without James seeing it. They declared that they had no idea of taking him alive, considering the undertaking suicidal.

The opportunity they had long wished for came this morning. Breakfast was over. Charlie Ford and Jesse James had been in the stable currying the horses preparatory to their night ride. On returning to the room where Robert Ford was, Jesse said:

"It's an awful hot day."

He pulled off his coat and vest and tossed them on the bed. Then he said:

"I guess I'll take off my pistols, for fear somebody will see them if I walk in the yard."

He unbuckled the belt in which he carried two .45 calibre revolvers, one a Smith and Wesson and the other a Colt, and laid them on the bed with his coat and vest. He then picked up a dusting brush with the intention of dusting some pictures which hung on the wall. To do this he got on a chair. His back was now turned to the brothers, who silently stepped between Jesse and his revolvers.

At a motion from Charlie both drew their guns. Robert was the quicker of the two, and on one motion he had the long weapon to a level with his eye, and with the muzzle not more than four feet from the back of the outlaw's head.

Even in that motion, quick as thought, there was something which did not escape the acute ears of the hunted man. He made a motion as if to turn his head to ascertain the cause of that suspicious sound, but too late. A nervous pressure on the trigger, a quick flash, a sharp report, and the well-directed ball crashed through the outlaw's skull.

There was no outcry — just a swaying of the body and it fell heavily backward upon the carpet of the floor. The shot had been fatal, and all the bullets in the chambers of Charlie's revolver, still directed at Jesse's head, could not more effectually have decided the fate of the greatest bandit and freebooter that ever figured in the pages of a country's history.

The ball had entered the base of the skull and made its way out through the forehead, over the left eye. It had been fired out of a Colt's .45, improved pattern, silver-mounted and pearl-handled pistol, presented by the dead man to his slayer only a few days ago . . .

Needless to say, Mrs. Jesse, little Jesse and Mary, and Mrs. Samuel were greatly grieved over the loss of their husband, father, and son respectively. The Ford brothers got only about $100 of the supposed $10,000 reward. And that's not all they didn't get. They expected to be hailed as conquering heroes. They even joined circus sideshows. But people simply did not care to pay their good money merely to see the "dirty little murdering cowards" — they were more interested in the dog-faced boy.

Three years afterward Charley Ford met Mrs. Samuel in Kansas City. She upbraided him for the murder of her son Jesse and he begged her forgiveness. She sternly replied, "If God can forgive you, I can."

And a year after this near Richmond, Missouri, they found Charley Ford's body in a patch of weeds, where, stricken by remorse, he had committed suicide. And about six years after this Bob Ford was killed by a former officer Kelly in Creede, Colorado, in jealousy over Nellie Watterson.

Robert Younger had served thirteen years as a model prisoner in St. Paul, Minnesota, when he died a natural death in the penitentiary hospital on September 16, 1889. He was about thirty years old.

On July 10, 1901, brothers Jim and Coleman Younger were paroled from the same penitentiary, after they had spent some twenty-five years there. Jim took to writing insurance policies after he and Cole had sold tombstones — of all things. Then, alas, Jim fell in love with a well-bred young Minnesotan but found he couldn't marry until fully pardoned. So his fiancée left him and he lost faith. He was found in his room in the Reardon Hotel in St. Paul one Sunday afternoon with a bullet through his brain and the revolver still in his hand.

Frank James, unlike most outlaws, died a natural death on February 18, 1915, on the very farm where he grew up, formerly belonging to his stepfather, Dr. Samuels. For many years after Governor Crittenden had pardoned him, he had led an exemplary life.

The very next year, Cole Younger, the last of the Jameses or Youngers, died on March 21, 1916, at his home at Lee's Summit. He succumbed from heart trouble.

Old Jim Cummins, the very last of the James-Youngers' associates was still alive in 1925 when Robertus Love wrote about the gang. Such was the decline of the most famous band of outlaws in the history of this country. They were the most protected band and the most hunted. Only two of the major members emerged to successful endings — Frank James and Cole Younger, and I strongly suspect that they would have told you that "crime does not pay."

* * * * * * *

There are many people today who will take issue with you if you say Billy the Kid was a criminal. And it's true that you or I might have done the same as he in sticking up for boss Tunstall and the Rev. McSween against the Murphy-Riley-Dolan faction. It was known that Tunstall was an honest, kind ranch owner and McSween a trustworthy, righteous store owner and minister; whereas at least Murphy indulged in buying rustled cattle and his faction attempted to freeze McSween out of business by one means or another — hook or crook.

You may recall the climactic burning of McSween's home and the dramatic, decisive battle of the feud in which McSween was murdered. Shortly after this epic event Murphy and Dolan were picked off by McSween's followers. Riley had married a Miss Fritz, the beneficiary of the Fritz insurance policy disputed between the feud factions; and the couple had moved away. In short, the feud was over, dead. All the leaders were dead or had moved. There was no longer a reasonable excuse to fight.

But Billy the Kid now became the inexcusable criminal, no longer the feudster. A handful of rustlers gathered round him, and they set off to harass the plains and canyons of Texas and New Mexico, stealing cattle right and left.

Big cattle concerns set out stock detectives after the Kid; and finally six-foot-four Pat Garrett, he of the Texas drawl and determination, was elected Sheriff of Lincoln County!

One cold, snowing night at old Fort Sumner, New Mexico, Garrett got detectives and deputies Lon Chambers, Barney Mason, and Jim East, and a Mexican or two together and formed a reception committee for the Kid and company, who Garrett knew would come to an old hospital where Charley Bowdre's Mexican wife lived.

Sure enough here they came. Garrett ordered them to halt, whereupon long Tom O'Folliard jerked his hand toward his gun. At that both Garrett and Chambers fired and O'Folliard went limp in his saddle, rocking to and fro as his horse jogged toward the rest of the outlaws. Garrett then fired at one outlaw but missed. Then all the deputies cut loose at all the gang who turned tail and galloped away, except O'Folliard, who was dying in his saddle. As the sheriffs approached him he begged for mercy. They took him off his horse and away to the old hosptial where he died within the hour.

For about another month Billy and Pat played hide and seek until the officer with posse found the Kid and company at Stinking Springs in an old abandoned house, with three of their horses hitched outside. The posse crouched behind an embankment and as Charley Bowdre came to the door they let him have it like a broadside salvo. Seven shots had broken the still of the night, several window panes, Bowdre's life blood, but not the Kid's defiant spirit. He shoved Bowdre into the yard, telling him to get an officer before he died. The posse held their fire while Bowdre stumbled forth saying, "I wish . . . I wish . . ." He fell dead and no one will ever know what he wanted.

Pat then shot one of the outlaw's three horses and the ropes with which the other two were tied, thus preventing an avenue of escape for the Kid as the animals wandered away from the house. Then the two parties of men exchanged compliments and banter. Pat was determined to sit it out or fight it out. And eventually it was his own stomach that captured Billy the Kid. After long hours Pat ordered bacon and eggs cooked to the windward of the house so that the surrounded outlaws would get the full benefit of the odor. One came out with hands up saying the rest wanted to surrender — anything to eat! So the Kid, Rudabaugh, Wilson, and one other outlaw were captured and taken to prison. (See books by Poe, Coe, Cunningham, and Burns).

Rudabaugh was sent to the Las Vegas jail, convicted of murder, sentenced to death; but he appealed and presently escaped and was never heard of again.

The Kid was also sentenced to hang and was put into the Lincoln County jail, formerly the Murphy store, to be kept there by Bell and Ollinger. We have seen how he escaped. He remained at large for several months and again Pat Garrett took up the scent. Now here is the peculiar part. Billy the Kid was free to ride out of the vicinity and could easily have escaped, just as Rudabaugh had done. His followers were all dead or captured. Why should he have hung around? No one knows, unless it was the lure of black eyes. Maybe he wanted to get his two more men (Pat Garrett and Governor Lew Wallace) before checking in his own chips. Maybe it was that he just felt at home in old Fort Sumner, where he did have many friends, especially señoritas — and one Pete Maxwell, whom we've mentioned before.

Pat knew that Pete might give him information of the Kid's whereabouts, so on the very ordinary night of July 13, 1881, Pat left deputies Poe and McKinney on Pete's doorstep while he slipped into Pete's dark bedroom to wake him up — Western friends were very informal in those days.

Just then who should step up on the porch outside but the Kid himself! He was barefooted, supposedly after a long ride, and he was returning from Pete's smokehouse with a strip of ham his *mamacita* was to cook for him. He barely noticed deputies Poe and McKinney. He thought they were merely Pete's friends and they surmised he was just another Mexican servant. The Kid said, *"Quien es?"* but didn't wait for a reply.

He ducked into Pete's dark bedroom where he saw the shadow of somebody sitting on Pete's bed. Pat had heard the *"Quien es?"* and thought he recognized the Kid's voice, and he was more convinced when he saw the Kid's dark silhouette against the silvery moonlight filtering through the door. But he was certain when the Kid again rasped, *"Quien es?"*

With that Pat without a word of warning jerked out his six-shooter and simultaneously shot Billy the Kid and ducked out of sight afforded by the moonlit window. He fired again; but dead shot that he was, this time he missed his mark by about ten feet, the bullet crashing into the wall. But the first shot was sufficient. The Kid with his usual left gun hand had drawn but was on his way to the floor half dead before he could have shot his six-gun.

Pete was now thoroughly awake, as he actively demonstrated when he flew out the front door. Poe and McKinney came in to view the prostrate remains of Billy the Kid, who had died at the age of twenty-one after killing supposedly a man for each of his chaotic years. There are still many people who claim that Billy the Kid was foully murdered — that he hadn't a fighting chance, but one wonders whether he deserved that fighting chance. Said George Coe, one of the Kid's former cohorts:

This final chapter in the Kid's life is one I have never fully understood. For the first and only time in his career he spoke first and shot last. He was doubtless afraid he would kill a friend of Maxwell's. Some critics have claimed it was cowardly of Garrett to kill the Kid without giving him the ghost of a chance. They are dead wrong. Garrett was anything but a coward. It took nerve, in no small package, to face danger as he did. He was the only man living that could have ever taken the Kid alive, and though I would have done anything reasonable to save the Kid, at the same time I must give Pat Garrett his due. I knew him well, and now feel no bitterness toward him for killing the Kid. It was some time, however, before I could be reconciled, as I was misinformed concerning the real facts. Once, while on a visit to Roswell, I chanced to have a long talk with John W. Poe, in whom I had absolute confidence, and he gave me all the details just as Garrett had told them, and relieved my mind and changed my attitude toward Pat Garrett. Garrett was assigned to a commission which he was going to perform if he died in the act. After several more eventful years, he was shot to death near Las Cruces by a man in his employ.

And with the Kid and his band of rustlers it was the same inevitable tale of woe in the ending. They were all, like all other gangs of Western outlaws, either killed or incarcerated. Civilization moved in and they moved out — it had to happen that way.

HANDS UP!

Many more bad men than you could shake a stick at were killed by officers of the law for resisting arrest. The officer was entirely blameless in carrying out his duty and making the arrest and shot merely in self-defense, once the outlaw refused to comply peacefully with his demands. Usually the outlaw was the first to reach for his irons. Then it was just a question of who killed whom and the officer was perfectly justified in shooting and shooting to kill.

Billy Breakenridge insisted that he could arrest a couple of young outlaws wanted for the murder of Mr. M. R. Peel of the Tombstone Mining Company at Charleston, Arizona, and for robbery of this company — their names were Zwing Hunt and Billy Grounds. Breakenridge was noted for the peaceful way he brought in dangerous criminals. But the authorities prevailed upon him to take a posse of officers, Gillespie, Young, and Allen, with him. The four officers rode out and Gillespie boldly and brashly burst into the youthful outlaws' cabin at Chandler's ranch, demanding their arrest; whereupon, they shot him dead and he fell flat on his face in the doorway. Then they shot officer Allen in the neck; he fell, seriously but not fatally wounded, just outside the cabin. Breakenridge and Young found refuge behind trees, shooting back through the still open door and hitting Billy Grounds, who fell dead across Gillespie. Breakenridge could see his boots through the door. While leaping for cover behind his tree, Young stopped a slug with his leg, but he stayed in the fight. Now Billy Breakenridge did a brave thing. While Young spat fire to cover him, he crawled up to unconscious Allen and pulled him to safety, where Allen soon revived and re-entered the fight.

Meantime a teamster who chanced along had been wounded by a stray bullet, and Breakenridge was again the Samaritan, hauling the teamster to a near-by house while the other deputies continued to relieve outlaw Hunt's boredom. Finally, Hunt made a run for freedom out the back door of the cabin, was wounded, and was found sprawled on the grass about thirty yards away. Billy Breakenridge, who had wanted to venture this thing alone, was the only one of the party uninjured. And Zwing Hunt, with the aid of his brother Hugh, escaped from the prison hospital but was killed later by Indians in a canyon subsequently named for him.

* * * * * * *

Out at the bloody old El Paso of long ago when Dallas Stoudenmire was still city marshal, an inquest was held concerning the murder of two Mexicans. Gus Krempkau, a former Texas Ranger, was court interpreter of evidence given by Mexicans, which seemed to implicate a Johnny Hale, he of questionable character. Of course, Johnny did not appreciate Krempkau's interpretations and told him so, once they were outside the courtroom. But Krempkau quietly and firmly insisted his translations were accurate, whereupon enraged Johnny whipped out his gun and promptly extinguished Mr. Krempkau. Stoudenmire, one-man charge-of-the-light-brigade, barged head on into the affair with guns drawn, coming right at Johnny. This sudden audacity stupified Johnny no end, as he stood there with his teeth in his mouth and gun .in his hand, without the presence of mind either to shoot or to yell surrender. Stoudenmire's first bullet struck a near-by Mexican, who evidently possessed the cat's curiosity but not its several lives. The second bullet killed Johnny Hale, who fell on top of his victim Krempkau. Then one George Campbell, Johnny's friend, who was near-by, drew his gun and backed away saying abjectly, "This is not my fight."

But there he was with gun drawn pointing at Stoudenmire, so how was he to know? So the intrepid officer ended Campbell's life with a third bullet.

Bang! bang! bang! bang! — one, two, three, four. That's how it happened — all in less than five seconds. And it was all so unnecessary. Hale had not yet been convicted and stood a fair chance for acquittal. If he or Campbell either had signified surrender by discarding their guns, they would have saved their lives, at least temporarily. But they say steel follows the lodestone.

* * * * * * *

At Hays City, Kansas, Wild Bill Hickok was officer of the law; and one bad man Strawhan was gunning for him because of an old grudge incurred at Ellsworth. Hickok "sided" into a saloon and pretended not to notice Strawhan. The latter, perceiving he was unobserved, meant to murder Wild Bill when he started to draw a bead; but Hickok was prepared. While Strawhan thumbed back his hammer, Wild Bill had drawn and shot him dead. Again Wild Bill had proved his psychological edge over the opponent.

* * * * * * *

At newly formed Perry, Oklahoma, Crescent Sam, a former Doolin gangster, appeared. Uncle Billy Tilghman told him to light a shuck. Deputy U. S. Marshal Fred Sutton was first-hand eye-witness to what took place between the two. In Sutton's own words:

"Hello, Crescent! When did you leave the Horseshoe outfit, and when are you going back?" asked Tilghman.

"I'm going back when I get good and ready, and not before," replied the outlaw.

Tilghman said, in his quiet way, "Crescent, I am marshal here. Don't let the setting sun find you on this town site."

"I'll be here after the sun goes down, all right," the outlaw answered.

"Don't do it, Crescent, that's all," Tilghman warned.

That night Tilghman and I strolled down an avenue between two rows of tents, toward the Buckhorn, a saloon and dance-hall under canvas, lighted by six large coal-oil lamps. As we neared it Crescent Sam stepped out of its door holding a six-shooter.

He fired twice at the moon and wailed: "I'm a wild wolf and it's my night to howl! If there's a hombre in this man's town can send me home till I'm ready to go, I'd like to see the color of his hair."

At that moment he spied Tilghman, and for a second or two they stood and eyed each other, Tilghman with a six-shooter in his hand, ready, and the outlaw with his.

Crescent fired first, from the hip. Tilghman fired so soon after that the two reports sounded almost like one. The outlaw fell. Tilghman blew the smoke from the barrel of his gun, shoved in another cartridge, raised his left arm and examined a hole where the bullet from Crescent's gun had gone through both coat and shirt, and then stepped over to where the dead bandit lay.

He looked down at him and said, "Poor fool! He belonged to a day that is passing. Today a new Oklahoma was born, and the day is coming when it will be a crime here even to carry a gun."

* * * * * * *

A woman was running away with an anonymous partner from her husband, a man named Tracy (not the aforementioned Harry Tracy of the 20th Century, West coast). Tracy was a desperate murderer from back East posing as an insipid telegraph operator somewhere in Arizona. He jealously traced the couple to Benson, Arizona, where he probably would have killed them both, had it not been for knight-errant Arizona Ranger Captain Harry Wheeler. The woman had asked his help so Harry lit out as Tracy followed the frightened couple to the train about to depart. Harry hadn't time to investigate the details; all he knew was that a lady was in danger and that was enough to any chivalrous Westerner.

He yelled at Tracy to stop, and without any warning the desperado whirled and shot the Ranger twice, in the stomach and foot. This would have disheartened an ordinary man, but not Harry Wheeler, who came from a long line of fighting soldiers. He retaliated with three shots; all took effect on Tracy, who went to his knees and shouted that his gun was empty. Wheeler naively pocketed his gun and went to haul the criminal to a place of safekeeping. But Tracy had lied. He still had two bullets. As he drew a bead, Wheeler stooped and threw a handful of sand into Tracy's eyes, causing him to miss by an inch. Then the Ranger dodged again, this time throwing a tin can into Tracy's face, causing the last bullet to go wide.

In a flash Wheeler was on Tracy and had wrestled away his gun, but both were too weak from the loss of blood to move until citizens came. Tracy was taken under care of a physician but died shortly. Wheeler actually walked to a hotel but was sick for a long time. His foot never completely returned to normality. He sent the $1,500 reward offered for capture of Tracy to the widow of the man Tracy had murdered back East. Knight-errant that he was, Captain Harry C. Wheeler died with more friends than he had dollars.

NECKTIE PARTY

By this time we already know the usual procedure in handling the murderer. He was usually the kind that gave no warning, shot from the back, killed someone unarmed, bushwhacked; in short, didn't abide by the code of the West. He was usually promptly hanged by impromptu vigilance committees.

Colonel Charles Goodnight and John Chisum were partners in the cattle business for about three years. Goodnight would drive herds from Texas to winter at Bosque Grande, where Chisum would join him; and later the two would deliver the cattle to Army contractors. Goodnight was an excellent citizen and he always wanted law and order and always hated a thief and murderer. He believed the foreman should accept moral responsibility for the conduct and lives of his trail drivers. So he usually signed a contract with them to the effect that in case of a death among the punchers along the trail the foreman would summarily appoint a vigilance committee to investigate. If it was found that someone had committed murder, he was to be hanged on the spot. Consequently, Goodnight never lost a trail driver because of a killing.

But Chisum did. While they were still partners, at Bosque Grande, one reputation-seeking Curly Tex slew one quiet, inoffensive Jingle Bob herder named James. Chisum was too busy to see that justice was done, so Goodnight took things into his own hands. He sent his most reliable gun fighter after Curly Tex, selected a jury, witnesses, prosecuting and defending "attorneys" — all from among his and Chisum's men. "Nigger" Frank, Chisum's horse-wrangler, had seen the killing and gave the most incriminating evidence. Curly Tex was found guilty and hanged on the spot.

Soon afterwards Goodnight and Chisum separated at the initiative of the Colonel, who had become disgusted with some of Chisum's practices.

Later Goodnight was President of the Canadian River Cattlemen's Association. It was he who sent John Poe to help Pat Garrett get Billy the Kid. It was he, also, who sent secretly to San Francisco for some extra strong marine night glasses. Ever so often afterwards in the dark night a rustler would just be ready to burn the JA brand when he would look up surprised at the barrels of a detective's gun. They never fathomed Goodnight's uncanny ability to detect them. It was also Goodnight who at one time probably owned more land and cattle than any other one man in this country — the JA Ranch, covering 650,000 acres around the beautiful Palo Duro Canyon in the Texas Panhandle, and nearly 100,000 head of cattle.

* * * * * * *

You may recall the brothers Harpe, among the very first "Western" desperadoes, who ravished the countryside of the then Western frontier of Kentucky, Virginia, and Tennessee long before the turn of the nineteenth century. Many another Western outlaw since their time might well have profited by the lesson afforded by the examples of their deaths. Little Harpe (Wiley) was posing as an anemic bookkeeper named "Mr. Shelton," when his long past bloody career caught up with him. Oh yes, they had detectives even in those dark days of history. He was then hanged in Gallows Field near Natchez, Mississippi.

Micajah Harpe had burned the home of a Kentucky settler named Stegall in his absence, killing Mrs. Stegall and their infant.

Just as McDuff cut off Macbeth's head and stuck it up in a public place as a warning to those who would aspire to be murderous, bloodthirsty, tyrannical dictators, so did Stegall hunt down Micajah Harpe, shoot him in the heart as he begged on his knees for the mercy which he never deserved, and finally severed the scoundrel's head and hung it high on a post over a public bridge. This was to serve as a warning of what would happen to all thieves and cutthroats of the then Western frontier. The place acquired the name of Harpe's Head, with which you may be acquainted.

* * * * * * *

In Boise City, Idaho, on April 3, 1865, a murder was commited which so irked the citizens that they rose in arms and broke

193

up the vicious Opdyke gang, whom they suspected of having murdered two old miners for their gold dust. John C. Clark, a bully rough and one of Opdyke's minions, disliked a citizen named Reuben Raymond, who had testified against him at a previous trial of Clark for horse stealing. He cornered Raymond and drew his gun. Said Raymond, as he bared his chest:

I am entirely unarmed, but if you wish to shoot me down like a dog, there is nothing to hinder you. Give me a chance, and I will fight you in any way you choose, though I have nothing against you.

Clark took deliberate aim and murdered Raymond. Citizens in wild excitement mobbed Clark and hanged him within a few minutes after Raymond's death.

David Opdyke threatened to burn the whole town in revenge for Clark's treatment; but when he saw every man and woman armed and vigilant throughout day and night, he changed his tune and lit a shuck. His cohort John Dixon joined him and they rode breakneck thirty miles to a cabin on the Rocky Ford Road, where they meant to spend the night. Vigilantes followed them, however; and before they knew it, they were captured. The vigilantes escorted them on to Syrup Creek next day and hanged them there.

MURDERED

In the month of June, 1862, at Florence in the Washington Territory, Boone Helm encountered the local tough man known only as Dutch Fred. Now Fred was not a murderer nor even a killer — merely a "tough." He could beat anybody in Florence in a good fist fight, but he was fair and honest. One night Fred's enemies plied Helm with liquor and shoved him at the Dutchman. Boone and Fred exchanged vocal barrages and eventually out came Boone's gun and Fred's knife, but disinterested parties disarmed the two, leaving the weapons with a bartender. Treacherous and murderous Helm then apologized to Fred and left. Later, however, he returned and retrieved his gun and shot at unarmed Dutch Fred. He missed; Fred stood up with arms folded squarely facing Helm, whose second shot took effect. Helm was arrested for this murder but escaped.

* * * * * * *

One of Joseph A. Slade's greatest offenses was the murder of old Jules René, the French-Canadian station keeper for the Overland, whose place Slade took. Jules had formerly put thirteen buckshot into Slade, who swore to get vengeance. The immortal Mark Twain was once supposed to have made Slade the Terrible's acquaintance. At least he lived in the time and section of the country when and where Slade's reputation was his herald. So let Mark Twain himself tell about Jules' sad demise:

In the fullness of time Slade's myrmidons captured his ancient enemy, Jules, whom they found in a well-chosen hiding-place in the remote fastnesses of the mountains, gaining a precarious livelihood with his rifle. They brought him to Rocky Ridge, bound hand and foot, and deposited him in the middle of the cattle-yard with his back against a post. It is said that the pleasure that lit Slade's face when he heard of it was something fearful to contemplate. He examined his enemy to see that he was securely tied and then went to bed, content to await till morning before enjoying the luxury of killing him. Jules spent the night in the cattle-yard, and it is a region where warm nights are never known. In the morning Slade practised on him with his revolver, nipping the flesh here and there, and occasionally clipping off a finger, while Jules begged him to kill him outright and put him out of his misery. Finally Slade reloaded, and walking up close to his victim, made some characteristic remarks and then despatched him. The body lay there half a day, nobody venturing to touch it without orders, and then Slade detailed a party and assisted at the burial himself. But he first cut off the dead man's ears and put them in his vest pocket, where he carried them for some time with great satisfaction. That is the story as I have frequently heard it told and seen it in print in California newspapers. It is doubtless correct in all essential particulars.

Later Slade was taken by vigilantes, tried, found guilty of murder, and sentenced to hang. But his wife came to see him, smuggled pistols to him, and the two came out shooting and escaped. Still later he was again threatened by miner vigilantes around Virginia City, and was warned by Judge Alexander Davis as much. So Slade unlimbered his derringer, pointed it at the Judge's head, and said he would hold the Judge as hostage and he reckoned the vigilantes wouldn't do anything about it then. But he was mistaken. When news of this reached them, some six hundred miners immediately stopped work and with all kinds of warlike instruments marched in and seized Slade the Terrible, who then became the lamb. He was so exhausted by tears, prayers, and lamentations that he could hardly stand upon the beam while vigilantes fitted the rope around his neck. He begged for just one last minute with his dear wife, which of course was refused since the last time he was granted such a liberty he had escaped.

His body went limp as his neck popped when they removed the beam upon which he was standing. Shortly afterwards up rode Mrs. Slade at full gallop, wailing tearfully at the sight of her hanged husband. She said they should have shot him rather than hang him like a dog.

This memorable event occurred on March 10, 1864. It is said that Mrs. Slade carried the body away and kept it in a tin coffin in alcohol until it was buried in Salt Lake.

* * * * * * *

Another bad man was murdered, one Arapaho Brown, formerly leader of the Johnson County (Wyoming) rustlers. After the war between the cattlemen and rustlers of this county had been quelled by U. S. Marshal Frank Clanton and several other officers, Arapaho got together a few thieves on Powder River and they formed a "small time" band of outlaws. But he double-crossed his own men, and they murdered him in a lonely cabin and cremated his body. In many murders of Western bad men it was merely "dog eat dog" and almost just as frequently it was just retribution for a vicious life of avarice.

Among the most famous murdered bad men of the old West were Wild Bill Hickok, shot in the back by Jack McCall; Jesse James, murdered from the rear by the Ford brothers; Phil Coe, shot from behind by none other than the "glorious, magnificent" Hickok himself; Sheriff Brady, shot from ambush by Billy the Kid; and "world's champion desperado" John Wesley Hardin, shot thrice from the rear by former officer John Selman.

BLOOD MONEY

Harry Head, Billy Leonard, and Jim Crane had tried to rob a Tombstone stagecoach laden with a Wells Fargo consignment box. They had killed the driver, named Philpot, but were driven off by shotgun messenger Bob Paul. County Sheriff Johnny Behan and his deputies Billy Breakenridge and none other than notorious Buckskin Frank Leslie rode out with U. S. Marshals Virgil and Morgan Earp as a posse after Head, Leonard, and Crane. But because of dissension between the U. S. and county officers,

196

they came back empty handed. Eventually Wells Fargo offered such a handsome reward for the three bandits that some ordinary cowboys at Hachita, New Mexico, killed them, seeking the blood money.

* * * * * * *

The Santa Fe offered $1,500 for the capture of Bitter Creek (George Newcomb) for the holdup of their train at Red Rock (Oklahoma), and the Rock Island Railroad offered $1,000 for the capture of Charley Pierce for the robbery of their train at Dover (Oklahoma).

The brothers Dunn — Dal, John, and Bill (themselves of questionable reputation) — decided to collect these rewards. They found the two train robbers asleep, murdered Pierce, and thought they had extinguished Bitter Creek. But his head had only been grazed, rendering him temporarily unconscious. Dal and John Dunn wrapped the bodies in a tarpaulin and threw them into a wagon to take them to claim the reward, while Bill Dunn remained to remove the signs of murder.

While the wagon rattled past a farmhouse, Dal noticed the tarpaulin moving and looked under to find Bitter Creek trying to load his gun. The outlaw begged for his life, but to no avail to the merciless Dunns. What shudders and shivers the outlaw must have experienced to awaken swathed in his own blood and lying face to face with his dead compatriot. In order not to arouse the farm folk, Dal struck the outlaw on the head with the butt of his gun, and once out of hearing again shot Bitter Creek and killed him. The Dunns collected the rewards but lost the respect of officers and outlaws alike.

BY THEIR OWN HANDS

As we have seen, a few of the bad men of the old West committed suicide. Train robber Grant Wheeler of Arizona, jail breaker Harry Tracy of Washington, murderer Charley Ford of Missouri met death by their own hands — Wheeler and Tracy because they feared the law and Ford because of a burning conscience. The redoubtable Tumlinson of South Texas was another desperado who valued his freedom more than his life. And you may recall that John Ringo killed himself probably because of melancholia. Jim Younger put a bullet through his brain because he couldn't marry the girl he loved.

Polk Wells, while in an Ohio penitentiary, made the acquaintance of Bill Norris, who was captured in Watertown, South Dakota, taken to Kansas, and tried for a robbery in Nortonville, and was sentenced to twenty-one years in the Leavenworth pen. But Bill's wild nature could not be tamed and would not stay cooped up for twenty-one years when it had been free as a bird, while he rode like the wind over the Midwestern prairies. So on the second day of his imprisonment, Bill butted his brains out against the cell walls.

And you may recall how the Apache Kid's cohorts, rather than be hanged by the white man's law, the night before the event was to occur, hanged themselves in their prison rooms. Colonel Dodge explained that the plains Indians believed that at death the soul escaped through the mouth. If choked or hanged, then, an Indian's soul would rot together with the corpse and there would be no way to escape to the happy hunting grounds.

* * * * * * *

—At Benton, Montana (then a Territory), Bill Hynson was suspected of having murdered a Chinawoman and having robbed her of $1,000. But he was given a job as night-watchman in spite of his reputation. Then he committed one offense after another. He aided a criminal named Charles Williams, doomed to hang, to escape. He slapped a Sheriff Morgan in the face in a quarrel over this escapade. He was thought to have knocked down a Mr. Robinson and robbed him in a dark street one night. Judge N. P. Langford, who was acquainted first-hand with the facts, tells about Hynson's suicide:

> On the morning of August 18 [1868], the same season, Hynson was observed to convey to a spot on a prairie, a mile or more distant from town, three pine-tree poles about twelve feet long and four inches in diameter. Tying one end of these three poles securely together, he raised them up in the form of a tripod. When they were stationed in a substantial manner, and to his liking, he went to a store and purchased a small coil of rope.
>
> "What is that rope for?" inquired a bystander.
>
> "To hang a man with," was his reply.
>
> The listeners understood this as a joke, and dismissed the subject with a laugh.
>
> Hynson next employed a Negro to go out and dig a grave near the tripod.
>
> "Who's dead, Massa Hynson?" inquired the man.
>
> "Never you mind," replied Hynson. "Go ahead and dig the grave. I'll furnish the corpse."

The negro obeyed and the grave was in readiness at nightfall.

The next morning the lifeless body of Hynson was found suspended from the tripod by the rope he had prepared.

The citizens flocked in crowds to the spot. Among them was the negro who dug the grave. When he saw the swaying form, and had scrutinized the ghastly face, he exclaimed,

" 'Fore God, dat's de gemman dat tole me to dig de grave, and said he'd furnish de corpse."

After the body was cut down, there was found in a pocket the following letter from the mother of Hynson:

> *My dear Son,* — I write to relieve my great anxiety, for I am in great trouble on your account. Your father had a dream about you. He dreamed that he had a letter from your lawyer, who said that your case was hopeless. God grant that it may prove only a dream! I, your poor, brokenhearted mother, am in suspense on your account. For God's sake, come home."

ACCIDENTAL

A very few bad men died accidentally. A wagon wheel ran over and broke Clay Allison's neck when he fell off the seat of the wagon he was driving home in a drunken stupor to his New Mexico ranch.

You may recall how Sam Bass' traitor Jim Murphy died. He went into a small town Texas drug store, lay down on a cot in the back, dropped some deadly poisonous eye medicine into his eyes. This lethal concoction trickled down his face to his lips and found its way to his stomach. He lay writhing in agony for hours before he finally succumbed. There were many sentimental Texans who believed this was a just death fit for Sam's squealer.

Out at Tombstone one of the Cochise County rustlers died an accidental death. Joe Hill had ridden through countless hails of bullets unscathed, only to get his neck broken in a fall when his horse stepped in a hole as he was tending herd one day.

THE EXCEPTIONAL

Few bad men died without their boots off; few died a natural death, in bed.

Ed Tewksbury and Doc Holliday died of consumption. Robert Younger died while in prison, Cole Younger died of heart

199

disease, and Frank James died on his farm in Missouri. Judge Roy Bean, "The Law West of the Pecos," passed away peacefully in the arms of his friend, Billy Dodd. With him went much of the spirit of the old West, the lawlessness he had unofficially helped to control. He died a natural death.

And probably so did Burt Alvord, who took, together with Bob Downing and Billy Stiles, $10,000 from a Union Pacific train near Willcox, Arizona, at the same time he was sheriff there. Downing, formerly with Sam Bass as Jackson, was killed by Arizona Ranger Speed when he went on a drunken spree and beat up a disreputable woman. Billy Stiles escaped to the Philippines, joined the Army there, returned to Nevada, and was actually made a sheriff there. He was killed while making an arrest. Burt Alvord buried his part of the loot, was captured, tried, sentenced. But he had double-crossed the Mexican desperado Augustine Chacon and had been instrumental in his capture by Captain Mossman, and so his term was cut short to seven years. He went out, upon his release, and dug up his treasure and rode away to the South, to Panama, where he died a few years later.

THEY SAID AND THEY DIED

Get six jolly cowboys to carry my coffin;
Get six pretty maidens to bear up my pall.
Throw bunches of roses all over my coffin;
Throw roses to deaden the clods as they fall.

—*From* Cowboy Lore

There's no telling what a bad man will say just before he leaps that unfathomable gulf into eternity.

"Let me go. The world is bobbing around," said Sam Bass just before he expired.

Usually the desperado revealed his courage or unconcern at the approach of death.

Tom Horn, just before hanging, said, "Ed, that's the sickest looking bunch of sheriffs I ever saw!" It is often said that they believed him innocent of the murder of the youthful sheepherder, Willie Nichols, for which he was hanged.

Doc Holliday had bet frequently that a bullet would win out over tuberculosis in his death; but he lost the bet, saying just before he succumbed, "This is funny."

Nearly all of Plummer's gang were hanged at the same time by vigilantes. They had caught Red Yager, who had made a full confession and had revealed the names and purposes of the whole gang. Then Red congratulated the vigilantes just before they hanged him, "Good-bye, boys, you're on a good undertaking. God bless you."

Later the vigilantes rounded up the entire outfit and conducted a mass hanging bee. Plummer himself, formerly a man of great daring and courage, now wept like a babe and implored the vigilantes to forgive him of his sins and to spare his life. Of course, they refused. He then requested that his brother and sister living in New York be spared the acquaintance of the wayward career he had lived and the manner in which he met his doom. Even Plummer's wife was ignorant of her husband's misdeeds until his death. The brother and sister found out about his crimes in spite of his request, to their great shock.

Just before Clubfoot George Lane reached the box to be hanged, he yelled to a friend peering through a crack in the wall, "Good-bye, old fellow," and sprang from the box. Johnny Cooper wanted a "good smoke" before his death on the scaffold. Bob Zachary prayed for the forgiveness of his executioners. George Shears said, "Gentlemen, I am not used to this business . . . Shall I jump off or side off?" When told to jump, of course, he replied, "All right, good-bye!"

Bill Bunton said, "I care no more for hanging than I do for taking a drink of water, but I'd like to have my neck broken. I'd like to have a mountain three hundred feet high to jump off from. Now, I'll give you the time: One — two — three. Here goes!"

Steve Marshland asked to be pardoned for his youth, but received the reprimand of one executioner that he should have considered his youth before the moment of his death. Hayes Lyons begged for his life, but being refused, requested at the last moment that his body be sent to his mistress to be buried. Cy Skinner, on the way to the scaffold, broke and ran, calling on his captors to shoot. They declined, and hanged him.

Incidentally, the Territory of Utah offered death by hanging, shooting, or beheading to its capital offenders; they invariably chose shooting. They probably believed it more honorable — a death on the field of battle killed by a bullet of the enemy, so to speak.

Very unusual was Bill Hunter, who while hanging by the neck, went through all the motions of drawing and firing his six-shooter six times. It was more than likely his reflexes, and not the man's will.

201

George Brown's last words, "God Almighty save my soul," might possibly further the idea that the bad man feared an inglorious death.

Alex Carter's last words were the password of Henry Plummer's gang," "I am innocent." It may have been that he hoped a last minute avenue of escape would present itself, but it didn't. And thus ended ingloriously the once powerful and impregnable (so they thought) gang of Henry Plummer. Again, it was the same old story — crime doesn't pay.

One Oklahoma bandit and murderer, sentenced to be hanged at twelve noon sharp, was delayed two minutes. He impatiently rasped, "Hurry up, I've got a date to lunch in hell!"

When asked if he had any last words, before being hanged, Cherokee Bill said, "No, I didn't come here to windjam; I come to die."

William Dowdle, of the Northwest mining camps, was shot by a man named Wohlgamuth. Expiring, he said, "Such is life, boys, in the days of forty-nine."

Arizona's Ranger Captain Harry Wheeler shot a bad man and, feeling remorseful, apologized to him. The man, dying, replied, "That's all right, pardner. There's no hard feeling on my part. You just beat me to it, that's all."

We have seen that the bad man dreaded a death with his boots on, which signified a life of crime for the outlaw. If he died with his boots on, that meant he died while in some act of outlawry, while being chased by officers or posses, or while being executed — a death of inglorious disgrace — an evil omen for an eternity.

U. S. Deputy Marshal Ed Short had in his custody one bandit Black-Face Charley (Bryant), whom he was escorting on a train to jail. Ed left Charley in care of an express messenger, who carelessly let the desperado get hold of a gun. Just them Ed returned, opening the door and getting a draft of wind and six-gun slug just above his heart. But he whipped out his own gun and shot Black-Face Charley; and by this time the two men closed in a grappling, catch-as-catch-can match. As the train drew up at Waukomis (Oklahoma) U. S. Deputy Marshal Fred Sutton was standing on the platform waiting to assist Ed Short and was surprised to see both officer and outlaw, soaking in blood and weak and fainting, fall out of the mail coach's door still struggling with each other. He separated the two, who died shortly. In Sutton's own words:

As he lay on the station platform Short said:
"I got that bandit, but he got me, too. I'm all in."
Within six feet of him lay Black-Face Charley, gasping for
breath and dying. He recognized me, and I knew him from the
scar on his face. I had heard, often, of Black-Face Charley, but
this was the first time I even suspected that my boy schoolmate,
Charley Bryant, was that outlaw. As he lay dying I thought of
him only as the boy I had known, and I asked:
"Can I do anything for you, Charley?"
"Yes, Fred, please pull my boots off, and don't tell the folks
back home," and those were his last words.

Wild Dick Yeager and George Black, who had robbed a Santa
Fe train near Enid (Oklahoma), were run down by a posse of marshals and sheriffs. As bullets began to fly and ricochet around the
two bandits, Black was hit and Yeager was away in a flash, getting
a slug in his hip on the run. George Black fell on his face, saying,
"Dick, pull my boots off, I'm dying." But it was too late; Dick was
long gone.

They found Dick next day several miles away, dead. He had
pulled off his boots, lain down in his stocking feet, and died.

Martin Barnhardt and Thomas Peasley fought a duel in Carson, Nevada, merely to ascertain who would be "chief" of the
township's roughs. As a result, neither became "chief" because
they were both killed. Judge N. P. Langford knew the facts first-
hand. In his words:

While Peasley was seated in the office of the Ormsby House
in Carson, engaged in conversation with some friends, Barnhardt
entered, and approaching him asked,
"Are you heeled?"
"For Heaven's sake," rejoined Peasley, "are you always spoil-
ing for a fight?"
"Yes," cried Barnhardt, and without further notice fired his
revolver. The ball passed through Peasley's heart. Seeing that
he had inflicted a fatal wound, Barnhardt fled to the washroom,
closing the windowed door after him. Peasley rose and staggered
to the door. Thrusting his pistol through the sash, he fired and
killed Barnhardt instantly. Falling back in the arms of his friends,
they laid him upon a billiard table.
"Is Barnhardt dead?" he whispered, as life was ebbing.
"He is," was the ready answer given by half a dozen sorrowing
friends.
" 'Tis well. Pull my boots off, and send for my brother Andy,"
and with the words on his lips he expired.

Peasley was supposed to be the original of Mark Twain's "Buck Fanshaw."

The owners and operators of "The Bucket of Blood" saloon at Laramie, Wyoming, were some cutthroats and murderers named Ace Moyer, Con Moyer, and Big Steve. Their pasts caught up with them and they were hanged by Laramie vigilantes. Big Steve's last request was, "Take my shoes off, will you? My mother always said I'd die with my boots on and I want to fool her."

When the smoke of the O. K. Corral battle cleared away, young Billy Clanton was one of the three dying outlaws killed by the Earps. Citizens carried Billy into a Dr. Goodfellow's office, where he whispered, "Pull off my boots. I promised my mother I'd never die with my boots on."

You may recall John Heath's hanging. He was the hold-up man whose gang robbed and murdered a Bisbee miner. A jury gave him the verdict, "murder in the second degree." Not satisfied with the verdict, a mob of angry Bisbee and Tombstone miners hanged him. The mob asked Heath if he had any last requests. "I wish," he replied, "you'd promise not to shoot my body full of holes after you swing me up." This promise was made and kept.

Texas bad man Bill Longley was hanged once and it didn't work. Friends came in and shot the rope in two and Bill's strong neck and his friends had saved him temporarily. Later, however, he was recaptured and re-hanged. This time it "took." When the sheriff asked him whether he had any last words, Bill spoke in a loud, clear voice so every one of the large crowd assembled could hear. And it was a good speech. He said he hadn't much to say, but that he hated to die surrounded by so many enemies and so few friends. He hoped everybody would forgive him for anything he had done, stating at the same time he had forgiven all that ever mistreated him. He believed that God had forgiven him. He knew that he had to die, and he hated it, but he had killed many men who, as he said, hated to die as bad as he himself did (various reports give the number from twenty-one to thirty-two). Thus Bill admitted his guilt and justified his hanging; he paid his debt to society.

If the bad man ever uttered a sensible remark throughout his lurid life, it was likely to be his last. He was usually very reasonable, truthful, or philosophical in his last requests. Bill went on to say that if he had any friends about him who thought of revenge, he hoped they would forget it, as it was wrong. He heard his brother Jim was in the crowd witnessing his hanging. He sincerely hoped not, but if he was he hoped he would let revenge alone and instead pray for him, as he asked all other to do. He had taken enough revenge himself and must be punished for it.

Then Bill took a few more puffs on his cigar and received the priest's blessing. And before permitting the black cloth to be tied around his head, he shouted in a loud, clear voice a last good-bye. And thus ended the life of a very courageous but foolhardy man, who might have been a good member of society had he been born thirty years ago instead of a hundred.

As we have already seen, frequently the bad man's last words (Phil Coe's, for example) were meant as a curse upon his slayer or executioner. Bill Dunn said, as he entered a small restaurant in Oklahoma, "Frank Canton, ———— ———— you, I've got it in for you." But those were his last words, because Canton shot him dead right there and then. At the largest hanging bee probably any vigilance committee ever effected, at the expense of Henry Plummer's gang, Jack Gallagher, George Ives, and Boone Helm blasphemed the air with curses upon their executioners.

Former frontier marshal Bat Masterson (at Dodge City) in his later years worked for a New York City newspaper. Just before slumping over his office desk from heart failure, he had scratched on a pad with his pencil, "Pretty good old world after all. The rich get their ice in the summertime; the poor in the winter."

Shortly before being shot by a drunken prohibition agent, Billy Tilghman, famed veteran officer, said to Fred Sutton, "Fred, if I don't get killed in the smoke I will have to go to bed to die and I can't do that." As before mentioned, the frontier officer, in direct contrast to the bad man, considered it quite an honor to die with his boots on, which signified an honorable death on the field of battle where he had died faithfully doing his duty by society.

BOOT HILL

Usually a bad man was buried unceremoniously in a local "boot hill," so called because most of those who were buried therein died with their boots on, and were even buried with them on. However, some had funerals; and tombstones with epitaphs marked their graves for some time, usually until souvenir hunters demolished them.

On Sam Bass' tombstone was engraved, "A brave man reposes

in death here. Why was he not true?" On Seaborne Barnes' gravestone was written, "He was right bower to Sam Bass."

Besides his name and dates, Cole Younger's tombstone had the words, "Rest in Peace, Our Dear Beloved." Perhaps Jesse James' complete epitaph should be given: "In Loving Remembrance of My Beloved Son, JESSE W. JAMES, Died April 3, 1882, Aged 36 Years, 6 Months, 28 Days Murdered by a Traitor and Coward Whose Name is Not Worthy to Appear Here." The coward referred to was Bob Ford who, as you recall, shot Jesse in the back while he was hanging a picture on the wall, very unusually unarmed.

Other than biographical information, Langford Peel's tombstone bore the inscriptions: "In Life, Beloved by his Friends, and Respected by his Enemies. Vengeance is Mine, Saith the Lord. I Know That My Redeemer Liveth. Erected by a Friend."

Most unusual of the epitaphs of bad men was that of Lame Johnny, of the enormous mouth, hanged by impromptu vigilantes and awarded the epitaph: "Lame Johnny. Stranger, pass gently o'er this sod. If he opens his mouth, you're gone, by God."

REINCARNATION

The saga of the Western bad man contains many precarious escapes from execution or from death in battle. Frequently stories are extant that such-and-such a bad man is still alive. Indeed, Curly Bills, Billy the Kids, and Jesse Jameses have popped up from nowhere in many places. These fabricated bad men are nearly always fakes, but the legends or superstitions that bad men "came back" are not always without grounds — some of them *did come back!*

Ygenio Salazar, a McSween fighter under Billy the Kid in the climactic fight of the Lincoln County war; Herbert M. Tonney, a Woodsdale warrior in the Stevens County (Kansas) war; and a Texan soldier named Sheppard, who drew one of the black beans in the Mier expedition — all three of these men were shot down with bullets clear through their bodies in several places, fell on the field of battle, and feigned death. In each case their enemies inspected the bodies, ruthlessly kicking each to see if life was extinct; the ruse succeeded in saving the lives of the three men, who escaped in the dark of the night. The next day, however, after the Mexicans had shot down the Texans who drew the black beans, Sheppard's body was missing and he had left a trail of blood. So the ruthless Mexicans tracked him down and killed him, just when a wild new hope for freedom and escape had found birth in poor Sheppard's tormented brain. However, Salazar and Tonney lived for many years after their escapes; and they thanked their lucky stars they were not detected.

We have seen how Bill Longley lived through his first hanging. Even after three doctors examined his dead body after the second hanging and pronounced him thoroughly deceased, there were many Texas Negroes who believed he was the devil incarnate and would return at any minute to descend upon their "holy-roly" meetings, marking his devastating course with death-dealing six-gun slugs.

Young Roy Bean was hanged by jealous California Mexicans and left for dead; they returned and found the rope but no Bean, who had been rescued by a pretty señorita. Likewise, Jesse James' stepfather was hanged by Kansas jayhawkers and left for dead, but was rescued by friends just before expiring.

There are many Californians even today who believe that Joaquin Murrieta was not killed by Ranger Harry Love in his surprise attack on the desperado's camp. There were three Murrietas. Now, who can say which was or were killed?

So convincing was the news that Polk Wells had been killed by a posse that his wife married a Mr. Warnica. When Polk reappeared in the flesh before his wife and their friends, they were greatly astonished.

Postcards signed "Jesse James" were sent to all of Jesse's friends saying that he was still alive, probably for no other reason than to cause a sensation. When things like these actually happened, it becomes more easily understood why many people superstitiously believed that a bad man sometimes "comes back" from the dead.

FADED AWAY INTO A MEMORABLE PAST

Civilization moved in while the Western bad man and his frontier moved out. The bad man had made his place in the sun and lost it. He brought about his own downfall because of his motives and methods which did not conform to the code of the West. He had his day of retribution. He had his part to play in the civilization of the West in making the pioneers of that section of the country realize that law and order must be preserved even on a frontier, and he forced them to coöperate to establish them.

He existed at the only time and place when and where he could have existed; probably never again in this country will there be such a situation as that in which he found himself.

He was an extreme individualist by nature and by necessity. Typically, he was a man among men. It does not seem likely that he will ever be forgotten — there never was and never will be another man exactly like the typical bad man of the West.

He has faded away into a memorable past. Although this is true, he will continue to live figuratively in the minds of the American people. The typical bad man of the West has evolved into a tradition in the literature, in the lore, and in the movies of this nation. Although his true character has been distorted or exaggerated, were his life truthfully portrayed it would still be very exciting, thrilling, and lurid.

For these reasons I dedicate this book

> to the place
> and the time
> and the spirit
> that never were
> anywhere else
> before nor since
> nor ever will be again.

APPENDIX

APPENDIX

TABLE I

Descriptions of the Western Bad Man

There appear in this book actual photographs of bad men never before having appeared in any kind of publication, but of some of the bad men it is impossible to obtain photographs or tintypes or portraits. For a great many of them it is impossible to obtain even accurate descriptions. But here are the fairly detailed descriptions of fifty-eight such characters, and they are quite representative of their lot. You will recall that we conjured up a vision of the typical bad man of the West in Chapter IV of this book, and that vision was based on the information given at the close of this table — "the composite bad man." The asterisk after a name indicates superior notoriety.

ALLISON, CLAY*:

Eyes:　clear, keen, cold, dancing blue.
Hair:　black.
Height:　6′ 2″.
Weight:　175 pounds.
Face:　"handsome as Apollo," large, hard, bronzed, high forehead, mustache and whiskers, heavy black eyebrows.
Demeanor:　polite, dominant, "seldom laughed," but "pleasant smile when not angry," honest and generous.
General:　"right foot lamed," raised hell and played tricks when drunk, a killer but not a murderer, "small woman-like hands."

ALVORD, BURT:

Hair:　black.
Weight:　big.
Face:　dark complexion, square jawed, "bull-dog pug nose."
Demeanor:　"domineering to the underdog," not trustworthy.
General:　at times cowardly; fought when odds were his; a half-breed — American-Mexican.

BART, BLACK:

Eyes:　blue.
Hair:　iron gray.

211

Face: mustache.
Demeanor: never drank, smoked, nor chewed, a poet, "a great reader of classics and Bible," a California stage robber.

BASS, SAM*:

Eyes: black.
Hair: brown.
Height: 5' 7".
Face: brown mustache, "showed teeth while talking," large white teeth.
Demeanor: quiet natured, liked to joke and "show off" in front of his companions, very liberal with money.
General: slovenly dressed, as a rule; not a killer until cornered; not given to drink.

BEAN, JUDGE ROY:

Eyes: cool blue.
Hair: gray.
Face: when young, a lady killer.
Demeanor: enjoyed a joke, especially on the other fellow; extremely mercenary at times and liberal at others.
General: when young, a dandy; not dangerous to a pacifist.

BONNEY, WILLIAM H. (Billy the Kid)*:

Eyes: shifty, foxy, red hazel spots, blue.
Hair: light brown, long.
Height: 5' 7½".
Weight: 135 pounds.
Face: asymmetrical, front teeth prominent (buck-teeth), thin faced, wolfish, tan.
Demeanor: light-hearted, wise-cracking, devilish grin — even while killing, cold blooded, a practical joker.
General: sang like a bird, cold blooded, healthy, hands and feet remarkably small, unusually strong for size, loyal to his friends, not given to drink.

BROCIUS, CURLY BILL*:

Eyes: black.
Hair: black, curly.
Weight: heavy set, burly.
Face: round, dimpled, swarthy, bull-neck, freckles.
Demeanor: good-natured, but strictly business and no romance, quiet, amiable.
General: panther-like in movements, not a killer — merely an Arizona rustler.

CASSIDAY, BUTCH* (alias George Le Roy Parker):
> Eyes: blue.
> Hair: tousled.
> Face: quick grin, shaven.
> Demeanor: good-humored.
> General: ordinary dress with derby, not a killer at all, train and bank robber, didn't drink.

CHRISTMAS, LEE:
> Eyes: blue.
> Hair: blond.
> Height: tall.
> Weight: big.
> Demeanor: dare-devil, swaggering.
> General: big-shouldered, Mexican revolution general.

CLANTON, OLD MAN:
> Eyes: blue, blazing.
> Face: full white beard, hard, wrinkled, tanned cheeks.
> General: compatriot of Curly Bill.

COLLINS, HENRY:
> Eyes: blue.
> Face: handsome, fine shapely forehead, fizzy burnsides.
> General: Sam Bass henchman.

COURTRIGHT, JIM:
> Eyes: steady, Indian-dark.
> Hair: long, black.
> Height: tall — 6'.
> Face: handsome, shapely.
> General: well-dressed; Ft. Worth's first gangster.

CUMMINS, JIM:
> Eyes: blue.
> Weight: small.
> Demeanor: meek, quiet-natured, loyal to friends, humorous.
> General: Jesse James' gang.

DALTON, BILL*:
> Eyes: blue.
> Hair: blond.
> Height: tall.
> Weight: "physically well favored."
> Face: all four Daltons are full-faced and square-jawed — pugnacious expression.

Demeanor: glib, quick-witted, cautious, tactful, oratorical.
General: member of the Dalton gang of train and bank robbers of Oklahoma.

DALTON, BOB*:

Eyes: blue.
Hair: blond.
Height: tall.
Weight: "physically well favored."
Face: full-faced, square-jawed, pugnacious expression.
Demeanor: pugnacity, well-directed, cool, deliberate, tenacious, fearless.
General: Chief of the Dalton band.

DALTON, EMMETT*:

Eyes: blue.
Hair: blond.
Height: tall.
Weight: "physically well favored."
Face: full-faced, square-jawed, pugnacious expression.
General: member of the Dalton gang.

DALTON, GRATTAN*:

Eyes: blue.
Hair: blond.
Height: tall.
Weight: "physically well favored."
Face: full-faced, square-jawed, pugnacious expression.
Demeanor: pugnacious — chip on shoulder, sensitive, joy in fighting.
General: member of the Dalton gang.

EVANS, JESSE:

Eyes: blue.
General: boon companion of Billy the Kid, later estranged.

FINK, MIKE:

Eyes: bluish gray.
Hair: long, red.
Height: 5' 9".
Weight: 180 pounds.
Face: large teeth, eyes wide apart.
Demeanor: braggadocian bully — the cock of the walk.
General: Mississippi River bully, fist fighter, rawhide cap, hairy chest, red shirt, knife belted jeans, strapping figure.

FISHER, J. K. (King)*:
Eyes: blue.
Height: tall.
Face: handsome.
Demeanor: unusual sense of humor.
General: friend of Ben Thompson, killed at the same event as as was Thompson — at San Antonio; at one time Deputy Sheriff Uvalde County, South Texas; at his death he was wearing excellent broadcloth suit, white shirt, black boots with high heels, his inevitable big white hat. Greatly feared but highly respected.

GRAHAM, GEORGE:
Weight: 200 pounds.
Face: very handsome.
General: well built, black coat and hat, looked like a Methodist preacher — had very little to do with feud.

GRAHAM, JOHN:
Eyes: brown.
Hair: brunette.
Face: well proportioned.
General: in the Graham-Tewksbury feud, Arizona.

GRAHAM, TOM:
Eyes: cold blue-gray.
Hair: brunette.
Height: tall.
Weight: large.
Face: bushy eyebrows, square jaw, forceful.
Demeanor: an ideal citizen except for feud, avoided bloodshed if possible, quiet.
General: honest, healthy, fine character — leader of the Grahams.

HARDIN, JOHN WESLEY*:
Eyes: sharp, blue, unsteady.
Hair: light.
Height: 5' 10''.
Weight: 150-155 pounds.
Face: devilish, reckless grin, babyish, innocent, mild-featured, large chin, light complexion.
Demeanor: talkative, boastful, restless, mild, when aroused one of the coldest blooded — shot before he thought, easily angered.

General: dandy, $25 hat, bright overcoat $100, polished boots, black broadcloth suit, plush sash around waist. "When on trial wore buckskin breeches," "highly ornamented saddlery," not given to drink, spurs size of dollar.

HARPE, MICAJAH:

Hair: black, short, curly.
Height: 6'.
Weight: heavy.
Face: hair over forehead, uncombed, full face.
Demeanor: gory, lustful, blood-thirsty, cold-blooded, killed for convenience.
General: straight build, "clothes of drab cloth," one of the earliest American desperadoes.

HARPE, WILEY:

Hair: black, straight.
Height: under 6'.
Weight: slight.
Face: scrawny, weazened, mean visaged, meagre, downcast, wolfish.
Demeanor: of the same nature as his brother.
General: Clothes of drab cloth; Kentucky, Tennessee, Virginia desperado — 1780-1800.

HELM, BOONE:

Weight: powerful, strong.
Demeanor: murderer, cannibal, robber, absolutely depraved, low, coarse, cruel, animal-like, ruffian, turbulent temper, brutal.
General: one of Plummer's gang, Idaho and Montana; sacrilegious, extreme secessionist.

HELMS, JACK:

Face: heavily bearded, handsome.
Demeanor: determined and unswerving.
General: deep-chested, black clothes, high boots, big spurs, fine figure, participated in Sutton-Taylor feud in Texas.

HENRY, DUTCH:

Eyes: steel blue.
Hair: blond.
General: a Texas rustler, put out of business by Goodnight. Operated mainly in Kansas, later a ranchman in Colorado.

HERNDON, ALBERT:

    Hair: dark brown.
    Height: 5′ 8″.
    Weight: 150 pounds.
    Face: brown mustache, handsome.
    Demeanor: good humored, even when captured.
    General: Sam Bass' henchman.

HICKOK, JAMES BUTLER (Wild Bill)*:

    Eyes: blue-gray.
    Hair: long blond silken curls.
    Height: 6′ 1″.
    Weight: 200 pounds.
    Face: yellow mustache, acquiline nose.
    Demeanor: quiet, meant what he said, revengeful, cold-blooded, fearless; "a mad old bull outstanding among herds," quiet even under fire.
    General: small hands and feet, perfect form, dress in fashion of the river gamblers — black and white broadcloth, long tail cutaway coat, fancy vest, $60 high heeled boots always polished, checkered pants, Prince Albert coat, silk white vest with embroidered flowers, cape over shoulders with silk lining, boots of patent leather with fancy designs, pleated white shirt. Perfect specimen — white slim hands.

HIGDON, COLONEL:

    Eyes: mild blue.
    Hair: gray.
    Demeanor: quiet, mysterious, stealthy, same under fire.
    General: an acquaintance of E. Cunningham — said to be very dangerous.

HILL, TOM:

    Face: swarthy, low-browed.
    Demeanor: braggart, cold-blooded killer, rough, loud-mouthed.
    General: associate of Billy the Kid; ignorant.

HOLLIDAY, JOHN H. (Doc)*:

    Eyes: gray.
    Hair: ash-blond.
    Height: 5′ 11″.
    Weight: 130 pounds; frail, slender.
    Face: haggard, fine nose, expressive mouth, lean, pox-marked, handsome contour, well proportioned, heavy eyebrows, trimmed mustache.

Demeanor: consumptive, fastidious, temperamental, witty, easily provoked, cold-blooded killer, loyal to friends, immaculate, expert blasphemer.

General: "dressed in typical river gambler's attire," always neat and immaculate, "quick on the draw."

IVES, GEORGE:
Eyes: lively blue.
Height: 6'.
Face: light complexion, shaven, innocent looking, youthful.
General: member of Plummer's gang.

JAMES, FRANK*:
Eyes: steel blue, restless, active.
Hair: sandy.
Height: tall.
Weight: 140 pounds.
Face: angular, sideburns, smooth chin, no resemblance to Jesse.
Demeanor: quiet, somber, given to deep thought.
General: intelligent, interested in politics, religious, angular body.

JAMES, JESSE*:
Eyes: steel blue, shifty, snappy.
Hair: short, brownish-black.
Height: 5' 10-11".
Weight: 165-170 pounds.
Face: granulated eyelids, disarming smile, full face, dark brown whiskers, roundish, stubby nose, fairly good looking, heavy dark lashes, fair complexion.
Demeanor: good natured except when excited, hot tempered, usually carefree but watchful.
General: religious, "an outlaw but not a criminal," missing finger-tip — wore gloves; business suit of cashmere dark brown, well fitting, spotless white shirt with collar and cravat — looked like business man (except when robbing), "small woman-like hands."

JENNINGS, AL:
Eyes: greenish-blue, fine, clear.
Hair: auburn.
Height: 5' +
Weight: 120 pounds.
Face: tan, sun-wrinkled, ruddy, wide brow, cleanly drawn nose, powerful jaw, wide firm mouth, scar on upper lip, gold teeth.

Demeanor: a consuming temper, intelligent.

General: numerous scars over body; Oklahoma desperado, reformed and was almost elected county attorney.

JOHN, DUTCH:

Eyes: fierce black.

Hair: black.

Height: tall.

Weight: large.

Face: browned by exposure, reflected dark passions of his heart, eyes full of malignity, matted whiskers; human gorilla, brutish.

Demeanor: sullen when captured.

General: Montana thief captured by Neil Howie (note Neil's description by contrast).

JOHNSON, ARKANSAS:

Eyes: blue.

Hair: light.

Weight: heavy.

Face: ruddy complexion, smallpox scars.

General: Sam Bass' henchman.

LESLIE, BUCKSKIN FRANK:

Eyes: gray.

Demeanor: fearless, cold-blooded killer, calm under fire, liked to show off ability with guns.

General: movements catlike and furtive, steel-wire toughness.

LONGLEY, BILL*:

Eyes: dark.

Hair: dark.

Height: 6'.

Weight: 200 pounds.

Face: large chin, not bad looking, not a repulsive feature.

Demeanor: fierce, hot tempered, lost his head easily, coldblooded; when peaceful, laughs and talks pleasantly.

General: Indian-like stooped shoulders; Texas Negroes were his meat.

OUTLAW, BASS:

Eyes: pale blue-gray.

Height: short.

Weight: little.

Face: receding chin.

Demeanor: highly irascible; the least interference and he shot.

General: killed a fellow Texas Ranger, and was killed by the Rangers. Given to drink.

PATTERSON, FERD:

Eyes: expressive, blue.
Hair: light with gray streaks.
Height: 6'.
Weight: 200 pounds.
Face: sandy whiskers, sad expression.
Demeanor: quiet mannered, not an extensive killer.
General: a Tennessee secessionist, who killed Sheriff Pinkham out West (note Pinkham's description).

PIPES, SAM:

Eyes: black.
Hair: black.
Height: 5' 10".
Weight: 175 pounds.
Face: black mustache.
Demeanor: good humored, jester even while captured.
General: Sam Bass' henchman.

PLUMMER, HENRY*:

Eyes: cold, expressionless, staring, "fish" gray.
Height: 5' 11".
Weight: 160 pounds.
Face: low brutish forehead, expressionless, immovable face, half-vacant stare, colorless complexion.
Demeanor: quiet, intelligent, "killing machine," cold-blooded, quiet even in his cups, monotonous voice, no bravado nor swagger, had well-keyed, strong nervous system, usually polite.
General: leader of worst band of cutthroats in West.

QUANTRILL, WILLIAM CLARKE*:

Eyes: blue.
Weight: 171 pounds.
Face: expressionless, gaunt, lean, deceiving, ordinary.
Demeanor: quiet, malicious, no natural affection, cold-blooded, degenerate, laughed and shouted in battle, lazy.
General: the all-time champion guerrilla chief — of Missouri border during Civil War.

RAYNER, BILL:

Demeanor: boastful, braggart, reputation seeking — a false alarm probably.

General: "the best-dressed Texas bad man" — black sombrero,. black Prince Albert coat, gray trousers pulled down over fine black boots, light gray gloves.

RINGO, JOHN*:
Eyes: pathetic, blue.
Height: 6' 2".
Face: pathetic, sad, morose expression; like Hamlet, darkly handsome, lean, saturnine, tragic countenance.
Demeanor: loyal to friends, moody, quiet, quarrelsome when drunk, brave, silent, mysterious, given to melancholy.
General: associate of Curly Bill at Tombstone, well educated, read extensively, sculpturesque physique.

SHORT, LUKE:
Eyes: blue.
Height: 5' 6".
Weight: 150 pounds.
Face: smooth.
Demeanor: soft-voiced, cool under fire.
General: immaculately clad; killed Courtright as by an accident.

SLADE, JOSEPH A.*:
Eyes: calm, Indian black.
Face: smile (even when shooting), pleasant though hard-countenanced, raw-boned, swarthy complexioned.
Demeanor: mild, courteous except when drunk, then a hell-raiser, pleasant, joking, personal magnitude.
General: kind husband, hospitable host, courteous gentleman.

SPOTSWOOD, TOM:
Eyes: blue.
Face: not too handsome; right eye larger than left; good whisker crop.

STARR, HENRY:
Eyes: very black.
Hair: jet black, straight.
Weight: slight.
Face: dark, Indian-like.
Demeanor: had Indian instincts, taciturn, low-pitched voice, interesting conversationalist.
General: abstained from liquor, tobacco, tea, and coffee; half Cherokee, half Irish; athletic physique, moved with aboriginal grace.

SUTTON, BILLY:

    Face: splendid looking young chap, hardly out of teens during feud.

    Demeanor: reckless air.

    General: flair for dress; leader of faction in Texas' Sutton-Taylor feud.

TAYLOR, JIM:

    Hair: dark.

    Height: 5' 10".

    Weight: 170 pounds.

    Face: dark complexioned.

    Demeanor: quiet, low, dull tone of voice.

    General: leader of faction in Texas' Sutton *vs.* Taylor-Hardin feud.

TEWKSBURY, EDWIN:

    Eyes: blue.

    Hair: black.

    Face: square jaw; ordinary looking except for high cheek bone, firm chin, and penetrating eyes.

    Demeanor: quiet.

    General: leader of faction in Tewksbury-Graham feud, Pleasant Valley, Arizona. Half-breed — Scotch-Indian.

THOMPSON, BEN*:

    Eyes: blue.

    Hair: black.

    Height: 5' 9".

    Weight: stocky.

    Face: square-jawed, black mustache, swarthy complexion, bulldog face.

    Demeanor: bulldog demeanor, described by Walton as kind-hearted and chivalrous; elsewhere as cold-blooded killer.

    General: thickset, the Texas cowboy protector at Abilene, Kansas — didn't like Hickok; friend of Phil Coe; a good husband; quite a dandy.

YOUNGER, COLE*:

    Eyes: blue.

    Hair: bald.

    Height: 6' +.

    Weight: 200 pounds.

    Face: round, full, pleasant.

    Demeanor: well modulated voice, intelligent.

General: religious, a good man except for robbing, cousin of
James boys, a good husband; reformed; figure of a
Bishop.

The Composite Bad Man:

Eyes		*Height*	
blue	38	Number not given	26
black	9	Number given	22
not given	11	tall	9
	—	short	1
Total	58		—
Hair		Total	58
blond	15		
brunette	19	av.	5′ 9½″
red	2	high	6′ 2″
not given	22	low	5′ +
Total	58		

Weight			
Number not given	22		
Number given	19	av.	169
heavy	12	high	200
light	5	low	120
Total	58		

TABLE II

Descriptions of the Pioneer Peace Officer

Likewise, not all of the good sheriffs, marshals, rangers, and deputies of the old wild West left behind pictures of themselves. But here
are descriptions of eighteen representative peace officers of the Western frontier. For "the composite good law officer," see the information
at the end of this table, or turn back to Chapter IV, wherein the bad
men are also described.

BEIDLER, X.:

Eyes: small, darting.
Height: short.
Weight: little.

Face: muddy complexion, puffy countenance, shaggy lashes, bristling long mustache over firm chin.
Demeanor: fiery.
General: thick body and legs.

EARP, MORGAN:

Eyes: blue.
Hair: light brown.
Height: 6' +.
Weight: 158 pounds.
Face: closely resembled brother, Wyatt; frequently mistaken for him.
Demeanor: of much the same temperament as brother, Wyatt; probably not quite as aggressive; not as much initiative.
General: the three Earp fighters (there were five brothers; the oldest and youngest did not figure as Western marshals) were frequently mistaken for one another.

EARP, VIRGIL:

Eyes: blue.
Hair: light brown.
Height: 6' +.
Weight: 156 pounds.
Face: closely resembled brother, Wyatt; frequently mistaken for him.

EARP, WYATT:

Eyes: blue.
Hair: light brown.
Height: 6' +.
Weight: 155 pounds.
Face: gaunt, eyes deep-set, pallor, long faced, square jaw.
Demeanor: no swashbuckling; strictly business.
General: loose limbed powerful frame, fearless; the leader of the Earp triumvirate.

GARRETT, PAT:

Eyes: gray.
Height: 6' 4½".
Face: eyes tragic expression, saturnine, asymmetrical face; pallor, lean.
Demeanor: drawling speech; dry, sly humor; at times taciturn; at others easy going; faced danger and praise with equal coolness.
General: killed Billy the Kid.

HOWIE, NEIL:
   Eyes: clear gray.
   Weight: medium, slight, small.
   Face: handsome, well proportioned.
   Demeanor: determined to do his duty, calm, gentle, in repose;
      commanding and powerful in excitement; quick moving.
   General: no uncommon strength — capturer of Dutch John
      in Montana.

HUGHES, CAPTAIN JOHN R.:
   Eyes: dark brown.
   Height: about 6'.
   Weight: about 180 pounds.
   Face: pleasing countenance and handsome.
   Demeanor: talked low, brave, religious, reserved.
   General: no drinker nor gambler, never turned back, fearless;
      Texas Ranger Captain. *(see* Foreword to this book).

KOSTERLITZKY, ?:
   Eyes: stern.
   Hair: clipped, short, Russian style.
   Demeanor: erect, always the soldier.
   General: carried sword like Cossack he was.

LOVE, HARRY:
   Eyes: black.
   Hair: long, black.
   Height: tall.
   Face: swarthy complexion.
   Demeanor: defiant swing.
   General: wore sword; sinewy, straight; easy of tread.

MASTERSON, BAT:
   Eyes: blue *(see* picture).

McDONALD, BILL:
   Eyes: gray-blue.
   Height: tall:
   Face: prominent nose, brown mustache.
   Demeanor: always alert and direct.
   General: angular, quick quiet movements, catlike; Texas Rang-
      er captain.

MOSSMAN, BURTON:
   Eyes: steel gray.
   Demeanor: quiet, soft-spoken.
   General: first Arizona Ranger captain — a leader of men.

OWENS, COMMODORE PERRY:

Eyes: steel blue. piercing.
Hair: blond, long.
Height: 5′ 10″.
Face: face without a hard line, looked too easy for a sheriff; good looking; high nose.
Demeanor: kept everyone at a distance; quiet.
General: steel-like muscles; sheriff, Holbrook, Arizona.

PINKHAM, ?:

Eyes: sharp, gray.
Height: 6′ +.
Weight: 200 pounds.
Demeanor: intensely alert; by no means a killer, slain by Patterson in Civil War controversy, agile, quick.
General: from Maine — a unionist.

REYNOLDS, CAPT. N. S.:

Eyes: blue.
Hair: blond.
Face: thin, long.
Demeanor: quiet; meant what he said; not excitable.
General: Captain of Texas Rangers; never backed down nor stopped.

SLAUGHTER, JOHN:

Eyes: hard, black.
Hair: black.
Height: 5′ 6″.
Weight: small.
Face: tanned, snappy, vigorous, thick neck.
Demeanor: grim, silent, strictly business.
General: big shoulders, Tombstone's law unto himself.

STOUDENMIRE, DALLAS:

Eyes: blue, small, deep-set, steel hard.
Hair: blond.
Height: 6′.
Weight: 200 pounds.
Face: drooping yellow mustache, chin like a rough-hewn oak block, very handsome.
Demeanor: quiet usually, but in his cups boisterous and overbearing.
General: Marshal of El Paso, later U. S. Marshal, ex-Confederate, killed in fight.

TILGHMAN, BILLY:
    Eyes: blue.
    Face: very handsome.
    Demeanor: quiet, gentle, soft-spoken, took chances, gentle-
        manly, never overbearing.
    General: abstained from drink, smoking, swearing. Didn't use
        gun except when absolutely necessary.

The Composite Good Law Officer:

Eyes		Hair	
blue	13	blond	6
black	2	brunette	2
not given	3	red	0
	—	not given	10
Total	18		—
		Total	18

Height		Weight	
given	8	given	5
not given	7	not given	10
tall	2	heavy	0
short	1	slight	3
	—		—
Total	18	Total	18
av.	6′	av.	174
high	6′ 4½″	high	200
low	5′ 6″	low	155

TABLE III

The Birth of the Bad Man of the West

From whence came the bad man? Here is the information about
the births of thirty-nine notorious characters of the old wild West.
Interesting is the fact that the median year of their births was 1851
and that eighteen were sons of the old South, as compared to twelve
from the North and only two from the new West. Does this mean anything? Turn back to Chapter I and perhaps you'll agree that it does.
The asterisk indicates superior notoriety.

AKE, JEFF:
    Date: 1845.
    Place: Arkansas.
    Where Fame was Gained: Texas.

BASS, SAM*:
Date: July 21, 1851.
Place: Mitchell, Lawrence County, Indiana.
Where Fame was Gained: Texas and Kansas.

BONNEY, WM. H. (Billy the Kid)*:
Date: November 29, 1859.
Place: New York City, New York.
Where Fame was Gained: New Mexico.

CASSIDY, BUTCH (George Le Roy Parker)*:
Date: 1865-1870.
Where Fame was Gained: Utah, Colorado, Wyoming.

CHRISTMAS, LEE:
Date: February 22, 1863.
Place: Baton Rouge, Louisiana.
Where Fame was Gained: Mexico (rebel leader).

COE, GEORGE:
Date: July 13, 1856.
Place: Brighton, Washington County, Iowa.
Where Fame was Gained: New Mexico.

COURTRIGHT, JIM:
Date: 1848.
Place: Iowa.
Where Fame was Gained: Texas.

DALTON, BILL, BOB, EMMETT, and GRATTAN*:
Date: 1859-1865.
Place: Missouri.
Where Fame was Gained: Oklahoma and Kansas.

GRAHAM, JOHN AND TOM:
Date: Near 1850.
Place: Boone, Iowa.
Where Fame was Gained: Arizona.

HARDIN, JOHN WESLEY*:
Date: May 26, 1853.
Place: Bonham, Fannin County, Texas.
Where Fame was Gained: Texas.

HELM, BOONE:
Place: Kentucky.
Where Fame was Gained: Montana, Idaho, Nevada.

HICKOK, JAMES B. (Wild Bill)*:
    Date: May 27, 1837.
    Place: Troy Grove, La Salle County, Illinois.
    Where Fame was Gained: Kansas and Montana.

HOLLIDAY, JOHN H. (Doc)*:
    Place: Valdosta, Georgia.
    Where Fame was Gained: Texas, Kansas, Arizona.

HORN, TOM:
    Date: 1861.
    Place: Memphis, Tennessee.
    Where Fame was Gained: Throughout the West.

IVES, GEORGE:
    Place: Ives Grove, Racine County, Wisconsin.
    Where Fame was Gained: Montana, Idaho, Nevada.

JAMES, ALEXANDER *FRANKLIN*:
    Date: January 10, 1843.
    Place: Centerville, Missouri (now Kearny).
    Where Fame was Gained: Kansas, Missouri, Wisconsin.

JAMES, *JESSE* WOODSON*:
    Date: September 5, 1847.
    Place: Centerville, Missouri.
    Where Fame was Gained: Kansas, Missouri, Wisconsin.

JENNINGS, AL:
    Date: During Civil War.
    Place: An abandoned Virginia schoolhouse.
    Where Fame was Gained: Oklahoma.

JOHNSON, ARKANSAS:
    Place: Missouri.
    Where Fame was Gained: Oklahoma and Texas.

LONGLEY, BILL*:
    Date: October 6, 1851.
    Place: Mill Creek, Austin County, Texas.
    Where Fame was Gained: Texas.

MASON, SAM:
    Date: Before 1800.
    Place: Pennsylvania.
    Where Fame was Gained: Ohio and Mississippi River.

OUTLAW, BASS:
Place: Georgia.
Where Fame was Gained: Texas.

PATTERSON, FERD:
Place: Tennessee.
Where Fame was Gained: Montana.

PLUMMER, HENRY*:
Date: 1837.
Place: Connecticut.
Where Fame was Gained: Montana, Idaho, Nevada.

QUANTRILL, WM. C.*:
Date: July 31, 1837.
Place: Canal Dover, Ohio.
Where Fame was Gained: Missouri and Kansas.

RINGO, JOHN:
Place: Texas.
Where Fame was Gained: Arizona.

SAGE, LEE:
Date: Late 1880's.
Place: At a robber's roost, dismal shack, southeast corner of
Utah.
Where Fame was Gained: Montana and Canada.

SHORT, LUKE:
Date: Before 1860.
Place: Arkansas.
Where Fame was Gained: Texas, Kansas, Arizona.

SLADE, JOSEPH A.*:
Place: Carlisle, Illinois.
Where Fame was Gained: Montana.

STINSON, BUCK:
Place: Greencastle, Indiana.
Where Fame was Gained: Montana, Idaho, Nevada.

TEWKSBURY, ED, JOHN, AND JIM:
Date: Near 1850.
Place: Humboldt country, California.
Where Fame was Gained: Arizona.

THOMPSON, BEN*:
    Date: 1843.
    Place, Yorkshire, England, or Lockhart, Texas.
    Where Fame was Gained: Texas.

WELLS, POLK:
    Date: June 5, 1851.
    Place: Missouri.
    Where Fame was Gained: Missouri.

	Year
Median date	1851

Place	
South	18
North	12
West	2

BIBLIOGRAPHY

BIBLIOGRAPHY

Primary Sources

(Note: Quotations from the bad men themselves and from the old-timers who knew them may be found in these references and are evident in my book. They vary from the so-help-me to the ridiculous fabrication, but they are interesting and do frequently enlighten and for that reason I have included them.)

Allen, Jules Verne. *Cowboy Lore,* The Naylor Company, San Antonio, Texas, 1934.

Baldwin, Joseph G., *The Flush Times of Alabama and Mississippi,* Bancroft-Whitney Company, San Francisco, California, 1901.

Breakenridge, William. *Helldorado,* Houghton Mifflin Company, New York, 1928.

Burns, Walter Noble. *Tombstone,* Garden City Publishing Company, Garden City, New York. 1927.

Canton, Frank M. *Frontier Trails,* Houghton Mifflin Company, New York, 1930.

Clark, O. S. *Clay Allison of the Washita,* Attica, Indiana, 1922.

Clemens, Samuel (Mark Twain). *Roughing It,* Vols. I and II, Harper Brothers Publishers, New York, 1913.

Coe, George. *Frontier Fighter,* Houghton Mifflin Company, New York, 1934.

Connelley, W. E. *Quantrill and the Border Wars,* The Torch Press, Cedar Rapids, Iowa, 1910.

Coolidge, Dane. *Fighting Men of the West,* E. P. Dutton and Co., New York, 1932.

Cunningham, Eugene. *Triggernometry,* Caxton Printers, Caldwell, Idaho, 1940.

Dalton, Emmett. *When the Daltons Rode,* Doubleday, Doran and Company, 1931.

Dodge, Richard Irving. *The Hunting Grounds of the Great West,* Chatto and Winders, London, 1877.

Gard, Wayne. *Sam Bass,* Houghton Mifflin Company, New York, 1936.

Hardin, John Wesley. *Life of John Wesley Hardin,* Smith and Moore, 1896. Reprinted by the *Frontier Times,* Bandera, Texas, 1937.

Hood, Thomas. "Gold," from *Power of Speech*, The Expression Company, Boston, Mass.

Hough, Emerson. *The Story of the Outlaw*, Grosset and Dunlap, New York, 1907.

Hunter, Robert Hancock. *The Narrative of Robert Hancock Hunter*, edited by Mrs. Beulah G. Green, Victoria, Texas, printed by Cook Printing Company, Austin, Texas, 1936.

Jennings, Al, and Irwin, Will. *Beating Back*, Houghton Mifflin Company, 1914.

Lake, Stuart N. *Wyatt Earp, Frontier Marshal*, Houghton Mifflin Company, 1931.

Langford, N. P. *Vigilante Days and Ways*, A. L. Burt Company, New York, 1912.

Love, Robertus. *The Rise and Fall of Jesse James*, St. Louis, Missouri, 1926.

Lloyd, Everett. *Law West of the Pecos*, The Naylor Company, San Antonio, Texas, 1936.

MacDonald, A. B. *Hands Up!*, A. L. Burt Company, New York, 1927.

O'Neil, James B. *They Die But Once*, Knight Publications, Inc., New York, 1935.

Otero, Miguel Antonio. *My Life on the Frontier*, The Press of The Pioneers, Inc., New York, 1935-39.

Poe, John W. *The Death of Billy the Kid*, Houghton Mifflin Company, New York, 1933.

Raine, W. M. *Famous Sheriffs and Western Outlaws*, Garden City Publishing Company, Garden City, New York, 1928.

Sabin, E. L. *Wild Men of the Wild West*, Thomas Y. Crowell Company, New York, 1929.

Sage, Lee. *The Last Rustler*, Little Brown, and Company, Boston, 1930.

Sutton, Fred. "They Died With Their Boots On, Saying . . .," *The Dallas Morning News*, Dallas, Texas, May 10, 1931.

Walton, W. M. "Life and Adventures of Ben Thompson," *Frontier Times*, Bandera, Texas, 1884, re-edited 1926.

Wells, Polk. *Life and Adventures of Polk Wells*, published by G. A. Warnica, Halls, Missouri, 1907.

Miscellaneous. Old newspapers and clippings, court records, collections in museums, all too numerous to list; as well as private conferences with "old-timers."

Secondary Sources

(Note: Anyone who has read these books finds that they, too, vary in all shades of truth. But no one will deny that the lore of the old wild West is a fascinating subject — and its "atmosphere" you have no doubt found permeated through the covers and leaves of this publication.)

Adams, Andy. *The Log of a Cowboy*, Houghton Mifflin Company, New York, 1931.

Boatright, Mody C. *Tall Tales from Texas Cow Camps*, The Southwest Press, Dallas, Texas, 1934.

Boatright, Mody C. *Folk Laughter on the American Frontier*, The Macmillan Company, New York, 1949.

Burns, Walter Noble. *The Robin Hood of El Dorado*, Coward-McCann, New York, 1932.

Burns, Walter Noble. *The Saga of Billy the Kid*, Grosset and Dunlap, New York, 1926.

Chisholm, Joe. *Brewery Gulch*, The Naylor Company, San Antonio, Texas, 1949.

Connelly, W. E. *Wild Bill and His Era*, The Press of The Pioneers, Inc., New York, 1933.

Crockett, David. *The Autobiography of David Crockett*, Charles Scribner's Sons, New York, 1923.

De Voto, Bernard. *Across the Wide Missouri*, Houghton Mifflin Company, Boston, 1947.

Dobie, J. Frank. *The Flavor of Texas*, Dealey and Lowe, Dallas, Texas, 1936.

Dobie, J. Frank. *A Vaquero of the Brush Country*, The Southwest Press, Dallas, Texas, 1929.

Dobie, J. Frank. *The Voice of the Coyote*, Little, Brown and Company, Boston, 1949.

Dobie, J. Frank, and Boatright, Mody C. *Straight Texas*, The Steck Company, Austin, Texas, 1937.

Duval, John C. *The Adventures of Big-Foot Wallace*, The Steck Company, Austin, Texas, 1935.

Forrest, Earle R. *Arizona's Dark and Bloody Ground*, The Caxton Printers, Ltd., Caldwell, Idaho.

Gann, Walter. *Tread of the Longhorns*, The Naylor Company, San Antonio, Texas, 1949.

Gardner, Raymond Hatfield. *The Old Wild West*, The Naylor Company, San Antonio, Texas, 1944.

Gillett, James B. *Six Years with the Texas Rangers*, Yale Univeristy Press, New Haven, 1925.

Haley, J. Everts. *Charles Goodnight, Cowman and Plainsman*, Houghton Mifflin Company, New York, 1930.

Hamner, Laura V. *The No-Gun Man of Texas*, Amarillo, Texas, 1936.

Hoover, J. Edgar. "No More Dillingers! You Can Prevent It! The Problem of Rural Youth," *Liberty*, August 13, 1938.

House, Boyce. *Cowtown Columnist*, The Naylor Company, San Antonio, Texas, 1946.

Life, Chicago, Illinois, July 20, 1938.

Lloyd, Everett. *Law West of the Pecos,* The Naylor Company, San Antonio, Texas, 1936.

London, I. R. *A Lady's Ranch Life in Montana,* 1887.

Martin, Jack. *Border Boss,* The Naylor Company, San Antonio, Texas, 1942.

Maxwell, Grant. "Cimarron," *New Mexico,* November, 1937.

McDaniel, Ruel C. *Vinegarroon,* Southern Publishers, Kingsport, Tennessee, 1936.

Ruxton, George F. *Wild Life in the Rocky Mountains,* The Macmillan Company, 1932.

Rynning, Thomas H. *Gun Notches,* Frederick A. Stokes Co., 1931.

Siringo, Charles A. *Riata and Spurs,* Houghton Mifflin Company, New York, 1927.

Smith, Honora DeBusk. "Cowboy Lore in Colorado," *Southwestern Lore,* Publication Number IX of the Texas Folk-Lore Society, Dallas, Texas, 1931.

Stewart, George R. *Ordeal By Hunger,* Henry Holt, 1936.

Townshend, R. B. *The Tenderfoot in New Mexico,* John Lane, The Bodley Head, Limited, London, 1923.

Webb, Walter Prescott. *The Great Plains,* Ginn and Company, New York, 1931.

Webb, Walter Prescott. *The Texas Rangers,* Houghton Mifflin, Boston, 1935.

Wharton, Clarence. *Satanta,* Banks Upshaw and Company, Dallas, Texas, 1935.

Wilstach, Frank J. *The Plainsman, Wild Bill Hickok,* The Sun Dial Press, New York, 1937.

Wilstach, Frank J. *Wild Bill Hickok, the Prince of Pistoleers,* Doubleday, Page and Company, New York, 1926.

Woodhull, Frost. "Folk-Lore Shooting," *Southwestern Lore,* Publication Number IX of the Texas Folk-Lore Society, Dallas, Texas, 1931.

SUPPLEMENTARY BIBLIOGRAPHY

Stanley Vestal recently paid this book about the highest possible compliment concerning any work of research. In his 1955 edition *The Book Lover's Southwest: A Guide to Good Reading,* he said that my book on the bad man of the west contained "little that is new, but much that is fresh."

I would guess that 95% of the materials of Shakespeare's plays contained little that was new to informed Elizabethan play-going patrons. What kept them coming to Shakespearean dramas time and time again was the freshness of the playwright's presentations. The stories Chaucer put together into *The Canterbury Tales* were already twice told and quite familiar to most British ears before he got hold of them. It was his fresh interpretation of the human element in these tales that has kept them popular for six centuries. Shakespeare and Chaucer are authentic in their portrayal of the human being for what he is. These two elements, freshness and authenticity, are the requisites for the immortality of a story, whether it be fictional or non-fictional.

Today widespread public interest in the bad man of the west is manifested in the number of books, both hardback and paperback, in the number of magazines such as *True West* and *Frontier Times,* and in the number of movies and television programs on the subject. At this writing such programs as "Maverick," "Cheyenne," "Sugarfoot," "Gunsmoke," "Trackdown," "Tales of Texas Rangers," "Tales of Wells Fargo," "The Californians," "Wagon Train," "The Restless Gun," "Tombstone Territory," and "Have Gun, Will Travel" are legion and have avid followers. Others propose to tell the adventures of such men as John Slaughter, Bat Masterson, Elfego Baca, and Bill Longley. I have a strong opinion that the life of these programs will be in direct proportion to their freshness and authenticity. Some have already deteriorated whereas others maintain a persistent appeal. The same is true concerning the number of editions of recent books and their longevity in print. If they are fictitious, they must still conform to the principles of freshness and authenticity. In J. Frank Dobie's words, "If this story isn't true to facts, it *is* true to life." Or as Mark Twain prefaced *The Prince and the Pauper,* "This tale may never have happened, but it *could* have happened."

In view of such widespread public interest in the bad man of the west, it seems wise to bring my bibliography up to date. In the following books, there may be little that is new to the veteran authority.

In some of them, however, there is freshness of insight into the characters of the old west. In all of them there is a blend of objectivity and subjectivity, the relative proportions of which the astute reader soon becomes aware. Viewers of myriad TV programs will have better discernment and more critical acumen for having read or examined the books in this supplementary bibliography. I have annotated those whose titles do not readily indicate their types of contents.

About the Bad Man

Adams, Ramon F.: *Six-Guns and Saddle Leather*: A Bibliography of Books and Pamphlets on Western Outlaws and Gunmen, University of Oklahoma, 1954. (This book has complete descriptions of 1,132 titles.)

Aikman, Duncan: *Calamity Jane and the Lady Wildcats*, Holt, 1927.

Anonymous: *The Dalton Brothers*, by an Eye Witness, Fell, New York, 1955.

Arnold, Oren: *Thunder in the Southwest*, University of Oklahoma, 1952.

Asbury, Herbert: *Sucker's Progress*, an Informal History of Gambling in America from the colonies to Canfield, Dodd, Mead, 1938.

Balcourt, Edgar D.: *The Dalton Brothers and Their Astounding Career of Crime*, Fell, New York, 1955.

Braddy, Haldeen: *Cock of the Walk*, University of New Mexico, 1955. (An amazing biography of Pancho Villa.)

Breihan, Carl W.: *The Complete and Authentic Life of Jesse James*, Doubleday, 1953.

Buel, James W.: *The Border Outlaws*, Historical Publishing Company, St. Louis, Missouri, 1881. (About the Jameses and Youngers.)

Burch, John P.: *Charles W. Quantrell*, True History of His Guerrilla Warfare on the Missouri and Kansas Border, Vega, Texas, 1923.

Bush, Niven: *Duel in the Sun*, Morrow, New York, 1944. (A novel in the bad man tradition, made into a movie.)

Castle Publishing Company: *Death Valley Scotty's Castle*. A Description of the Castle and Its Furnishings, Death Valley, n.d.

Cody, William F.: *Autobiography*. Illustrated by N. C. Wyeth. Cosmopolitan, 1924.

Clark, Thomas D.: *The Rampaging Frontier*, Bobbs-Merrill, Indianapolis, 1939.

Corle, Edwin: *Billy the Kid*, Duell, Sloan and Pearce, 1953. (A novel based on the life of the outlaw.)

Crichton, Kyle S.: *Law and Order, Ltd*. The Rousing Life of Elfego Baca of New Mexico, Santa Fe., 1928.

Croy, Homer: *He Hanged Them High*, Duell, Sloan and Pearce, 1952. (An account of Judge Isaac C. Parker, the "hanging judge" of the Arkansas Territory.)

Cunningham, Eugene: *Texas Triggers*, Sundial, 1948.

Davis, Britton: *The Truth About Geronimo*, Yale University, 1929.

Dimsdale, Thomas J.: *The Vigilantes of Montana*, University of Oklahoma, 1953. (A reprint of a book first published in 1866.)

Donald, Jay: *Outlaws of the Border*. A Complete and Authentic History of the Lives of Frank and Jesse James and the Younger Brothers and Their Robber Companions including Quantrell and His Noted Guerrillas. Cincinnati, 1883.

Douglas, Claude L.: *Famous Texas Feuds*, The Turner Company, Dallas, 1936.

DuPuy, William A.: *Baron of the Colorados*, Naylor, 1958. (The fascinating story of a mule-skinner who decided to make a fortune.)

Dykes, J. C.: *Billy the Kid*: The Bibliography of a Legend, University of New Mexico, 1952. (This book contains 437 references.)

Edwards, William B.: *The Story of Colt's Revolver*, Stackpole, Harrisburg, Pennsylvania, 1953.

Farber, James: *Texans with Guns*, Naylor, 1958.

SUPPLEMENTARY BIBLIOGRAPHY

Ferguson, Erna: *Murder and Mystery in New Mexico*, Merle Armitage, Albuquerque, 1948.

Forrest, E. R. and Hill, E. B.: *Lone War Trail of Apache Kid*, Trail's End Publishing Company, 1947.

Fortune, Jan I.: *Fugitives*: The Story of Clyde Barrow and Bonnie Parker, The Ranger Press, Dallas, 1952.

Gard, Wayne: *Frontier Justice*, University of Oklahoma, 1949.

Gardner, Raymond H.: *The Old Wild West*, Naylor, 1944.

Garrett, Pat F.: *Pat F. Garrett's Authentic Life of Billy the Kid* (ed. Maurice G. Fulton, Macmillan, 1927. This book was reprinted by the University of Oklahoma Press in 1954.)

Glasscock, C. B.: *Man-Hunt*: Bandits and the Southern Pacific, Grosset and Dunlap, n.d.

Harkey, Dee: *Mean as Hell*, University of New Mexico, 1948.

Harrington, Fred H.: *Hanging Judge*, Caxton Printers, Caldwell, Idaho, 1951. (Another book about Judge Isaac C. Parker of the Arkansas Territory.)

Havighurst, Walter: *Annie Oakley of the Wild West*, Macmillan, 1954.

Henry, Will: *Death of a Legend*, Random House, 1955. (Another book about Jesse James.)

Holbrook, Stewart H.: *The Rocky Mountain Revolution*, Holt, 1956. (The story of Harry Orchard, the bad man responsible for much of the violence in Western mining areas around the turn of the century.)

Holloway, Carroll C.: *Texas Gun Lore*, Naylor, 1952.

Horan, James D.: *Desperate Men*, Putnam's, 1949. Also published by Avon Books in 1952. (Revelations from sealed Pinkerton files.)

Horan, James D.: *Desperate Women*, Putnam's, 1953.

Horan, James D. and Paul Sann: *Pictorial History of the Wild West*, Crown, 1954.

Hunt, Frazier: *The Tragic Days of Billy the Kid*, Hastings House, 1956. (This book is based on forty years' research, but it is subjective.)

Hunter, J. Marvin and Noah H. Rose: *The Album of Gunfighters*, Published by authors, 1951 and 1955. Contact Warren Hunter, 504 Villita Street, San Antonio. (This is a museum piece, probably the best collection of photographs of its kind.)

Jackson, Joseph H.: *Bad Company*, Harcourt Brace, 1949. (This is mostly about California Stage robberies.)

Jackson, Joseph H.: *Tintypes in Gold*, Macmillan, 1939.

Jahns, Pat: *The Frontier World of Doc Holliday*, Hastings House, 1957.

Kane, Harnett T.: *Gentlemen, Swords and Pistols*, Morrow, 1951. (History of celebrated American duels from Virginia to California.)

Kane, Harnett T.: *Pistols for Two*, Morrow, 1951. (Duelling in America — mostly about the South — but two chapters on how and why the duel got to the Southwest and the far West.)

Keleher, William A.: *Violence in Lincoln County, 1869-1881*, University of New Mexico, 1957. (Reputedly the most unbiased treatment of the role of Billy the Kid.)

Ketchum, Phil: *The Night of the Coyotes*, Ballantine, 1956. (An unusual paperback in that it explores the subsurface motives of a fictitious western bad man.)

Lea, Tom: *The Wonderful Country*, Little, Brown, and Company, 1952. Reprinted as a Bantam Giant book in 1954. (Though the fictitious hero is a pistoleer, this book is more than a mere story of a bad man. It is a classic.)

Lewis, Oscar: *Sagebrush Casinos*, Garden City, Doubleday, 1953. (The story of legal gambling in Nevada.)

Locke, Charles O.: *The Hell Bent Kid*, Norton, 1957. (A story of a boy who could have been John Wesley Hardin.)

Lockley, Fred: *Vigilante Days at Virginia City.* Personal Narrative of Colonel Henry E. Dosch, Member of Fremont's Body Guard and One-Time Pony Express Rider. Reprinted from the *Oregon Historical Quarterly*, Eugene, Oregon, 1923.

MacDonald, W. C.: *Bad Man's Return,* Doubleday, 1958.

Manfred, Frederick: *Riders of Judgment,* Random House, 1957. (Another book about the Johnson County, Wyoming war of 1892.)

Martin, Charles L.: *A Sketch of Sam Bass, the Bandit,* University of Oklahoma, 1956.

Martin, Douglas D.: *Tombstone's Epitaph,* University of New Mexico, 1951.

Mercer, A. S.: *Banditti of the Plains,* Cheyenne, 1894; reprinted 1935 by the Grabhorn Press, California, 1935; reprinted by the University of Oklahoma Press, 1954. (An eye-witness account of the Johnson County, Wyoming war of 1892.)

Monaghan, Jay: *The Great Rascal,* Little, Brown and Company, 1951. (Lively biography of Ned Buntline, for whom the special six-gun was named. His real name was Edward Z. C. Judson.)

Myers, John M.: *Doc Holliday,* Little, Brown and Company, 1955.

Neider, Charles: *The Authentic Death of Hendry Jones,* Harper, 1956. (An introspective biography of a mythical bad man known as The Kid, a kind of archetype.)

Nordyke, Lewis: *John Wesley Hardin, Texas Gunman,* Morrow, 1957. (A crowded 269 pages about a man who lived a crowded life.)

Otero, Miguel: *The Real Billy the Kid,* Wilson-Erickson, Elmira, New York, 1936.

Parkhill, Forbes: *The Law Goes West,* Alan Swallow, Denver, 1956. (The legalities and litigations concerning both bad men and other denizens of the old wild west.)

Poe, John W.: *The Death of Billy the Kid,* Houghton Mifflin, 1933.

Pond, Fred E.: *Life and Adventures of Ned Buntline,* The Cadmus Book Shop, New York, 1919.

Quinn, John Philip: *Gambling and Gambling Devices,* Canton, Ohio, 1912.

Raine, William M.: *Guns of the Frontier,* Houghton Mifflin, 1940.

Raine, William M.: *On the Dodge,* Houghton Mifflin, 1938. (Any novel by this author and about the bad man is likely to be both fresh and authentic, because of his background of years of research into the subject.)

Rascoe, Burton: *Belle Starr,* Random House, 1941.

Rascoe, Burton: *The Dalton Brothers,* Frederick Fell, 1954.

Richter, Conrad: *Tracey Cromwell,* Knopf, 1942. (A novel by a first-rate fictionist, in the bad man tradition.)

Ridge, John Rollin (Yellow Bird): *The Life and Adventures of Joaquin Murrieta,* University of Oklahoma, 1955.

Rockwell, Wilson: *Sunset Slope,* Big Mountain Press, Denver, 1956. (A series of accounts about various bad men living on the western slope of the Rockies in Colorado from about 1850 to about 1925.)

Rowan, R. W.: *The Pinkertons: A Detective Dynasty,* Little, Brown and Company, 1931.

Russell, Carl P.: *Guns on the Early Frontiers:* A History of Firearms from Colonial Times Through the Years of the Western Fur Trade, University of California (Berkeley), 1957.

Sanders, Helen F.: *X. Beidler, Vigilante,* University of Oklahoma, 1957.

Schmitt, J. A.: *Fighting Editors,* Naylor, 1958.

Sell, Henry B. and Victor Weybright: *Buffalo Bill and the Wild West,* Oxford, 1955.

Shirley, Glenn: *Law West of Fort Smith,* Holt, 1957. (Still another book about Judge Isaac C. Parker.)

SUPPLEMENTARY BIBLIOGRAPHY

Sonnichsen, C. L. and W. V. Morrison: *Alias Billy the Kid,* University of New Mexico, 1955. (The account of one Brushy Bill Roberts, who claimed to be the real Kid.)
Sonnichsen, C. L.: *Billy King's Tombstone,* Caxton, 1942.
Sonnichsen, C. L.: *I'll Die Before I'll Run,* Harper, 1951.
Sonnichsen, C. L.: *Ten Texas Feuds,* University of New Mexico, 1957. (These last two books present feuds as they should be — impartially and truthfully.)
Streeter, Floyd B.: *Ben Thompson: Man With a Gun,* Fell, 1957.
Valentine, Alan: *Vigilante Justice,* Reynal, Santa Fe, 1956.
Vestal, Stanley: *Queen of Cowtowns, Dodge City,* Harper, 1951. Also a Pennant Book, 1954.
Waters, William: *A Gallery of Western Badmen,* Americana Publications, Box 746, Covington, Kentucky, 1954.
Wenck, H. E.: *Phantoms of Old Tombstone,* Arizona Silhouettes, 1730 E. Greenlee, Tucson, Arizona, 1958.
White, Owen P.: *Them Was the Days,* Minton, New York, 1925.
White, Owen P.: *Lead and Likker,* Minton, New York, 1932.
White, Owen P.: *My Texas 'Tis of Thee,* Putnam's, 1936.
White, Owen P.: *Trigger Fingers,* Putnam's, 1937.
Williamson, Harold F.: *Winchester: The Gun that Won the West,* Combat Forces Press, Washington, 1953.

About the Peace Officer

Aten, Ira: *Six and One-Half Years in the Ranger Service,* J. Marvin Hunter, Bandera, Texas, 1945.
Bell, Horace: *Reminiscences of a Ranger, or Early Times in California,* W. Hebberd, Santa Barbara, California, 1927. (First printed in Los Angeles, 1881.)
Box, Michael J.: *Captain James Box's Adventures and Explorations in New and Old Mexico,* J. Miller, New York, 1869. (Captain Box was a Texas Ranger.)
Coolidge, Dane: *Jess Roundtree, Texas Ranger,* Dutton, 1933. (A novel based on the life of a Texas Ranger.)
Croy, Homer: *Trigger Marshall,* Duell, Sloan and Pearce, 1958. (The only full-length biography of the Danish-born Oklahoma peace officer Chris Madsen).
Cunningham, Eugene: *Buckaroo, A Tale of the Texas Rangers,* Houghton Mifflin, 1933.
Cunningham, Eugene: *Texas Sheriff, A Novel of the Territory,* Houghton Mifflin, 1934. Also a Triangle Book, 1948.
Cunningham, Eugene: *Whistling Lead,* Houghton Mifflin, 1936.
David, Robert D.: *Malcolm Campbell, Sheriff,* Casper, Wyoming, 1932. (Campbell participated in the Johnson County war.)
Douglas, Claude L.: *The Gentlemen in the White Hats,* Southwest Press, Dallas, 1934. (Sketches of famous Texas Rangers.)
Gillett, James B.: *The Texas Ranger,* World Book Company, New York, 1925.
Greer, James K.: *Texas Ranger and Frontiersman, The Days of Buck Barry in Texas,* Southwest Press, Dallas, 1932.
Greer, James K.: *Colonel Jack Hays,* Dutton, 1951.
Grinstead, J. E.: *Texas Ranger Justice,* Dodge Publishing Company, New York, 1941.
Haley, J. Evetts: *Jeff Milton, A Good Man with a Gun,* University of Oklahoma, 1948.
Harrison, Benjamin S.: *Fortune Favors the Brave: The Life and Times of Horace Bell, Pioneer Californian,* The Ward Ritchie Press, Los Angeles, 1953.
Henderson Henry M.: *Colonel Jack Hays, Texas Ranger,* Naylor, 1954.

Hunt, Frazier: *Cap Mossman: Last of the Great Cowmen,* Hastings House, New York, 1951. (Biography of the Arizona Ranger Captain, foreman of the Hash-Knife Outfit, and capturer of the desperado Augustine Chacon.)

Jennings, N. A.: *A Texas Ranger,* Southwest Press, Dallas, 1930.

Lackey, B. Roberts: *Stories of the Texas Rangers,* Naylor, 1955.

Lee, Nelson: *Three Years Among the Comanches: The Narrative of Nelson Lee, the Texas Ranger,* University of Oklahoma, 1958. (This book was first published in 1859.)

Maltby, W. Jeff: *Captain Jeff,* Whipkey Printing Company, Colorado, Texas, 1906. (An autobiography of a Texas Ranger.)

Martin, Jack: *Border Boss,* Naylor, 1942. (A biography of Texas Ranger Captain John R. Hughes.)

Mason-Manheim, Madeline (ed.): *Riding for Texas,* Reynal and Hitchcock, New York, 1936. (This book contains "the true aventures of Captain Bill McDonald of the Texas Rangers as told by Colonel Edward M. House to Tyler Mason.")

O'Connor, Richard: *Bat Masterson,* Doubleday, 1957.

Paine, Albert B.: *Captain Bill McDonald, Texas Ranger,* Gammel, 1905. (Also published by Little and Ives, New York, 1909.)

Pike, James: *Scout and Ranger,* Princeton University Press, 1932. (Pike was a Texas Ranger. This is a reprint from an edition of 1865 edited by Carl L. Cannon.)

Raymond, Dora Neill: *Captain Lee Hall of Texas,* University of Oklahoma, 1940.

Reid, Samuel C.: *Scouting Expeditions of the McCulloch's Texas Rangers,* Bradley, Springfield, Mass., 1859. (This book was originally published by G. B. Zeiber, Philadelphia, 1847. Its most recent reprinting is by the Steck Company of Austin, Texas, 1935.)

Reid, Mayne: *Wild Life; or, Adventures on the Frontier,* Robert M. DeWitt, New York, 1859. (Reid was a Captain in the Texas Rangers.)

Roberts, Dan W.: *Rangers and Sovereignty,* Wood Printing and Engraving Company, San Antonio, 1914. (Another treatment of the Texas Rangers by one of their Captains.)

Rohan, Jack: *Yankee Arms Maker,* Harper, 1948. (Despite the title, the book concerns Texas Rangers.)

Sowell, Andrew J.: *Rangers and Pioneers of Texas,* San Antonio, 1884.

Tilghman, Zoe A.: *Marshal of the Last Frontier; Life and Services of William Matthews (Bill) Tilghman, for Fifty Years One of the Greatest Peace Officers of the West,* A. H. Clark, Glendale, California, 1949.

Webb, Walter Prescott: *The Story of the Texas Rangers,* Grossett and Dunlap, 1957. (Written for youthful readers, but appealing to grownups as well.)

Webb, Walter Prescott: *The Texas Rangers; a Century of Frontier Defense,* Houghton Mifflin, 1935. (The same subject from the more scholarly standpoint.)

INDEX

245

INDEX

ABOUT THE AUTHOR

George D. Hendricks was born near Midlothian, Texas, on November 2, 1913. He was valedictorian at Kerens High School in 1931. At The University of Texas, where he received his B.A., M.A., and Ph.D. degrees, he was a member of three honorary scholastic fraternities: Phi Eta Sigma, Phi Delta Kappa, and Phi Beta Kappa. He did graduate work also at The University of Colorado and at The University of California at Berkeley. He was a Teaching Assistant at The University of California, and a Teaching Fellow at The University of Texas. He has also taught in the public schools at Harlingen, Fort Worth, and Austin, Texas. At present he is Professor of English at North Texas State University where he has been since 1951.

Mr. Hendricks served in the United States Army five years during World War II. He was an enlisted man in the 132nd Field Artillery Battalion of Texas' 36th Division and later an officer in the 359th Field Artillery Battalion of the 95th Division. He was a Battery Commander for three years until his release from active duty. His Battery received the Meritorious Service Wreath and Plaque for its battle record, and he was personally awarded the Bronze Star Medal for meritorious service in combat. He is now a colonel in the Ready Reserves.

Mr. Hendricks has published magazine articles and book reviews in the following journals:

> The Phi Delta Kappan
> Journal of American Folklore
> Publications of the Texas Folklore Society
> Western Folklore
> Arizona Quarterly
> Southern Folklore Quarterly
> Sing Out
> Pennsylvania Archaeologist
> True West

He is the author of the first Paisano Book of the Texas Folklore Society, entitled *Mirrors, Mice, and Mustaches*, issued by the S.M.U. Press, 1966, and has contributed three folklore items to the new edition of the *World Book Encyclopedia*, a Marshall Fields publication. In the capacity of folklorist he has appeared on television programs sponsored by the Texas State Education Agency. He is a past president of the Texas Folklore Society, and a councilor of the American Folklore Society. He is actively engaged in compiling a cumulative bibliography of the life and literature of the Southwest, which subject he instructs at North Texas State College. At present this bibliography numbers over 8,000 items. Mr. Hendricks is listed in *Who's Who in American Education, Directory of American Scholars, Who's Who in the Southwest, Contemporary Authors, Who's Who in Texas Today,* and *Dictionary of International Biography.*

He finds time somehow to sponsor the Epsilon Upsilon Chapter of the Kappa Sigma social fraternity (of which he was an undergraduate member at Texas) on the NTSU campus, to be a deacon at the First Christian Church of Denton, and to play an occasional amateur game of golf, swim, do his own yard work, entertain his children, and attend a summer two-week tour of active duty in the Army Reserves. Mr. Hendricks is also a member of Phi Eta Sigma, Phi Delta Kappa, and Phi Beta Kappa, honorary scholastic fraternities.

A DUEL ON HORSEBACK

THE JAMES GANG HOLDS UP A TRAIN

FRANK ANTHONY STANUSH